CORELDRAW in easy steps

Stephen Copestake

In easy steps is an imprint of Computer Step
Southfield Road . Southam
Warwickshire CV33 OFB . England

Tel: 01926 817999 Fax: 01926 817005
http://www.computerstep.com

Third edition, 1998

Notice of Liability

Every effort has been made to ensure that this book contains accurate and current information. However, Computer Step and the author shall not be liable for any loss or damage suffered by readers as a result of any information contained herein.

Trademarks

Corel® is a registered trademark and CorelDRAW™ is a trademark of Corel Corporation. Microsoft® and Windows® are registered trademarks of Microsoft Corporation. All other trademarks are acknowledged as belonging to their respective companies.

Printed and bound in the United Kingdom

ISBN 1-84078-000-2

Contents

Chapter One

First Steps

This chapter gets you started with CorelDRAW quickly. It shows you how to launch CorelDRAW and create new (or open existing) documents at the same time. You'll learn how to specify which toolbars and roll-ups display, and how to work with different document views. You'll also discover how to use features which are new in versions 4 to 8 to make your work even more efficient.

Covers

Starting CorelDRAW

This screen is slightly different in version 6.

To launch CorelDRAW, click the Start button on the Task Bar at the base of the Windows screen. Then click Programs. In the Program menu, click the relevant entry (e.g. CorelDRAW 8). In the sub-menu, select the relevant entry (e.g. CorelDRAW 8).

When they launch, versions 6-8 of CorelDRAW produce a special screen. Do either of the following:

In versions 3-5, this screen does not launch. Instead, CorelDRAW immediately launches a new blank document.

Click here to create a blank DRAW file

Or here to open an existing file

If you elected to open an existing file, do the following:

If you want to see what a file looks like *before* opening it, ensure the Preview box is ticked. Then click Open to open it.

Double-click the file you want to open

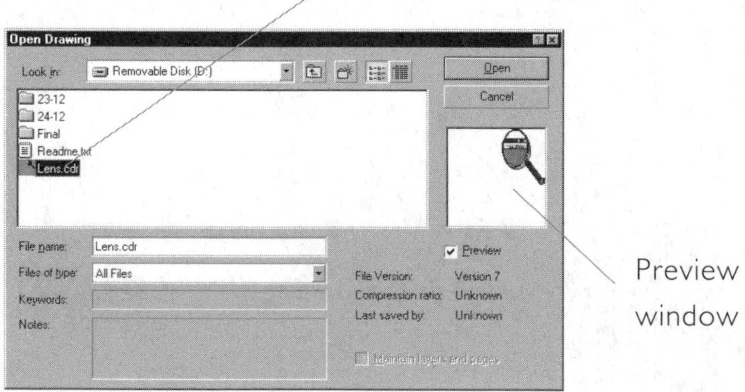

Preview window

The CorelDRAW screen

The other components are common to most or all Windows programs. See your Windows documentation for how to use them.

The screen in versions 3-5 is simpler. Below is the version 5 screen:

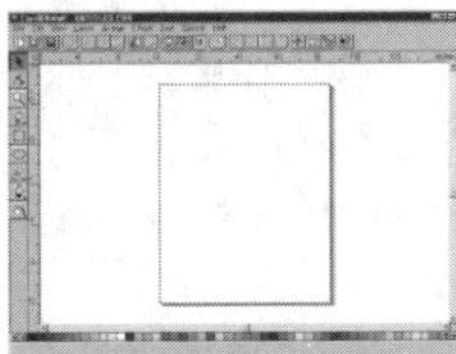

Note that the basic components are unaltered.

The commands available in the Property Bar vary according to which object (text or otherwise) is selected. See the 'Using the Property Bar' topic later.

Whether you create a new CorelDRAW document or open an existing one, the result will look like this:

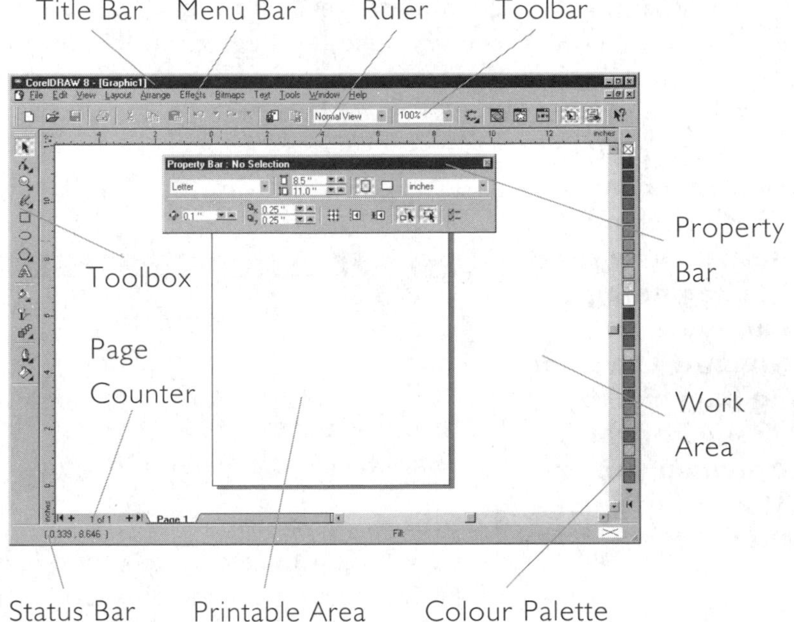

The following are details of CorelDRAW-specific screen components:

Toolbars New to version 5

Toolbars are collections of icons. By clicking an appropriate icon, you can launch a specific feature. This saves you having to pull down menus. CorelDRAW provides a variety of toolbars.

Work Area & Printable Area

You can work anywhere in the Work Area, but only the objects placed on the Printable Area can be printed.

Property Bar New in version 7

The Property Bar is a special on-screen toolbar which displays commands in a convenient and easily accessible format.

Page Counter New in version 6

CorelDRAW lets you create multi-page documents. The Page Counter displays the total number of pages in a document, and tells you which page is currently active. You can also use the Page Counter to move from page to page very easily: simply click the relevant page tab, or click the Page Forward or Page Back arrows.

When you're on the first page of a document, the Page Back arrow changes to a "+": click on it to insert a new page at the beginning of the active document. The same thing happens to the Page Forward arrow when you are on the last page of a document.

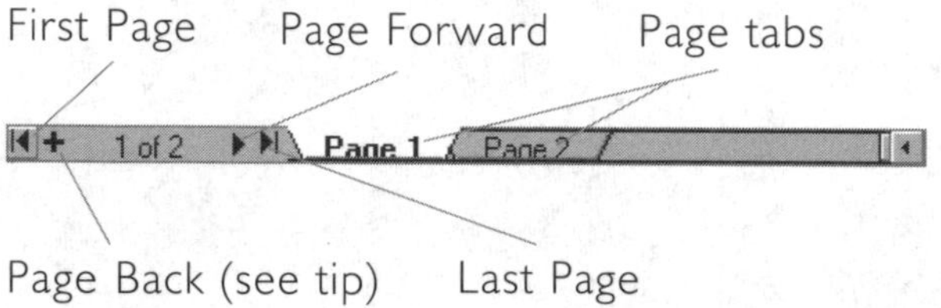

Colour Palette

You use the Colour Palette to apply colours to object fills.

Toolbox

The Toolbox provides access to an assortment of special tools. By clicking the appropriate icon (and occasionally by selecting from a subsidiary flyout, too), you launch the relevant tool. Tools are discussed as they occur.

In versions before 7, the Toolbox has fewer available tools e.g. the Polygon, Interactive Transparency, Interactive Fill and Interactive Blend tools are not present.

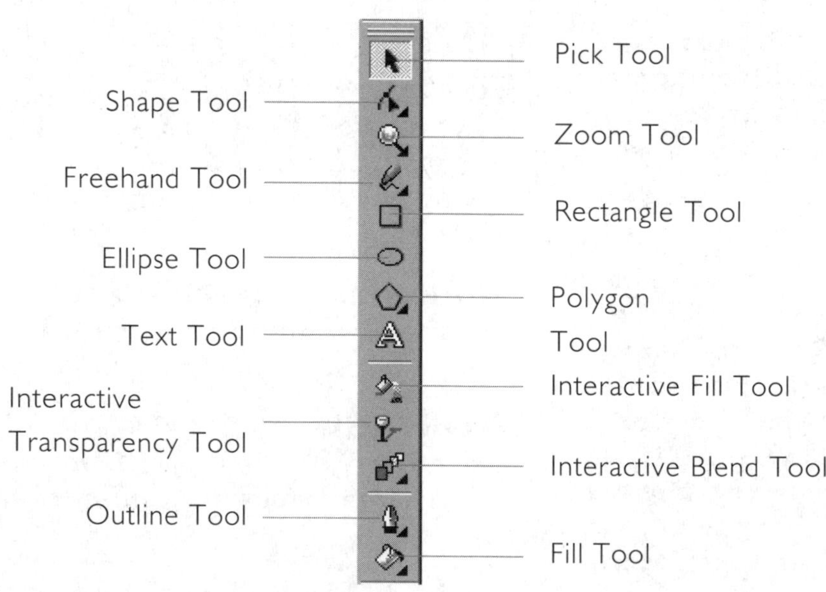

Document Info New in version 7

CorelDRAW documents can quickly become complex. To help you find your way around them, you can use a feature called Document Info. Document Info lists document components, under the following headings:

File	Filename/address details
Document	Document statistics (e.g. page count, paper size)
Graphic Objects	Details of graphic objects (e.g. lines)
Text Statistics	Text information (e.g. paragraph/word counts and fonts used)
Bitmaps	Details of included bitmaps
Styles	Details of styles used
Effects	Details of effects
Fills	Details of fills and colours used
Outlines	Details of outlines used

Using Document Info

Pull down the File menu and click Document Info. Now do the following:

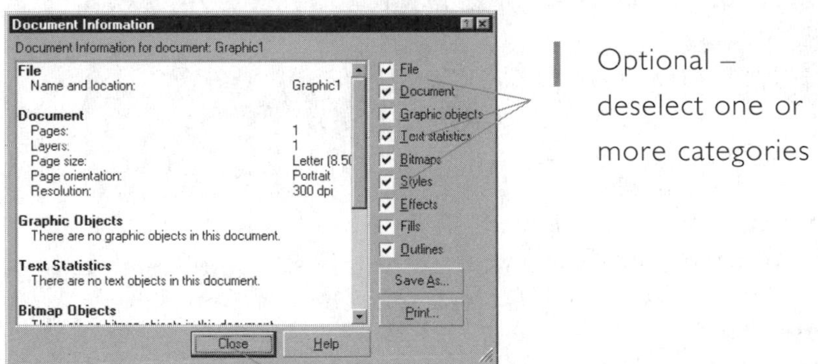

1 Optional – deselect one or more categories

2 Click here to close Document Info when you've finished

Using templates New in version 4

Users of versions 7 and 8 can also select 'Template' from CorelDRAW's Welcome screen to create a new document based on a template. (See page 8.)

Users of versions 4-5 should use an abbreviated procedure.

Follow step 1 (but note that the File menu is rather different). In the New From Template dialog, select a template. Click OK.

Users of version 6 should use a slightly different procedure.

Pull down the File menu and click New, From Template. In the New From Template dialog, select a template. Click Open.

Templates are collections of formatting and drawings. Their advantage is that they save you time and effort. When you create a new file based on a template, you automatically have access to all the associated formatting and drawings.

Creating a new document based on a template

Pull down the File menu and do the following:

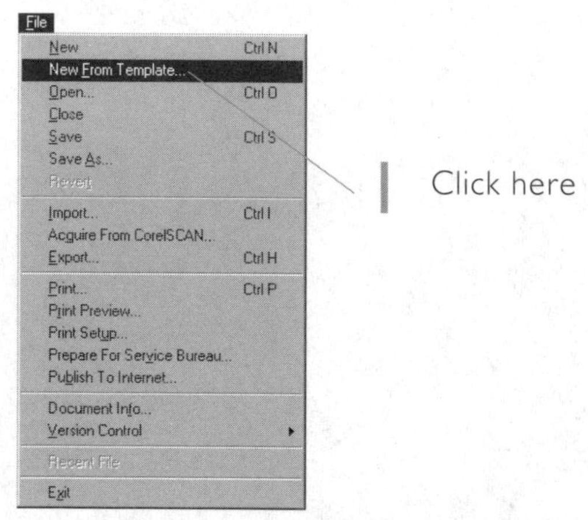

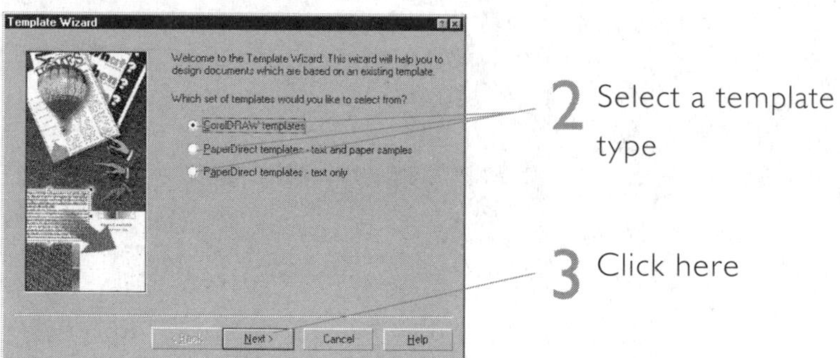

Now complete the additional dialogs which launch, selecting a specific template.

Working with toolbars New in version 5

Users of versions from 5 can select which toolbars display. You can also copy or remove icons, and reposition toolbars on the screen.

Selecting Toolbars

Pull down the View menu and choose Toolbars. Now do the following:

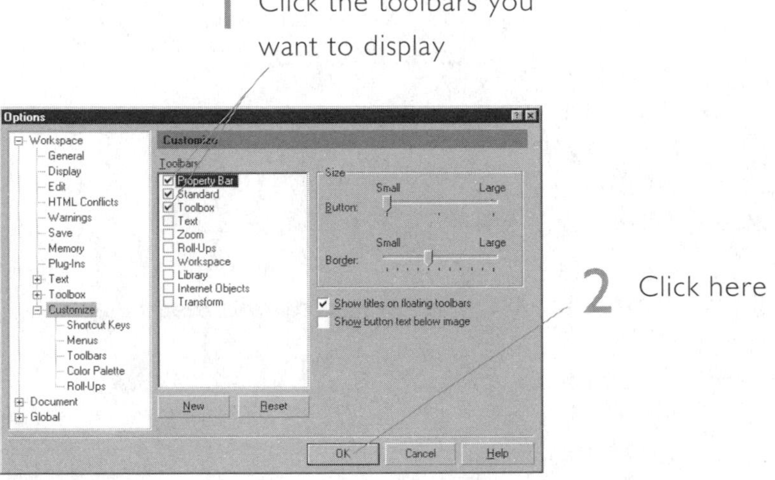

Adding icons

To add a new icon to an on-screen toolbar, click Toolbars in the Customize list on the left of the Options dialog. In the Commands section, click a command category/sub-category combination; CorelDRAW displays icons on the right of the dialog. Drag the appropriate icon to the relevant toolbar.

Removing icons

To delete an icon from an on-screen toolbar, click Toolbars in the Customize list on the left of the Options dialog. Drag any icon off an on-screen toolbar (anywhere except onto a toolbar). When you release the mouse button, the icon vanishes.

To move a toolbar, simply click in its border during normal on-screen editing and drag it to a new location.

Toolbars in version 5 are at an embryonic stage: the operations described here can only be carried out in versions 6-8.

Version 6 and 7 users should follow a different procedure.

Click Toolbars in the View menu. To specify which toolbars display, click them in the Toolbars section.

To add or remove icons, click the Customize button. Now follow the appropriate actions on the right.

Finally, click OK.

Using the Property Bar New in version 7

The Property Bars shown as examples here have been 'resized' – see below.

The Property Bar displays commands on-screen. It does so in a format which is immediately accessible, and – even more usefully – it only displays commands which relate to the currently selected object. This means that the Property Bar can have incarnations which change quite dramatically:

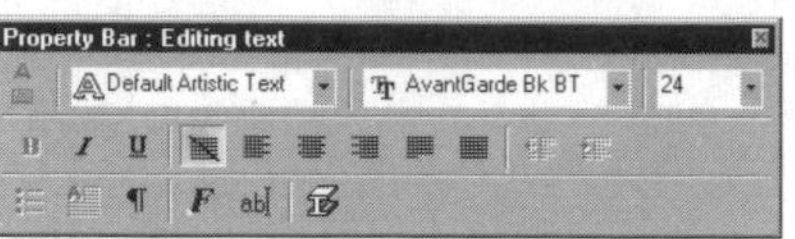

Property Bar when text is selected

Version 7's Property Bar has a slightly different look . . .

Property Bar when a polygon is selected

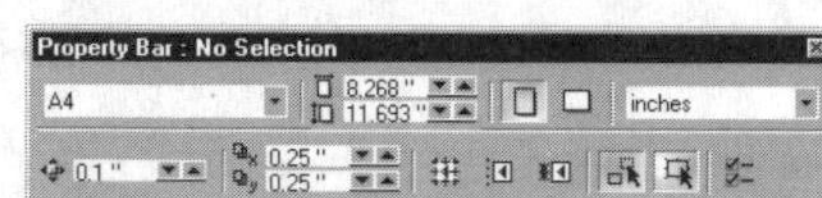

Property Bar when no object is selected – i.e. it displays Page Setup commands

If (when an object is selected and the Property Bar is on-screen) you click a tool in the Toolbox, CorelDRAW updates the commands in the Property Bar accordingly.

Launching the Property Bar

If the Property Bar isn't already visible, pull down the View menu and click Property Bar.

Closing the Property Bar

Click the Close button – ☒ – in the upper right-hand corner of the Property Bar.

Customising the Property Bar

The Property Bar acts like a toolbar. This means you can:

- position it on the top, bottom, left or right of the screen. To do this, drag the Property Bar's Title bar to the correct location
- resize it, using normal Windows techniques

Fixing the Property Bar on the edge of the screen is called 'docking'.

Working with roll-ups

Roll-ups are specialist dialog boxes which can be left on screen so that their functions are always available. You can 'shrink' roll-ups (with the result that only their title bars display) to conserve space.

Launching roll-ups

Pull down the View menu and click Roll-Ups. In the sub-menu, select the relevant roll-up (e.g. Blend).

When minimised, roll-ups look like this:

Shrinking roll-ups

To minimise a roll-up, follow step 1 below. Repeating this restores a roll-up to full size.

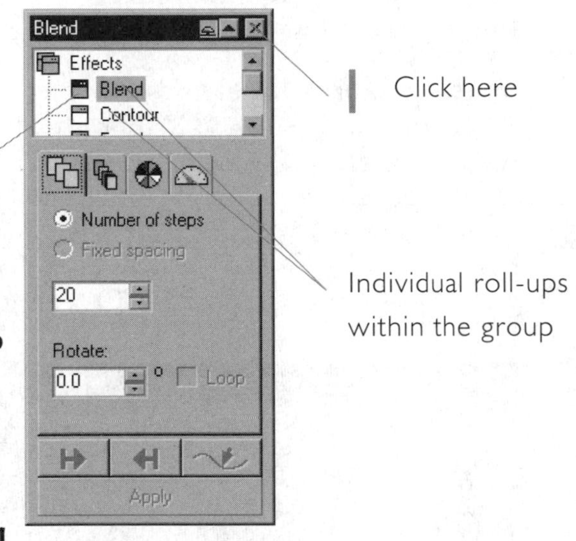

To ungroup a roll-up, move the mouse pointer over an individual roll-up icon and drag it off the group.

REMEMBER

Grouping/ungrouping roll-ups can only be carried out in versions 6-8.

Version 6 users should hold down the Ctrl (not Alt) key.

Grouping roll-ups

You can combine more than one roll-up into a single group. The Blend roll-up above is an example of this; by default, it forms one component of an overall roll-up group. Other components are: Contour, Envelope, Extrude, Lens.

Grouping roll-ups saves even more space.

To do this, open the relevant roll-ups. Hold down Alt and drag one roll-up onto the title bar of the second.

Using Undo and Redo

You can even undo undos. DRAW calls this 'redoing'. Simply click Redo in the Edit menu.

A very useful feature in CorelDRAW is the ability to reverse editing actions. Most changes can be undone; the main exceptions are:

- any change of zoom level
- opening or saving files (version 8 users, however, can undo changes irrespective of the number of save operations performed)

In version 3, you can't perform multiple undos: you can only undo the last editing action.

CorelDRAW lets you set the number of undos. You can have as many as your computer's memory permits.

Undoing the last action

Press Ctrl+Z, or Alt+Backspace.

Setting Undo levels

By default, CorelDRAW 8 allocates 99 undo levels (versions before 7 allocate fewer). If you want more (or fewer), pull down the Tools menu and choose Options. Then follow the procedures below.

In versions 4 and 5, do the following instead.
Pull down the Special menu and click Preferences. In the Undo Levels field, type in the no. of undos you want. Click OK.

1 Click both locations

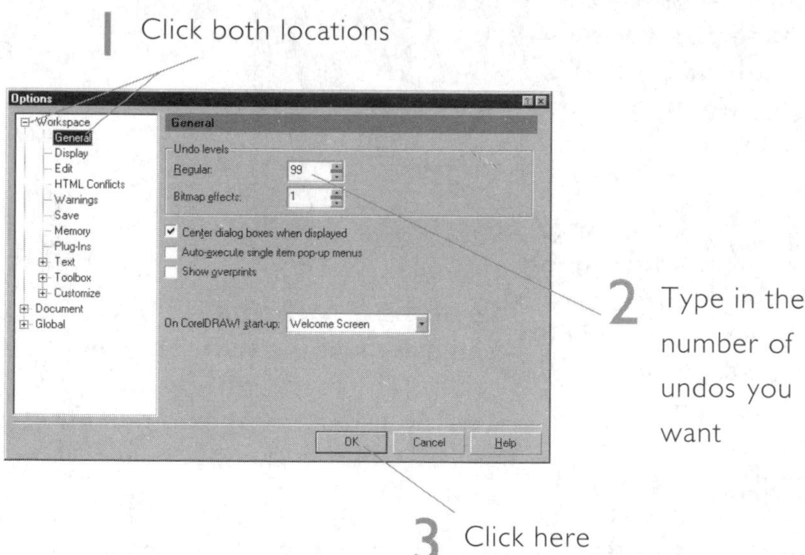

2 Type in the number of undos you want

3 Click here

Using views

CorelDRAW lets you work with documents in various 'views'. These are specialised ways of looking at your work.

In versions before 5, Full Screen Preview is called Preview.

Full Screen Preview

Sometimes, it's useful to view your work without any of the screen components we discussed on pages 9 and 10 being visible. Use Full Screen Preview to achieve this. Full Screen Preview provides a clearer idea of what your drawing will look like when printed.

To preview your work, press F9.

Note that if you're using a PostScript printer, Full Screen Preview may display some features inadequately.

A CorelDRAW graphic in Full Screen Preview

These views only affect the way CorelDRAW objects display on-screen; they have no effect on image content.

To return to your normal view, press F9 again (or the Spacebar).

Simple Wireframe New in version 7

This view hides just about all complex object properties (including fills, extrusions, and intermediate blend shapes) although black-and-white bitmaps display. Simple Wireframe view displays only the outlines of objects. This can make editing your drawings a lot easier and quicker, especially if they're complex.

To enter Simple Wireframe view, pull down the View menu and click Simple Wireframe.

HANDY TIP

These views only affect the way DRAW objects display on-screen; they have no effect on image content.

Wireframe

This view is somewhat less Draconian than Simple Wireframe. Fills and outlines do not display; instead, drawings are shown in 'skeleton' form, but with rather more detail. Like Simple Wireframe, Wireframe view can make editing your drawings a lot quicker.

To enter Wireframe view, pull down the View menu and click Wireframe.

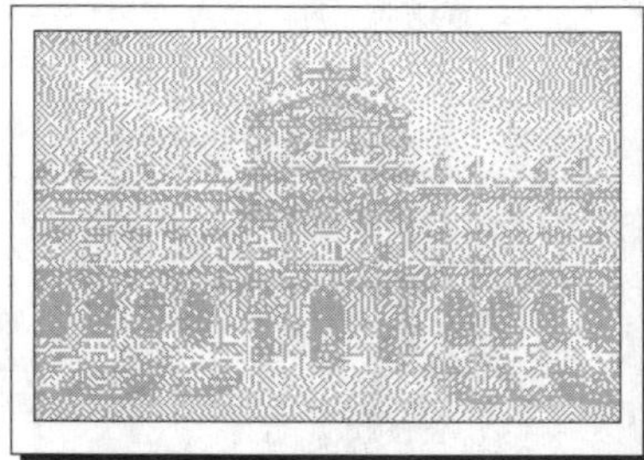

The image from page 17 in Wireframe view

Draft New in version 7

This view displays most fill types (e.g. solid and fountain fills) but not high-resolution textures.

Versions 3 and 4 only have one special view (apart from Preview): Wireframe.

To launch this, pull down the Display menu and click Edit Wireframe.

To return to Normal view, repeat the procedure.

To enter Draft view, click Draft in the View menu.

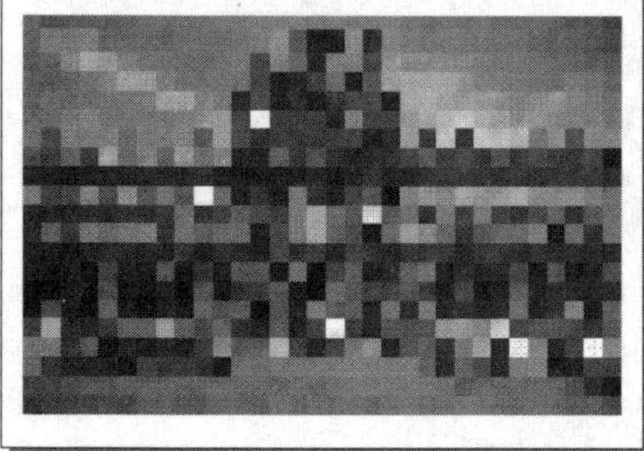

The same image in Draft view

Normal and Enhanced New in version 7 views

Both Normal and Enhanced views display all object properties (but Enhanced does so even more effectively).

To enter Normal or Enhanced view, pull down the View menu and click Normal or Enhanced.

Using Zoom

In versions before 6, the relevant Zoom functions are to be found in the Zoom tool in the on-screen Toolbox.

Often, it's important to be able to view sections of your drawings in close up ('zoom in'). On other occasions, you'll want to take an overview ('zoom out'). CorelDRAW lets you do both very easily.

First, make sure the Zoom toolbar is visible (for how to do this, see page 13). Now do any of the following:

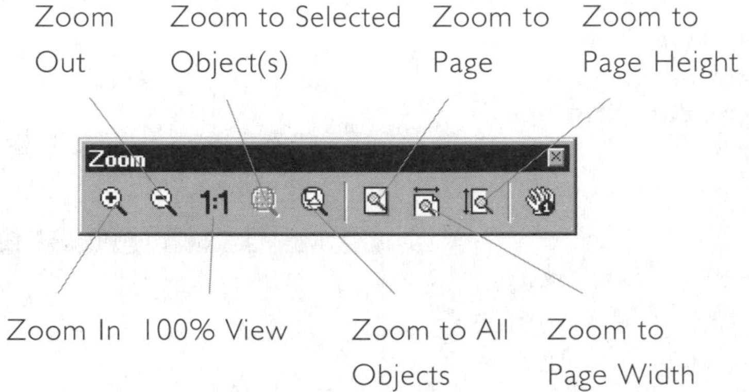

To close the Zoom toolbar, click the Close button: ☒ in the upper right hand corner.

Users of versions 7 and 8 can also use the Property Bar to set zoom levels. First, ensure it's on-screen (for how to do this, see page 14). Then click the Zoom Tool in the Toolbox. This is the result:

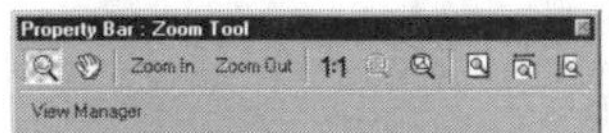

Now use any of the commands listed under 'Using the Zoom toolbar' on the right.

Using the Zoom toolbar New in version 6

When you click the Zoom In button, the mouse pointer changes to a magnifying glass. Move this over the part of your drawing whose zoom level you want to increment and left-click.

To zoom out, click the Zoom Out button. Position the pointer over the part of the drawing whose zoom level you want to decrease and right-click.

Click the 100% View button to view your drawing at the dimensions it will have when printed.

Click Zoom to Selected Objects to have selected objects fill the screen, or Zoom to All Objects to view all objects, whether selected or not.

Click Zoom to Page to view all of the printable page.

Click Zoom to Page Width to view the document width-wise, or Zoom to Page Height to view it length-wise.

Using View Manager New in version 6

View Manager is a specialist adaptation of CorelDRAW's Zoom feature. It lets you allocate names to specific views of an open document. Once you've named a view, you can return to it very easily.

You can also use the native Zoom buttons to fine-tune the view *before* carrying out step 1.

Creating a view

First zoom in on the object(s) you want to save as a view. Press Ctrl+F2. Then carry out the following actions:

1 Click here

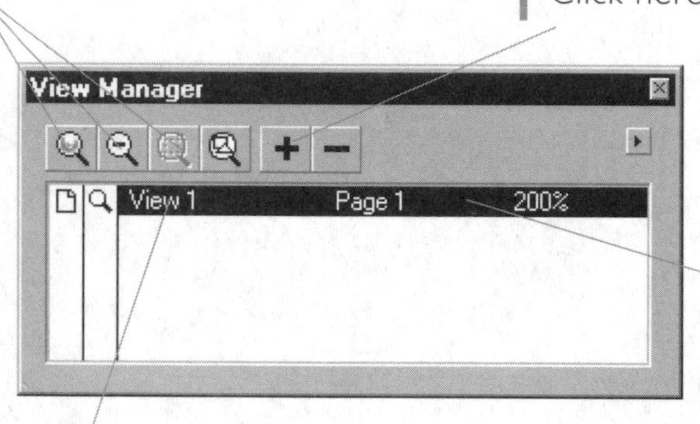

View Manager creates – and names – the view

Use View Manager to move around quickly and easily in especially complex or multi-page documents.

2 (Optional) Click here. Delete the standard name and type in your own. Press Enter

Repeat this procedure as often as necessary.

Jumping to a view

When you've created multiple views, double-clicking on a view's entry in the View Manager (but not the name section) takes you straight to it.

To close the View Manager roll-up when you've finished with it, click this button – ☒ – in the upper right-hand corner.

In version 8, the View Manager may display 'docked' on the right of the screen:

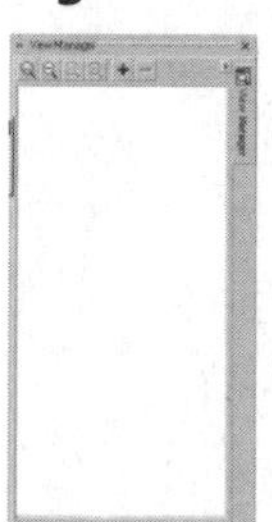

Using workspaces New in version 8

In version 8 of CorelDRAW, you can:

- customise many aspects of the way you use CorelDRAW
- save the customisation details as a 'workspace'
- apply the workspace/customisation details with a few mouse clicks

In this way, you can – in effect – create and apply different versions of CorelDRAW, with settings specific to given purposes.

We've already seen (on page 16) how to customise one aspect of the way you use CorelDRAW; other aspects you can customise include:

— the way CorelDRAW's display operates

— the way CorelDRAW handles text

— the way CorelDRAW handles internal memory

Creating a workspace

Pull down the Tools menu and carry out the following actions:

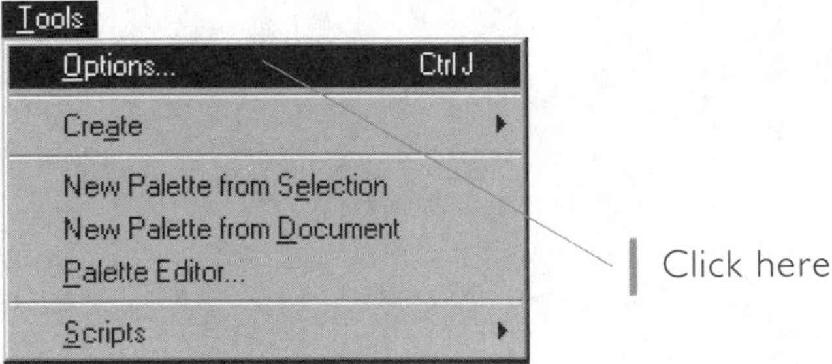

Now perform the additional steps on page 22.

Before you carry out step 2, do the following.

In the drop-down list, select a program area; complete the dialog on the right of the list. Repeat as often as necessary. Finally, carry out step A again, then perform steps 2-6 on the right.

Now perform the following steps (but see the HANDY TIP on the left):

2 Ensure this is selected

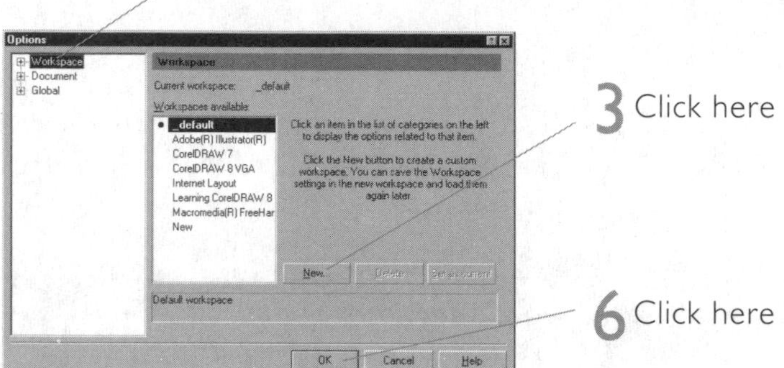

4 Name the new workspace

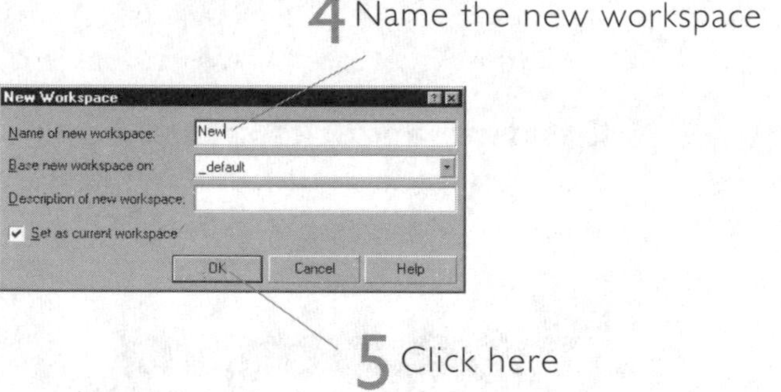

5 Click here

Applying a workspace

Follow step 1 on page 21, and step 2 above. In the Workspaces available: field in the Options dialog, highlight the workspace you want to apply. Click this button:

Now carry out step 6 above.

Chapter Two

Basic Drawing

This chapter gets you started with CorelDRAW quickly. We'll look at some specialist CorelDRAW selection techniques. Then you'll learn how to create simple shapes. Finally, you'll also learn about shortcuts which allow you to align the objects you create, easily and conveniently.

Covers

Selection techniques

CorelDRAW makes use of standard Windows selection procedures. For instance, with the Pick tool in the Toolbox activated, clicking on a drawing object's outline 'selects' it (this means that any editing actions you undertake apply solely to this object). However, there are other selection routes which are more or less specific to CorelDRAW...

Using marquees

In versions after 5, holding down the Alt key as you define a marquee automatically selects objects which merely intersect it.

This is a very useful technique for selecting one or more objects at a time. Make sure the Pick tool is activated. Then simply move the mouse pointer to one corner of the (imaginary) rectangle which contains the object(s) you want to select. Click and hold down the left mouse button as you drag out a dashed rectangle that completely surrounds the objects. When you release the button, all the enclosed objects are selected.

Selected objects are surrounded by eight black rectangles – see page 25.

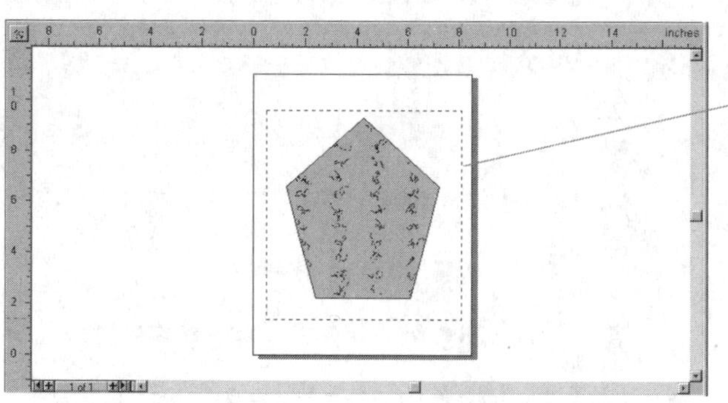

Marquee just before the mouse button is released

Using Shift

Another way to select several objects is to activate the Pick tool and hold down one Shift key as you click sequentially on the object outlines.

Selecting all objects automatically

You can have CorelDRAW select all objects on the current page within the active document. To do this in versions 5-8, double-click the Pick tool. (Alternatively, in all versions before 8, pull down the Edit menu and click Select All).

Working with selected objects

When you select an object in CorelDRAW, it's surrounded with black handles:

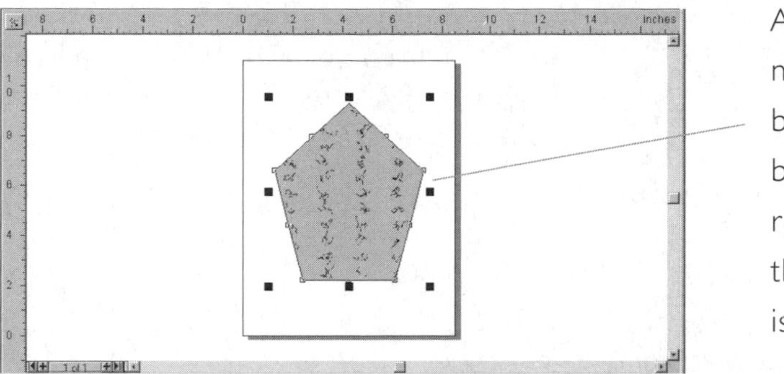

After the mouse button has been released; the object is selected

HANDY TIP

If you hold down one Ctrl key as you resize or stretch an object, changes are made in 100% increments.

If you hold down one Shift key as you resize or stretch an object, changes are made from the centre outwards.

You can combine the above keystroke enhancements.

You can perform a variety of operations on selected objects. These include:

- moving/resizing
- reshaping/rotation
- filling
- customising outlines

Moving and resizing are undertaken with more or less standard Windows techniques (i.e. dragging a centre handle stretches objects, thus disrupting their height/width ratio, while dragging on a corner handle resizes them proportionally). We'll be looking at the use of outlines, reshaping/rotation and fills in later chapters.

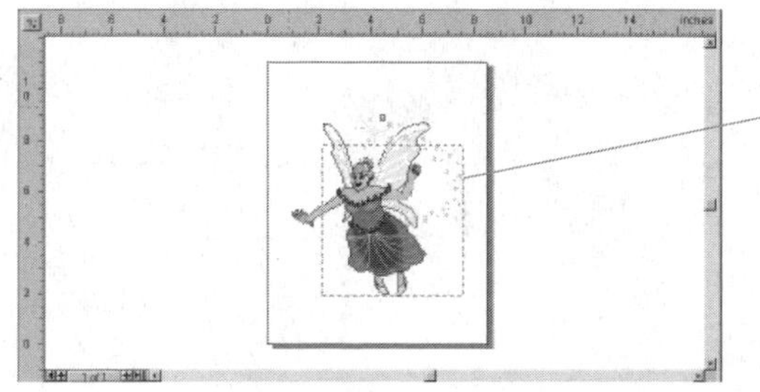

A graphical object in the course of being resized

Object locking New in version 8

When you've created complex documents in CorelDRAW (that's to say, documents with numerous object components and/or objects which are themselves complex), it can sometimes happen that objects which you don't wish moved or resized can be affected inadvertently. To prevent this, version 8 users can opt to 'lock' specific objects to the underlying drawing area. Locked objects cannot be:

— moved or resized

— filled

— deleted

Nearly all objects can be locked in version 8 – the main exceptions are:

- text
- blended or extruded objects
- objects with drop shadows

Locking one or more objects

Use the techniques discussed on page 24 to select one or more objects. Pull down the Arrange menu and do the following:

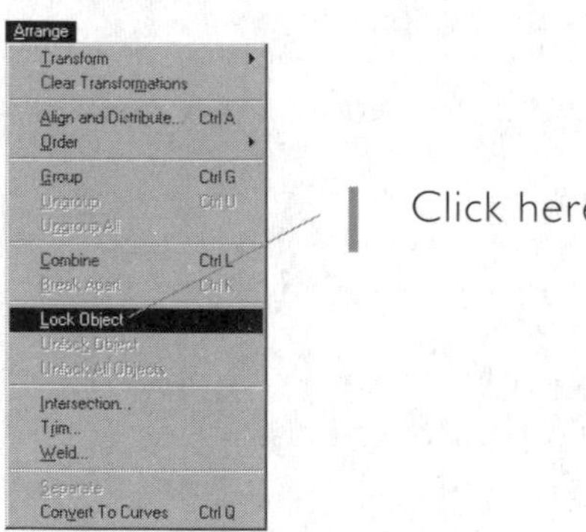

Click here

To unlock one or more locked objects, first select them. Then pull down the Arrange menu and click:
Unlock Object
or
Unlock All Objects
as appropriate.

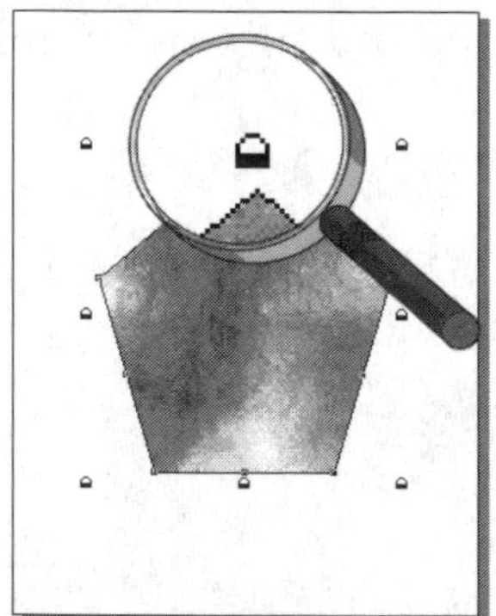

A locked object – notice the transformed handles

Digger selection New in version 8

Another feature of complex documents in CorelDRAW is the inability to find specific objects which are hidden under others. Version 8 users have a way round this: digger selection

Look at the next illustration:

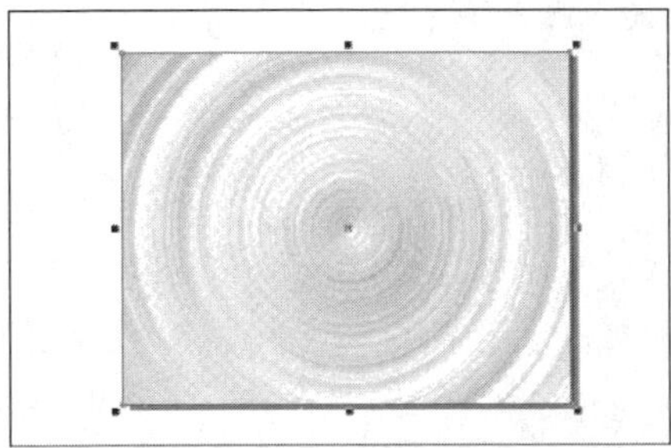

Here, a large textured object sits on top of another, smaller object (currently unseen). The visible object has been selected; the problem is, how to select the lower object. In this instance, it would be simple enough merely to drag the large object to one side. However, if there were a multiplicity of objects, the problem would be more difficult. The answer is to use digger selection.

Using digger selection

REMEMBER

This is the hidden object's centre X icon:

Hold down the Alt key while you click varying locations on the uppermost object. Eventually, this is the result:

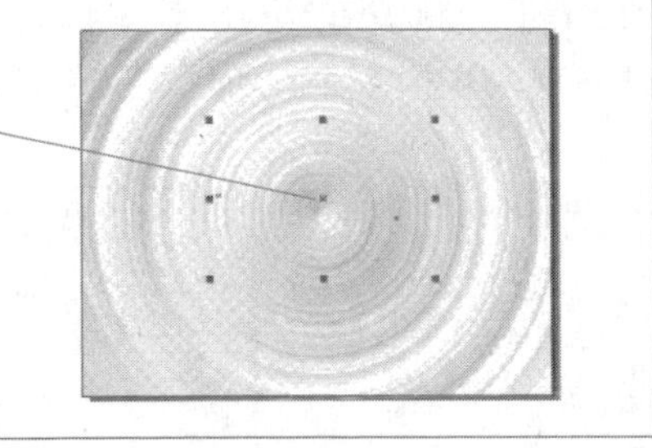

The hidden object's selection handles appear in green

Move the mouse pointer over the centre X and drag the hidden object out.

Working with lines

The Toolbox looks different in earlier versions of CorelDRAW.

Versions 3 and 4 have a joint Freehand/ Bezier tool:

Follow step 1, then 2 OR 3. Now follow the relevant instructions on the right.

If you define additional segments, click as close to the line-end as possible.

If you hold down the Ctrl key as you define lines with the Freehand tool, they're constrained to 15 degree increments.

Many drawing operations are undertaken with the help of the Freehand or Bezier tools. These are accessible from within the Toolbox. Follow the procedure below.

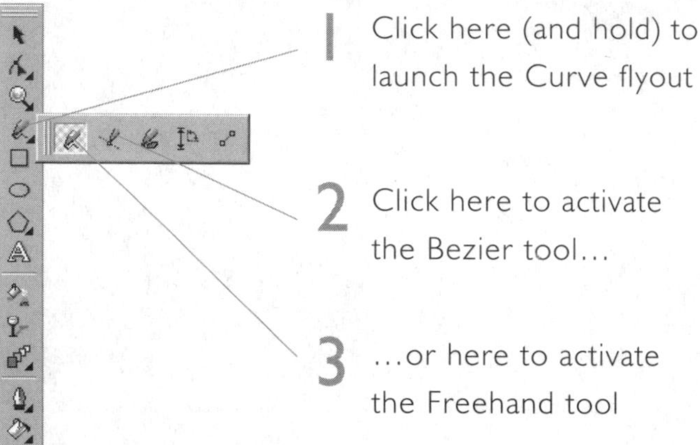

1. Click here (and hold) to launch the Curve flyout
2. Click here to activate the Bezier tool...
3. ...or here to activate the Freehand tool

Using the Freehand tool

The Freehand cursor is a cross with a wavy line. Click in your drawing where you want the line to start. Then click where you want it to end. If you want the line to continue, click one line-end and draw another segment. Repeat this as often as necessary.

Using the Bezier tool

The Bezier cursor is a cross with a *circled* wavy line. Click where you want the line to start. Then click where you want it to finish. If you want the line to continue, click where you want the next line to end. Repeat this as often as necessary. Press the Spacebar twice when you've finished (or activate another tool by clicking on it in the Toolbox).

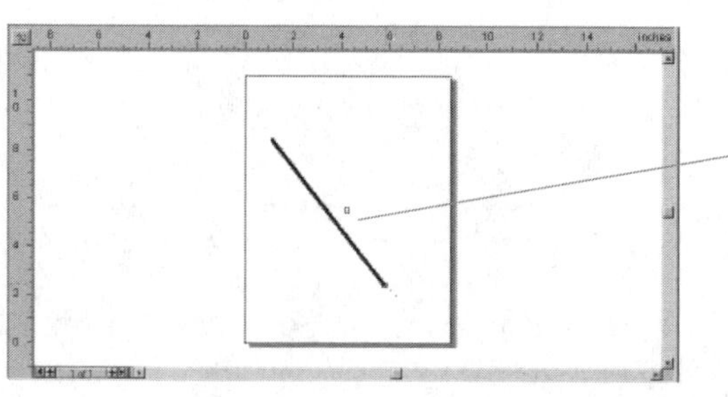

A Bezier line which has just been created

Working with freehand curves

Version 3 and 4 users should activate the joint Freehand/ Bezier tool:

To use it, follow steps 1-4.

You can easily erase part of a freehand curve *before* you carry out step 4. Simply hold down one Shift key while you drag backwards over your curve. Release Shift to resume drawing.

If you define additional curves, click as close to the endpoint as possible.

Drawing freehand curves

Drawing freehand curves is one of CorelDRAW's least user-friendly operations, in the sense that using it effectively requires some artistic ability. In fact, it's probably the feature you'll use least of all. However, freehand drawing in CorelDRAW can create highly original effects. Think of it like using a pencil, or an Etch-a-Sketch.

To draw curves with the Freehand tool, launch the Curve flyout (see page 28 for how to do this). Then select the Freehand tool. Perform the following operations:

1. Place the mouse pointer where you want your curve to start.
2. Hold down the left mouse button.
3. Drag out the curves you need.
4. Release the mouse button when you've finished.

Joining curves

If you want to create a new curve and join it to an existing one, place the mouse pointer over the endpoint of the original. Then follow steps 2 to 4 above.

The illustration shows a typical CorelDRAW freehand curve:

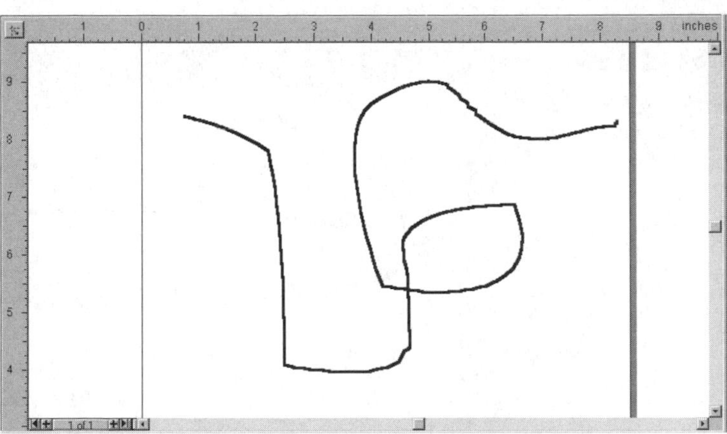

Working with ellipses

REMEMBER

The Toolbox looks different in earlier versions of CorelDRAW. For example, there are fewer buttons.

CorelDRAW makes creating ellipses easy.

Drawing an ellipse

In the Toolbox, click the Ellipse tool.

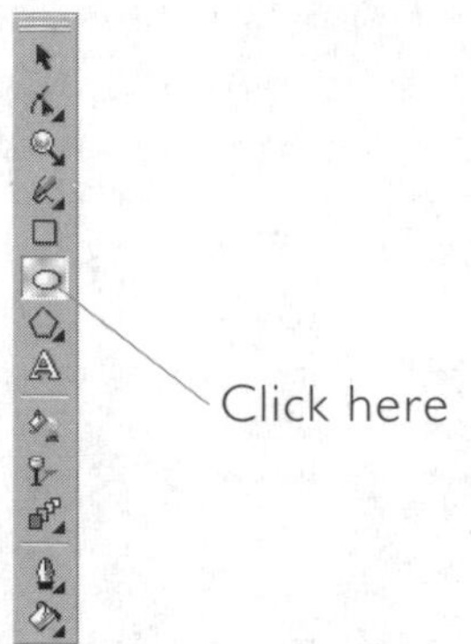

Now carry out these steps:

1. Place the mouse pointer at the location where you want one corner of the ellipse to begin.
2. Click and hold down the left mouse button.
3. Drag to create the ellipse.
4. Release the mouse button.

You can create an ellipse from the centre outwards. Simply hold down one Shift key as you carry out steps 2-4.

The following is an example of a CorelDRAW ellipse.

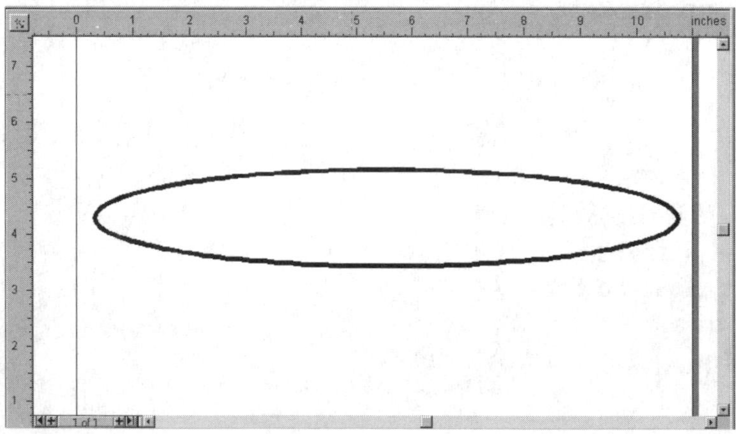

Working with circles

CorelDRAW lets you create perfect circles very easily, with the minimum of expertise. You can also create circles outwards, from the centre.

Drawing circles

In the Toolbox, click the Ellipse tool. (For how to do this, see page 30.)

Now carry out these steps:

1. Place the mouse pointer at the location where you want one corner of the circle to begin
2. Hold down one Ctrl key
3. Click and hold down the left mouse button
4. Drag to create the circle
5. Release the mouse button
6. Release the Ctrl button

HANDY TIP **To create a circle from the centre outwards, simply hold down one Shift key (as well as Ctrl) as you carry out steps 2-6.**

The following is an example of a CorelDRAW circle:

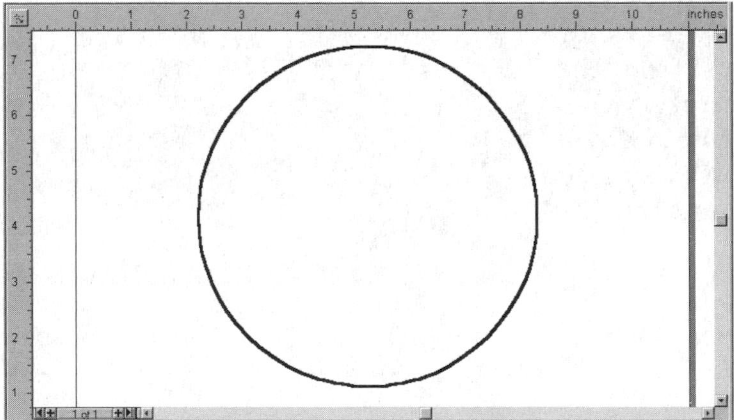

Working with rectangles

You can easily create rectangles in CorelDRAW.

Drawing a rectangle

In the Toolbox, click the Rectangle tool.

The Toolbox looks different in earlier versions of CorelDRAW. For example, there are fewer buttons.

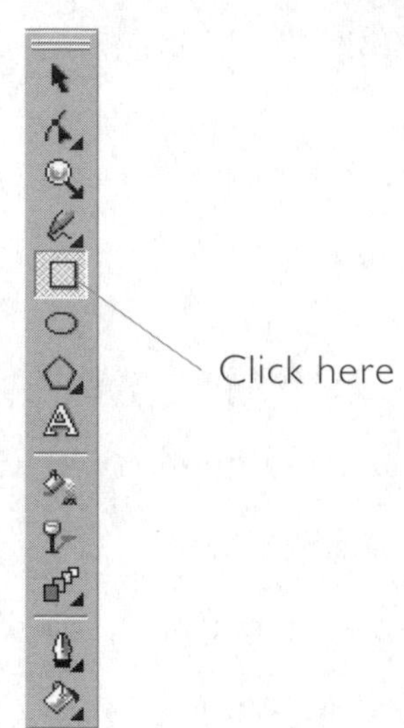

You can create a rectangle from the centre outwards. Simply hold down one Shift key as you carry out steps 2-4.

Now carry out these steps:

1. Place the mouse pointer where you want one corner of the rectangle to begin.
2. Click and hold down the left mouse button.
3. Drag to create the rectangle.
4. Release the mouse button.

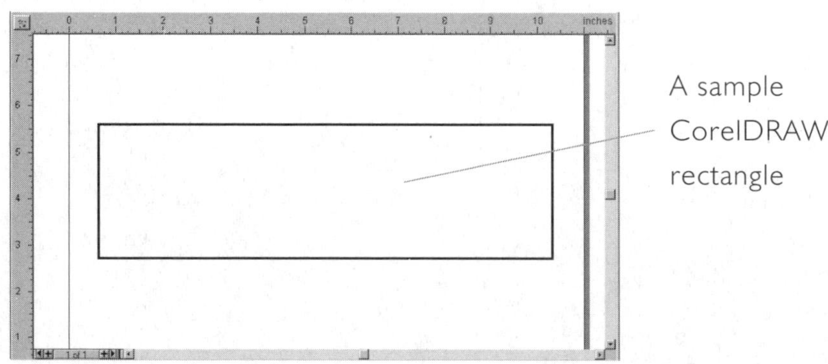

Working with squares

In the same way that the use of the Ellipse tool can be extended to produce perfect circles, the Rectangle tool can produce squares.

Make sure you release the Ctrl key *after* you've released the left mouse button.

You can create a square from the centre outwards. Simply hold down one Shift key (as well as Ctrl) as you carry out steps 2-6.

Drawing a square

In the Toolbox, click the Rectangle tool. For how to do this, see page 32.

Now carry out these steps:

1. Place the mouse pointer at the location where you want one corner of the square to begin.
2. Hold down one Ctrl key.
3. Click and hold down the left mouse button.
4. Drag to create the square.
5. Release the mouse button.
6. Release the Ctrl button

The following is an example of a CorelDRAW square.

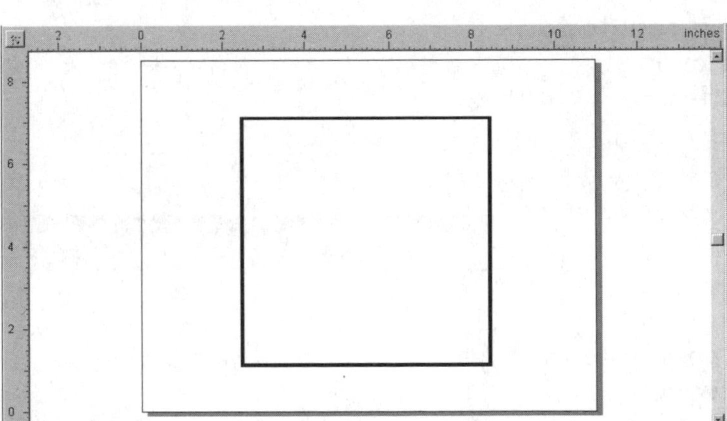

Using grids

Users of versions 6 and 7 should carry out a different procedure.

Pull down the Layout menu and click Grid & Ruler Setup. In the resultant dialog, activate the Grid tab. Enter the relevant point frequencies. Click Show Grid. Finally, click OK.

Users of versions 3, 4 and 5 should do the following respectively:

- click Grid Setup in the Display menu
- click Grid Setup in the Layout menu
- click Grid Setup in the Display menu

Now complete the dialog which appears. Finally, click OK.

CorelDRAW provides several aids which allow you to align objects you create automatically and precisely (this is also useful when you resize objects). One of the foremost of these is grids.

Grids consist of a uniform arrangement of points to which objects can be 'snapped' i.e. aligned automatically.

Setting up a grid

Press Ctrl+J. Then carry out the following steps:

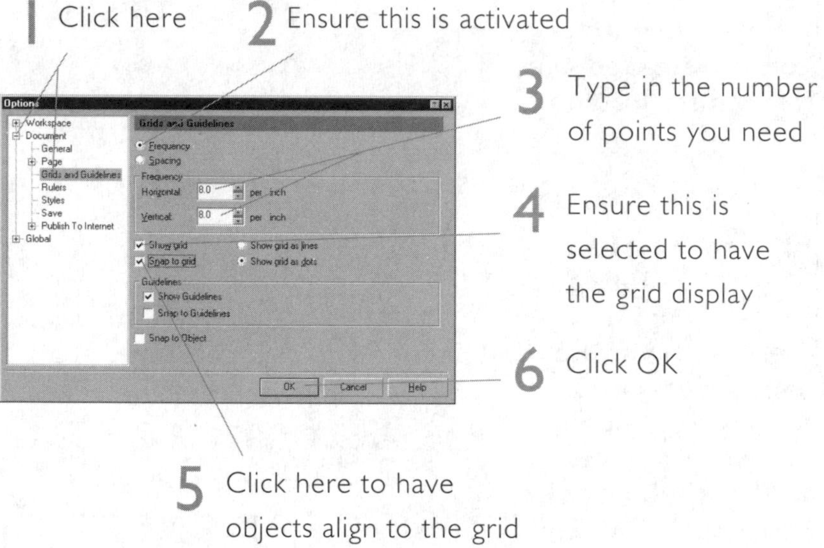

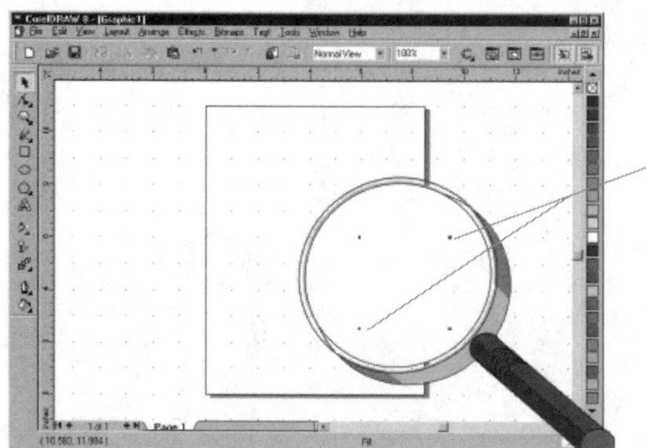

Specifying grid structure New in version 8

Users of CorelDRAW 8 can specify an additional grid parameter: they can opt to have grids display as:

— dots

— lines

By default, as we saw on page 34, grids display as dots. However, it's sometimes useful to have grids defined as lines, so that they resemble graph paper.

A grid displayed as dots

When grids are displayed as lines, the intersections represent grid dots.

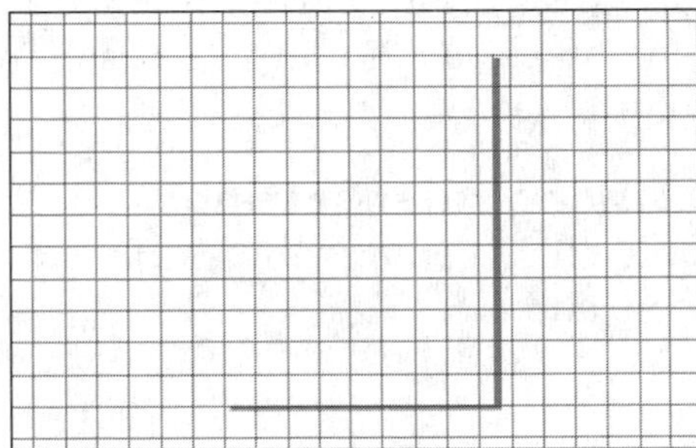

A grid displayed as lines

Customising grid format

Double-click a ruler. On the left of the Options dialog, click Grids and Guidelines. Click one of the following:

- Show grid as lines
- Show grid as dots

Finally, click OK.

Using the ruler

Users of version 4 onwards can move rulers onto the page. To do this, move the mouse pointer over a ruler. Hold down Shift; left-click and drag it to a new location.

Rulers are another aid to aligning objects. Both horizontal and vertical rulers are flexible, on-screen calibrations which you can use to size and position drawing components.

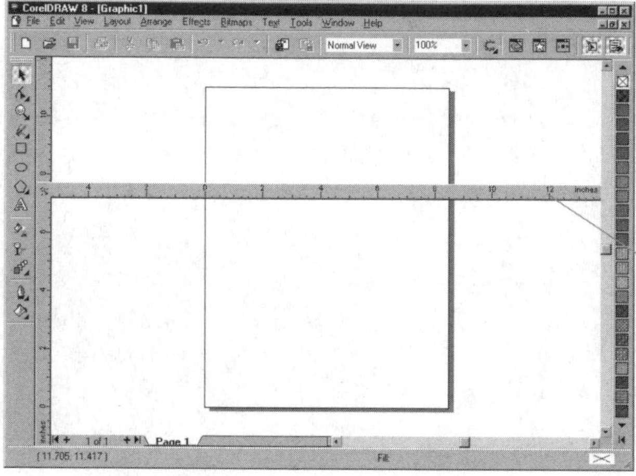

Repositioned ruler (see the HANDY TIP)

Users of versions 3 and 4 should click Show Rulers in the Display menu.

Users of versions 6 and 7 should ignore step 1. Instead, complete the Grid & Ruler Setup dialog in line with steps 2-4.

Displaying the rulers

If the rulers aren't currently displaying, pull down the View menu and choose Rulers. (But see the higher REMEMBER tip on the left).

Specifying ruler settings

Double-click a ruler. Now perform the following steps, as appropriate:

In versions before 6, the dialog which launches *appears* to relate only to grids. However, the Grid Frequency and Grid Origin fields implement ruler settings, as well.

1 Click here

2 (Optional) Click the arrows and choose new ruler units

3 (Optional) Enter new values here to reset the ruler origin point

4 Click here

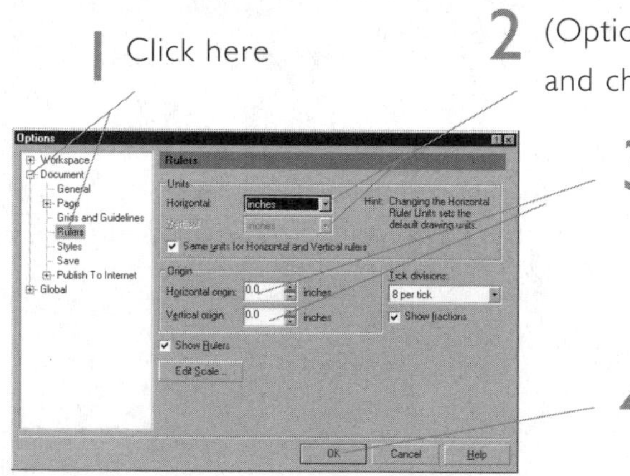

Using guidelines

Guidelines are saved with the document which contains them.

Whereas grids can be used to position all the objects within a particular drawing, you use guidelines to position *individual* objects. Guidelines are movable, non-printing lines on screen. You can create as many guidelines as you need.

Creating a horizontal guideline

Move the mouse pointer over the horizontal ruler. Click and hold down the left mouse button. Drag onto the page. Release the button when the guideline is correctly positioned.

Creating a vertical guideline

Move the mouse pointer over the vertical ruler. Click and hold down the left mouse button. Drag onto the page. Release the button when the guideline is correctly positioned.

To make objects (when created or repositioned) align to guidelines, users of versions 5-8 should pull down the Layout menu and click Snap To Guidelines.

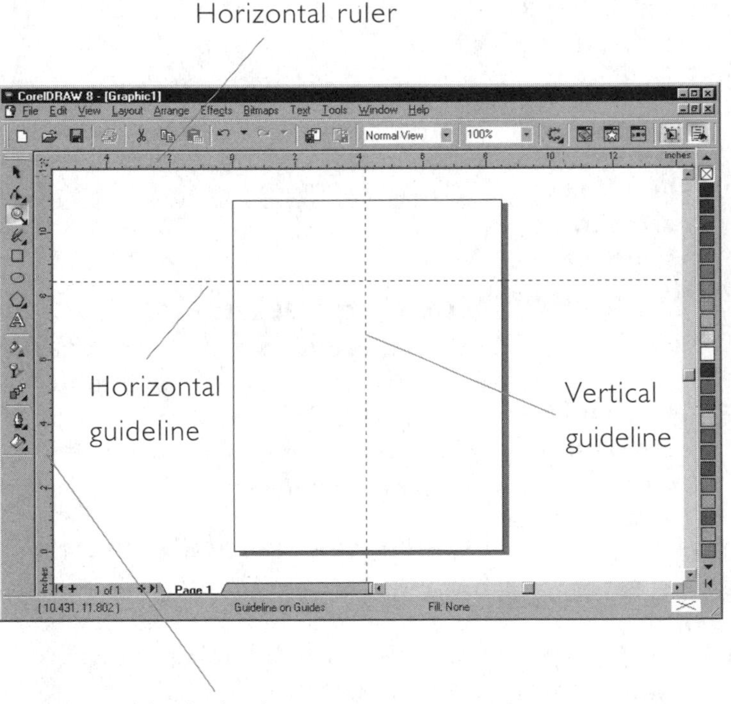

Users of version 3 should click Snap to Guidelines in the Display menu, instead.

Version 4 users should click Snap To, Guidelines in the Layout menu.

Creating a slanting guideline New in version 6

A feature which is currently lacking in just about any other program is the ability to define *sloping* guidelines. These are useful for positioning objects whose shape is nonstandard.

Version 6 and 7 users don't need to click guidelines twice to reveal the handles.

To create a slanted guideline, first create a vertical or horizontal guideline (see 'Creating a horizontal guideline' and 'Creating a vertical guideline', on page 37). Then move the mouse pointer over the guideline and click twice. Drag one of the guideline handles until the angle is correct. Then release the mouse button.

Remember that once you've slanted a guideline, you can only convert it back again if you're using version 7 or 8.

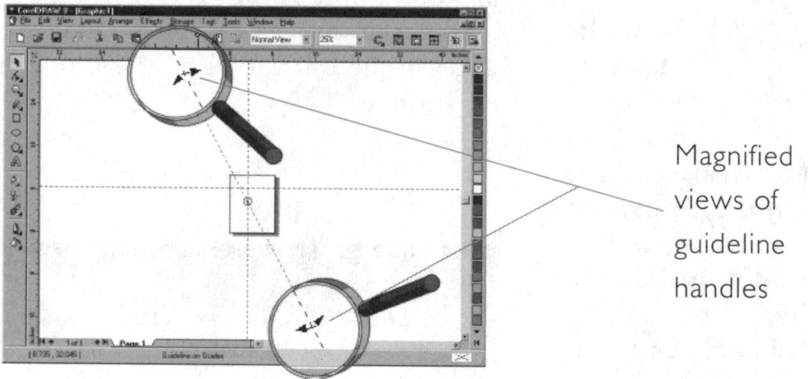

Magnified views of guideline handles

Guideline handles are shown slightly differently in earlier versions.

Moving guidelines

You can easily reposition guidelines you've already created. To do this, move the mouse pointer over the guideline. Click and hold down the left mouse button; drag the guideline to its new location. Release the mouse button to confirm the move.

To delete a *slanting* guideline, double-click it. In the Guidelines Setup dialog, click the Slanted tab. Select the guideline in the box and click Delete. Click OK.

Deleting horizontal/vertical guidelines

Place the mouse pointer over the guideline you want to remove. Click and hold down the left mouse button; drag the guideline back to the horizontal or vertical ruler (it doesn't matter which). Release the mouse button to confirm the deletion.

Advanced guidelines New in version 8

In version 8 of CorelDRAW, guidelines are themselves objects. This means that you can:

- select them
- deselect them
- print them

Selected guidelines are red, unselected guidelines blue.

Selecting guidelines

To select a guideline, ensure the Pick tool is active and then simply click it. To select more than one guideline, hold down one Shift key as you click them.

Deselecting guidelines

With the Pick tool selected, click away from the guideline(s).

Printing guidelines

By default, guidelines do not print. However, you can rectify this if you want.

To close the Object Manager, click this button:

in the top right-hand corner.

Pull down the Layout menu and click Object Manager. Carry out the following steps:

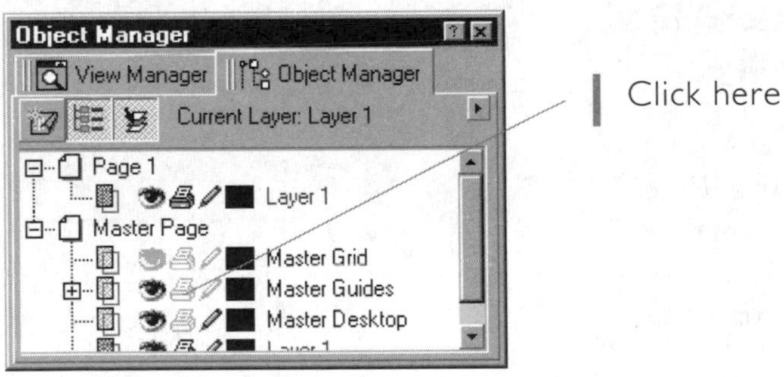

Click here

When the print icon looks like this:

printing is enabled.

Now begin printing in the normal way.

Snapping to objects

There is a snap hierarchy: Snap To Objects takes precedence over Snap To Grid or Snap To Guidelines.

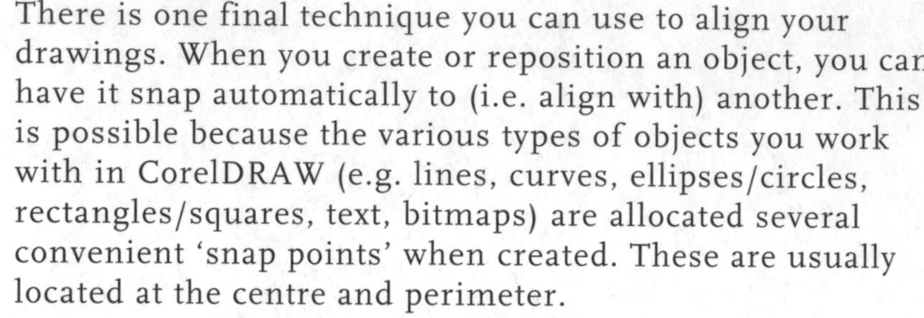

There is one final technique you can use to align your drawings. When you create or reposition an object, you can have it snap automatically to (i.e. align with) another. This is possible because the various types of objects you work with in CorelDRAW (e.g. lines, curves, ellipses/circles, rectangles/squares, text, bitmaps) are allocated several convenient 'snap points' when created. These are usually located at the centre and perimeter.

Users of version 3 should click Snap to Objects in the Display menu, instead.

Version 4 users should click Snap To, Objects in the Layout menu.

Turning on Snap to Objects

To have objects you create or change snap to existing objects, pull down the Layout menu and click Snap To Objects.

Viewing snap points New in version 6

To see an object's snap points, first make sure Snap to Objects is enabled. Then launch the Curve flyout (see page 28 for how to do this) and do the following:

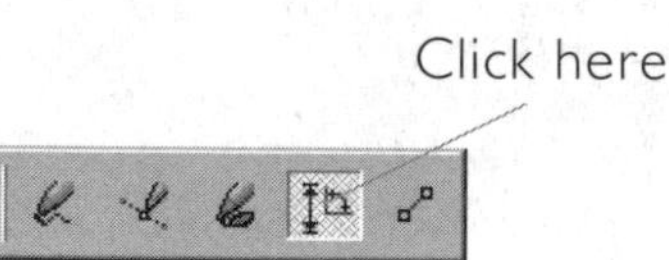

In version 6, click the following tool:

within the Toolbox. Use any tool in the resultant flyout to reveal snap points.

Now move the mouse pointer over the object. CorelDRAW reveals snap points when the pointer encounters them.

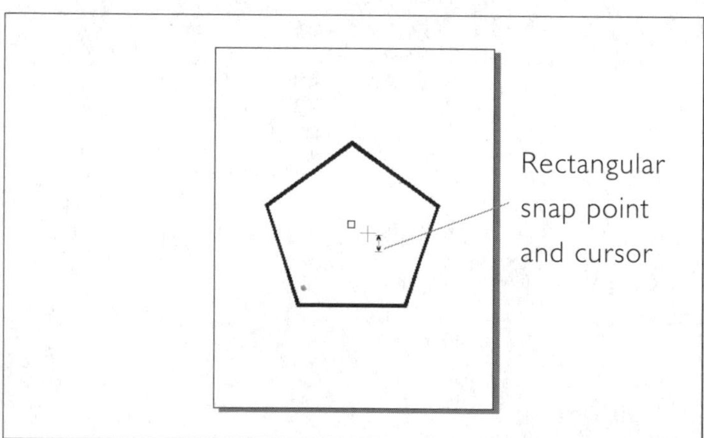

Activating the Snap To Objects feature has no effect on the alignment of *existing* objects.

Chapter Three

Advanced Drawing

This chapter shows you how to create complex Bezier curves and variable-sided polygons. We'll also discuss ways to manipulate objects, create specialised lines and work with nodes.

Covers

Working with Bezier curves

In Chapter 2, we looked at how to create Bezier lines. However, CorelDRAW also lets you create Bezier curves. These are much more useful (and easier to draw) than freehand curves. When you create Bezier curves, you click to define the start and end points, and drag to define the extent of the curve; CorelDRAW does the rest.

Creating a Bezier curve

First, carry out the following actions:

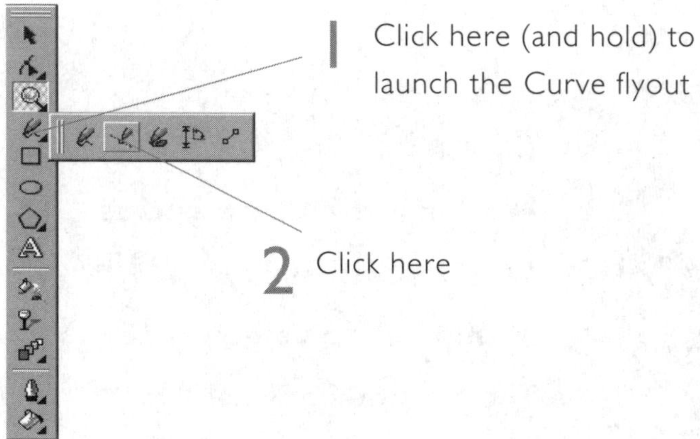

Versions 3 and 4 have a joint Freehand/ Bezier tool:

Follow steps 1 and 2 to select the Bezier component. To use it, follow the relevant instructions on the right and on page 43.

Then click in your drawing where you want the curve to start. Hold down the mouse button and drag. CorelDRAW creates a central node and two control points.

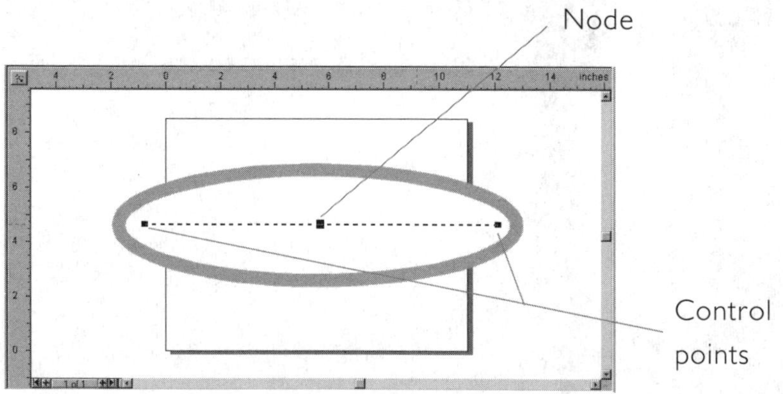

Magnified view of first stage

Bear in mind the following:

- The depth of the curve is regulated by the distance between the control points and the node.
- The slope of the curve is regulated by the control point angle.

Holding down one Ctrl key as you define Bezier curves constrains them to 15° increments.

Release the mouse button. Now click where you want the curve to end, and drag. The result will look something like this:

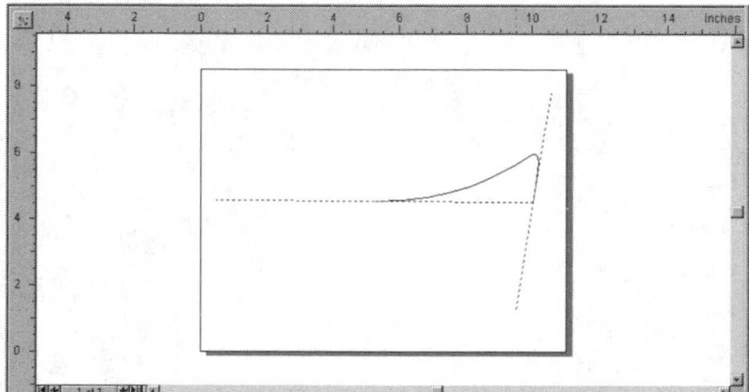

Release the mouse button. Repeat this procedure if you want to create more curves. Press the Spacebar twice when you've finished defining the curve. Or click another tool in the Toolbox.

The next illustration shows our completed curve.

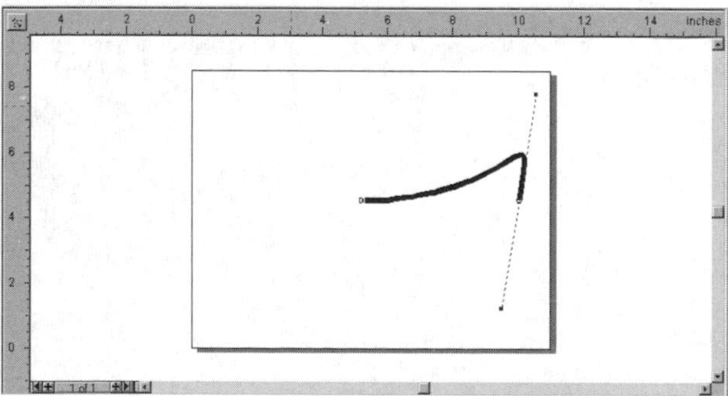

Working with polygons New in version 6

CorelDRAW lets you create polygons quickly and very easily. By default, CorelDRAW creates 5-sided polygons; however, you can also specify how many sides the polygon should have. Additionally, you can create stars and spirals.

Holding down one Ctrl key as you define polygons, stars or spirals stops them from being stretched out of shape.

Holding down one Shift key as you define polygons, stars or spirals creates them from the centre outwards.

In versions 6 and 7, the Options dialog is somewhat different.

Creating a pentagon

Refer to the Toolbox and carry out steps 1 and 3 below:

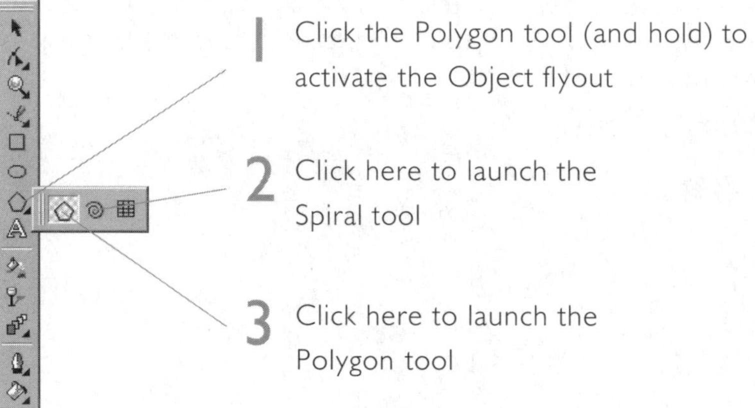

Place the cursor where you want one corner of the pentagon to appear. Hold down the left mouse button and drag to define it. Release the button when you've finished.

Creating a polygon with more or fewer than 5 sides

Follow steps 1 and 3 above. However, before you start to draw the polygon, double-click the Polygon tool in the Toolbox. Then do the following:

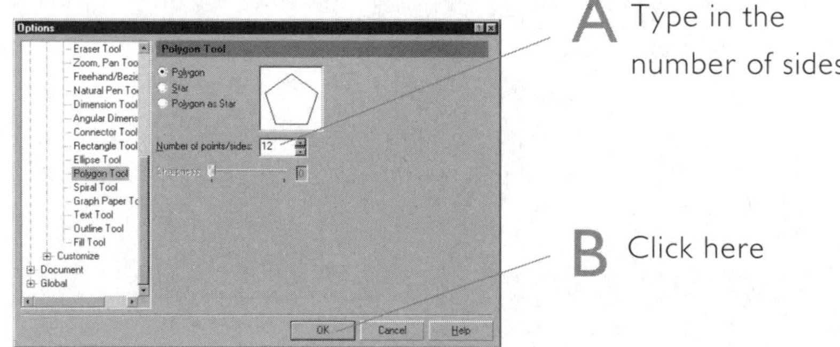

Finally, place the cursor where you want one corner of the polygon to appear. Hold down the left mouse button and drag to define it. Release the button when finished.

By default, DRAW creates spirals with 4 revolutions. If you want more or fewer, double-click the Spiral tool:

in the Toolbox *after* you've carried out steps 1 and 2 on page 44. In the Options dialog, type a revised number in the Number of revolutions field. Click OK. Now define the spiral.

Creating a star

Follow steps 1 and 3 on page 44. However, before you begin to create the star, double-click the Polygon tool in the Toolbox. Then do the following:

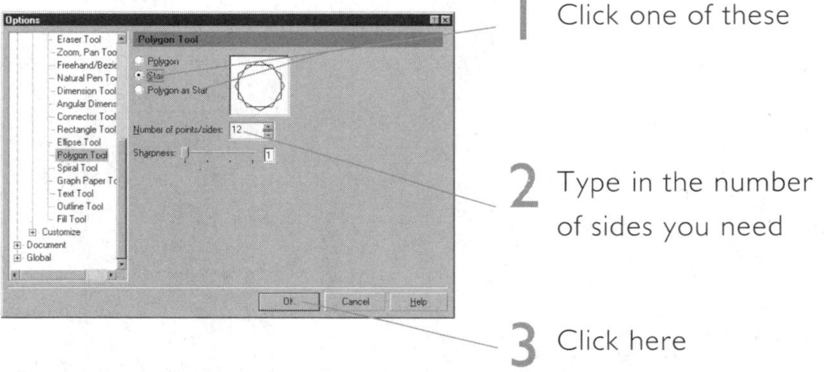

1 Click one of these

2 Type in the number of sides you need

3 Click here

Creating a spiral

Carry out steps 1 and 2 on page 44. (However, if you want your spiral to have more or fewer than four revolutions, see the Remember tip on the left before creating it.)

If you're using versions 7 and 8, you can create logarithmic spirals. Launch the Options dialog (see the tip above); choose Logarithmic. Click OK. Finally, create the spiral in the normal way.

Place the cursor where you want the spiral to start. Hold down the left mouse button and drag to define it. Release the button when you've finished.

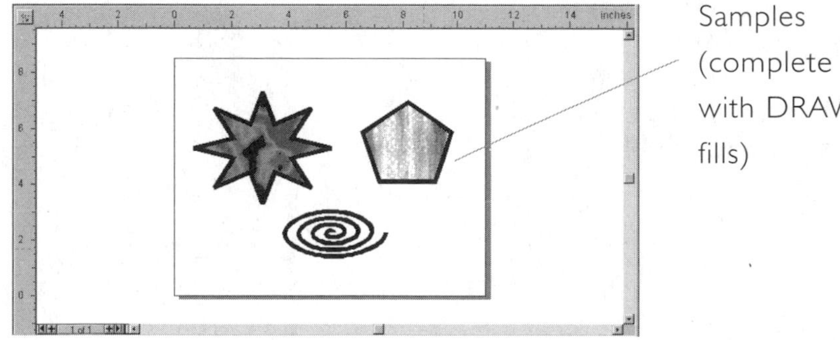

Samples (complete with DRAW fills)

Manipulating objects

Once you've created drawing objects, CorelDRAW lets you amend them in a variety of ways. We've already discussed resizing. However, you can also skew and rotate them. Skewing distorts objects horizontally or vertically, while rotation moves them around their centre point.

Skewing an object

Double-click the outline of the object you want to skew. CorelDRAW surrounds it with two-way arrows.

Magnified view of rotation handle

Magnified view of skew handle

If you right-click *before* you release the left mouse button, DRAW creates a skewed copy of the object, and leaves the original intact.

Move the mouse pointer over one of the side arrows. Click and hold down the left mouse button; drag to skew the object. Release the mouse button.

To constrain skew or rotation to 15° increments, hold down one Ctrl key as you drag.

The same image, skewed

Rotating an object

Double-click the outline of the object you want to rotate. Move the mouse pointer over one of the corner arrows (see the illustration on page 46). Click and hold down the left mouse button; drag with a circular movement to rotate the object. Release the mouse button.

If you right-click *before* you release the left mouse button, DRAW creates a rotated copy of the object, and leaves the original intact.

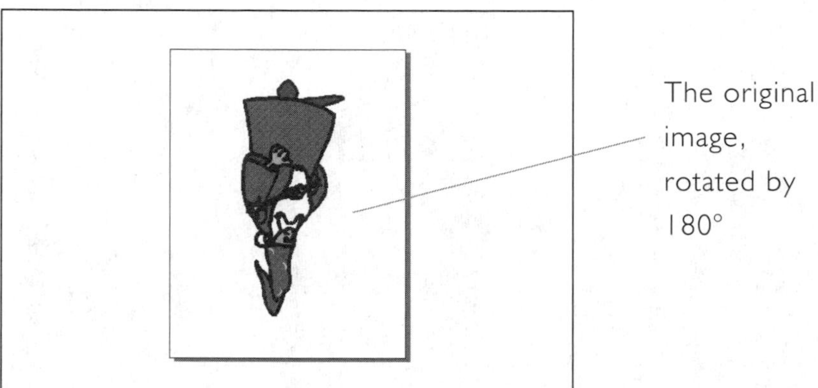

The original image, rotated by 180°

Rotation moves objects around a specific point, normally in the centre of the object. However, if you want you can move this point prior to rotation (this varies the effect of rotation dramatically). Simply double-click the object to reveal the rotation handles. Then position the mouse pointer over the rotation point and drag it to a new location.

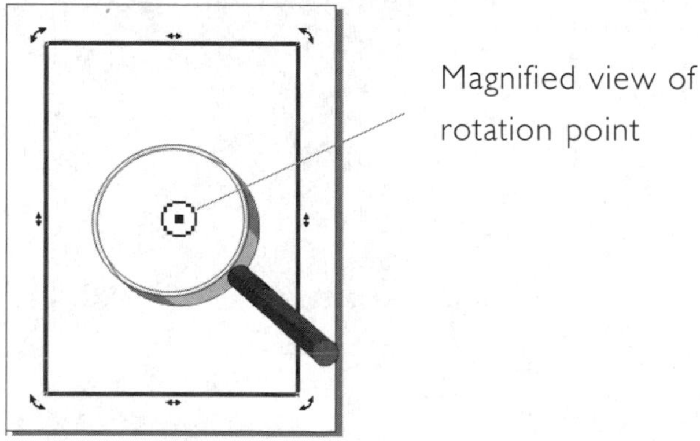

Magnified view of rotation point

Rotate the object in the way we've just discussed.

The Natural Pen tool New in version 5

With CorelDRAW, you can create curves whose thickness varies from end to end.

Versions 5 and 6 called these curves PowerLines.

Creating variable-thickness curves in versions 7 and 8

In the Toolbox, do the following:

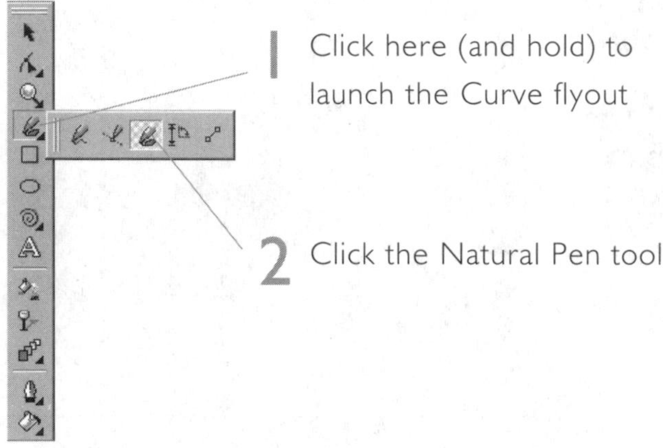

Now double-click the Natural Pen tool *in the Toolbox*. Carry out the following steps:

Re. step 1 – choose Presets (pre-defined PowerLines) if you want a shortcut approach. If you do, carry out the following in step 2:

Click here; choose a preset in the list

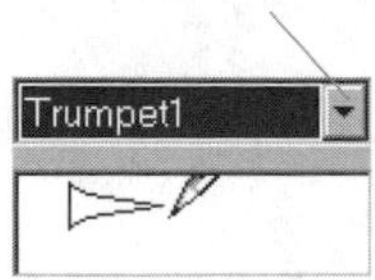

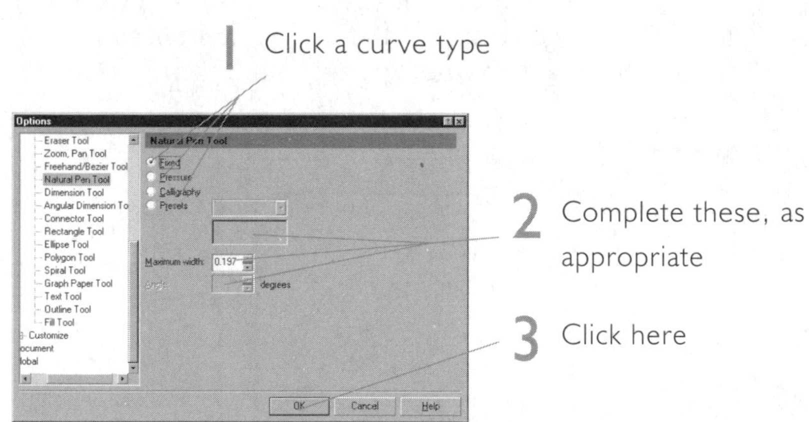

Now perform the following operations:

A. Place the mouse pointer where you want your curve to start.

B. Hold down the left mouse button.

C. Drag out the curve

D. Release the mouse button when you've finished.

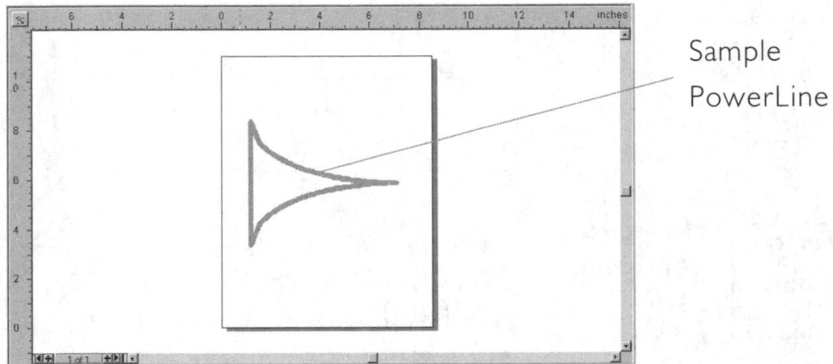

Creating variable-thickness curves in versions 5 and 6

Pull down the Effects menu and click PowerLine. Now do the following:

After step 4, activate the Freehand tool:

in the Toolbox. Now follow steps A-D above.

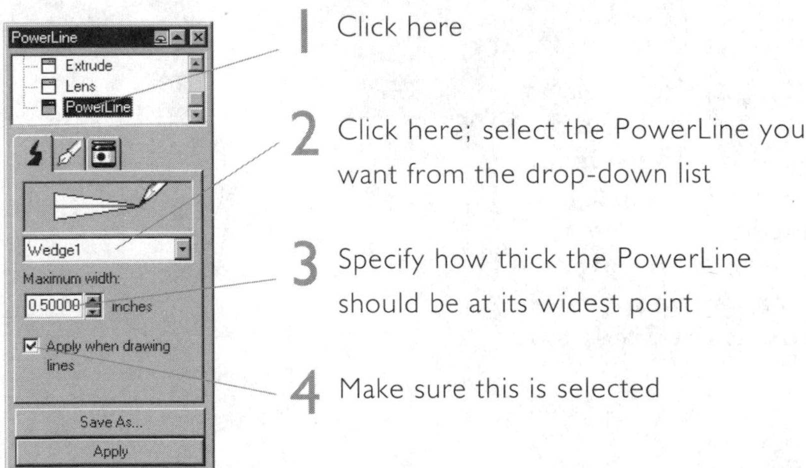

Working with nodes

So far, we've looked at techniques which you can use to define or edit *whole* lines or curves. However, CorelDRAW also lets you amend line and curve sections. You can do this because, when you create objects, CorelDRAW inserts 'nodes' automatically. Look at the following Bezier curve:

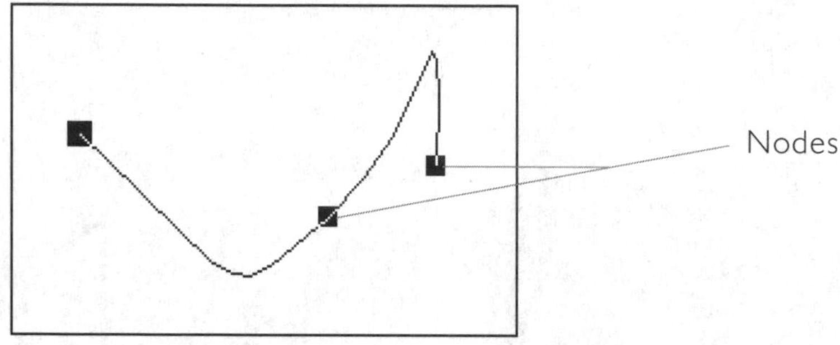

However, version 8 users can edit nodes without using the Shape tool **– see pages 55 and 56.**

CorelDRAW inserts nodes whenever a curve changes direction (however imperceptibly). Although some nodes are visible when an object is selected with the Pick tool, to work with nodes you need to activate the Shape tool. You can drag nodes to reshape curves. You can also add your own nodes or delete existing ones.

Reshaping lines or curves

First, do the following in the Toolbox:

In versions 3,4 and 5, there is no Shape flyout.

Instead, simply click the Shape tool icon in the Toolbox.

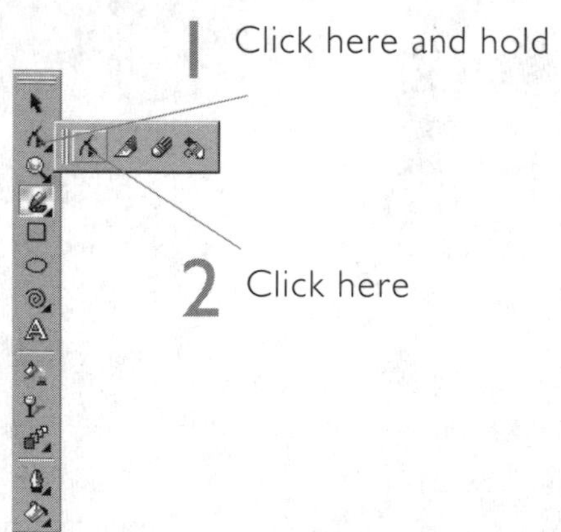

The cursor changes to a black triangle. Move it over the node which you want to move. Left-click and drag the node. When you release the mouse button, the curve is redefined.

If the existing nodes aren't in the right place, or if there aren't enough, you can create your own – see page 52.

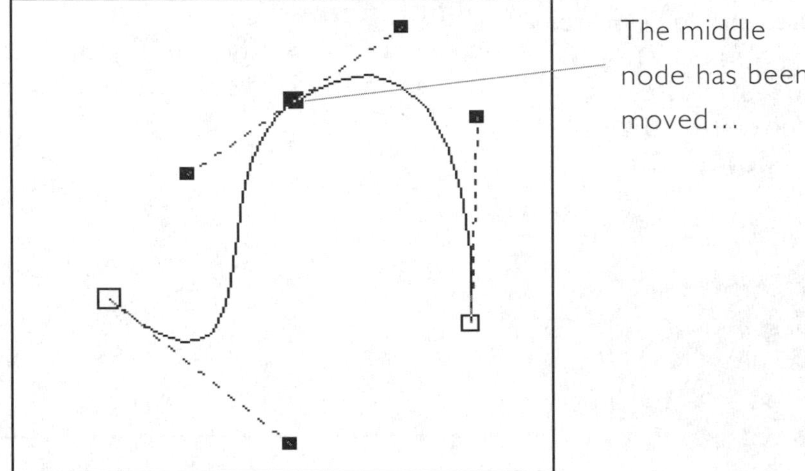

The middle node has been moved...

Another method

Another way to reshape curves is to use the Shape tool to drag the curve itself. This is useful, though less so than working with nodes.

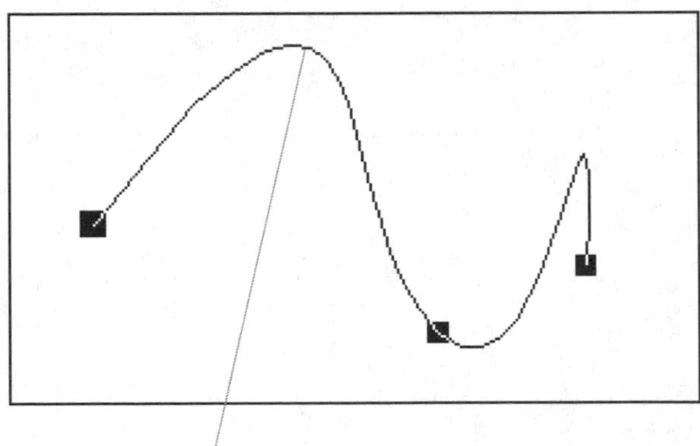

Here, the curve itself has been dragged to a new location

Adding and deleting nodes

Versions 3-7 require a different procedure. Double-clicking a line/curve produces a special dialog (it varies slightly according to the version):

A Click here

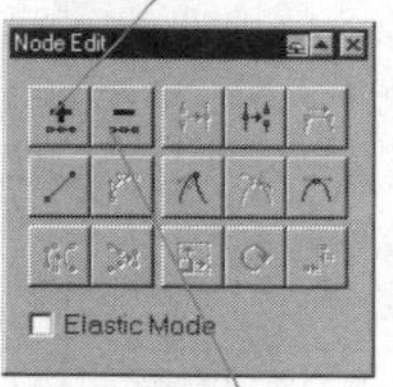

B Click here

Carry out step A to add a node, step B to delete one. (In version 3, though, click Add or Delete respectively).

If you can't reshape a curve in the way you want by using the existing nodes, or by simply dragging directly on the curve itself, you need to add one or more nodes. Fortunately, this is easy to do. You can also delete nodes.

Adding a node

Make sure the Shape tool is activated. Double-click the location in the curve where you want the new node added.

Deleting a node

Make sure the Shape tool is activated. Double-click the node you want to remove.

The original curve. A new node has been added...

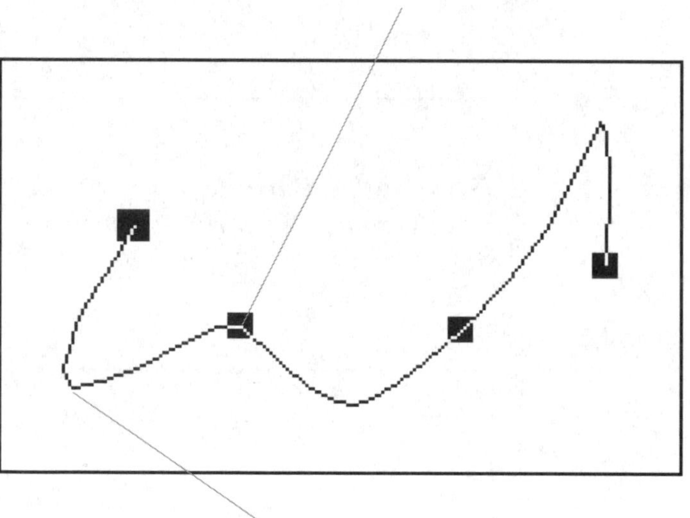

...and the curve has been redefined

You can use the Shape tool to 'marquee' select multiple nodes. (See page 24 for an explanation of marquee selection).

Rotating/skewing nodes New in version 6

Versions 6 and 7 require a different procedure.

Double-clicking a line/curve produces a special dialog (it varies slightly according to the version):

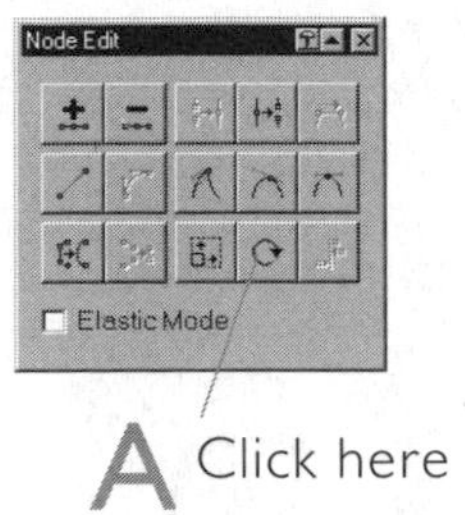

Carry out step A above to launch rotation/skew handles.

A useful feature is the ability to rotate or skew curve nodes. This can produce some unique effects.

Rotating/skewing a node

Make sure the Shape tool is activated. Select the nodes along the curve you want to skew. In the Property Bar, do the following (if the Property Bar isn't currently on-screen, pull down the View menu and click Property Bar):

CorelDRAW surrounds the curve with rotation/skew handles:

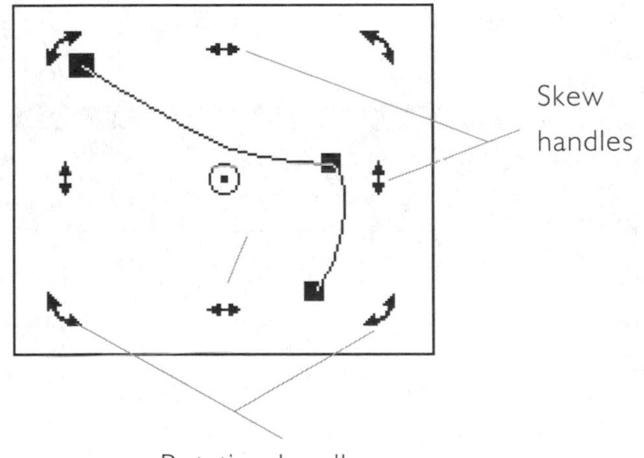

For how to use rotation/skew handles, see pages 46 and 47.

Other node tips

You can carry out the actions listed on the right simply by moving the Shape tool cursor over a node, double-clicking and dragging.

However, if you want to reshape squares/rectangles and circles/ellipses in more depth, you have to convert them to curves first. To do this, select the object(s), then press Ctrl+Q (Ctrl+V in version 3). Finally, use any of the techniques discussed on pages 50-53 to amend the objects' nodes.

Versions 3-7 do not use the Property bar. Instead, double-clicking a line/curve with the Shape tool produces the Node Edit dialog.

Simply click the appropriate icon.

CorelDRAW's nodes are a complex subject which can only be covered briefly here. However, the following tips should be helpful when allied to practice.

Reshaping rectangles and circles

Objects created with the use of the Freehand and Bezier tools can be reshaped using the techniques discussed on pages 50-53. However, the extent to which you can amend some objects with the Shape tool is restricted:

squares/rectangles	the corners can be rounded
circles/ellipses	they can be turned into arcs and wedges

Other actions

The Property Bar (when the Shape tool is active) can be used to carry out some fairly intricate node operations. The next illustration shows some of these:

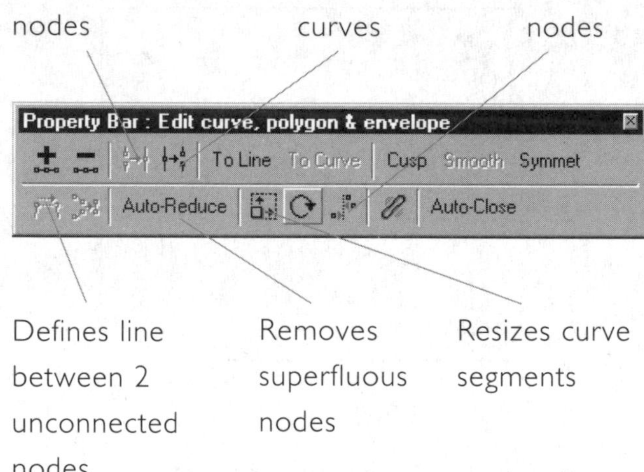

The best way to become familiar with these is to try them out.

Node editing shortcuts New in version 8

Because node editing is such an intrinsic part of work with CorelDRAW, version 8 now enables users to:

- enter the node-editing state from within any creation tool (Rectangle, Ellipse, Polygon etc.)
- enter the node-editing state directly from within the Pick tool

Using either of these methods (described below and overleaf) saves time and effort: it is no longer necessary to activate the Shape tool directly.

1. Entering node-edit mode from any creation tool

Do the following in the Standard toolbar (if this toolbar isn't currently on-screen, pull down the View menu and click Toolbars. In the Toolbars section of the Options dialog, click Standard. Click OK):

This button in the Standard toolbar is a toggle: clicking it successively alternately activates and deactivates node-edit mode.

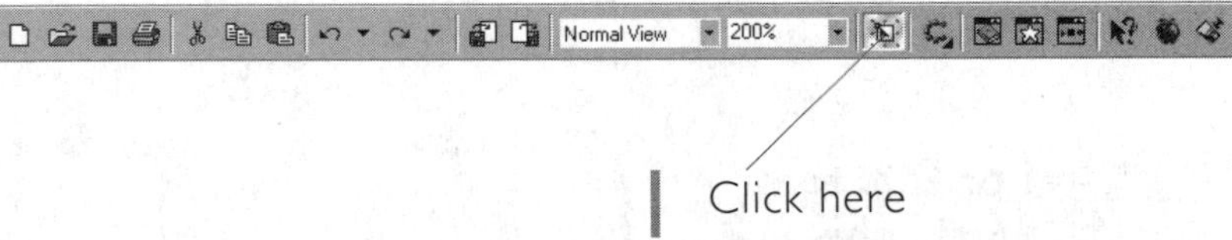

2. Entering node-edit mode via the Pick tool

Ensure the Pick tool is active, then double-click any line or curve.

Double-clicking a line or curve selects the object and activates the Shape tool.

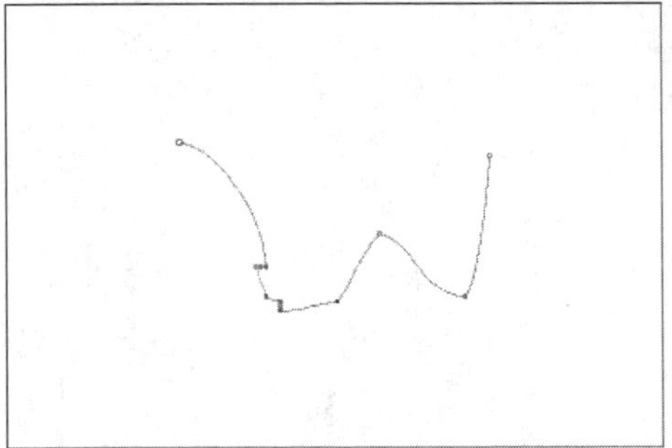

The result of double-clicking a curve: the nodes are now visible

Shortcut 2. on page 55 may appear to be less useful than shortcut 1.

However, since the Pick tool is the most used tool, the ability to enter node edit mode simply by double-clicking a line/curve (and omitting the requirement to activate the Shape tool directly) is useful.

For this to work, the Enable Node Tracking toggle in the Standard toolbar must be active – follow step 1 on page 55 if it isn't.

Node-edit mode in action

The examples below illustrate the advantages of using shortcut 1. described on page 55.

In the first illustration, two Bezier lines have just been created.

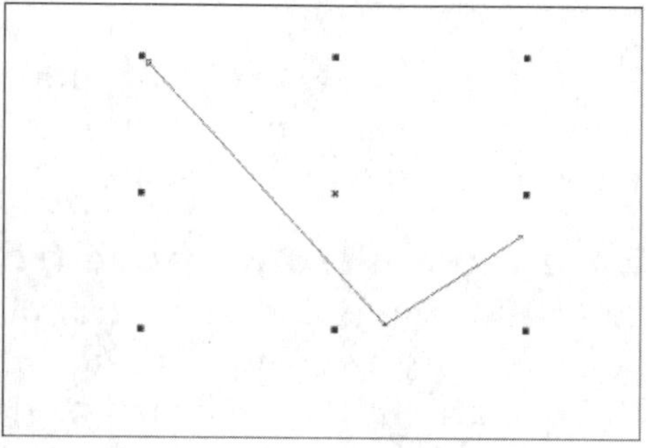

Normally, if you needed to reshape the lines, the normal procedure would be to:

1. click the Shape tool in the Toolbox
2. reposition the mouse pointer over the relevant node prior to redefining the line

However, there is now no need to undertake step 1. Instead, simply follow step 2. This is the result:

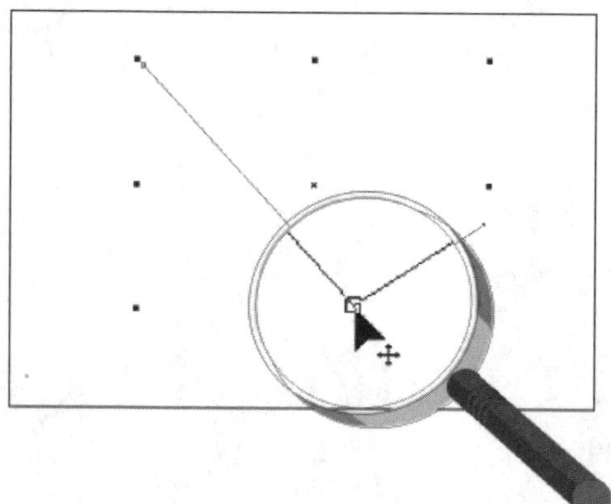

The mouse pointer automatically changes into the node-editing tool

Chapter Four

Basic Text Work

In this chapter, you'll learn how to create artistic and paragraph text. You'll also learn how to change basic text formatting (typefaces, type sizes, alignment, spacing and shift/rotation) with and without the use of CorelDRAW's Text editor. Version 8 users will also discover how to use various text shortcuts.

Covers

The Text tool

Versions before 7 have two separate text tools:

- The Paragraph Text tool
- The Artistic Text tool

Although these have been incorporated into an overall Text tool in versions 7 and 8, artistic and paragraph text still work in the same way.

Artistic text is often referred to as a text 'string', and paragraph text as a text 'frame'.

When you use the Text tool in versions 7 and 8, CorelDRAW automatically detects the underlying text type.

CorelDRAW lets you work with text – a vital component of design work – with the Text tool. You can use the Text tool to enter two kinds of text:

Artistic text

Artistic text is designed to handle relatively short amounts of text (up to 32,000 characters in version 8). It's the most artistically versatile, and the quickest to use because it's more intuitive: if you want, you can simply click where you need the text to be inserted and start typing straight away.

Use artistic text for single lines of text (e.g. titles or headings), or if you want to apply any of CorelDRAW's special effects (e.g. drop shadow) to text.

Paragraph text

Paragraph text, on the other hand, adopts a more structured approach: text is created in frames. These allow features such as columns, drop caps and tabs/indents which are missing in artistic text.

Use paragraph text for large, formalised blocks of text.

Features in common...

Whichever text type you use, certain features are held in common. For instance, you can:

- amend the typeface and type size
- amend the style (bold, italic etc.) and alignment
- adjust the spacing (between lines, words and characters)
- carry out kerning (reposition characters within words)
- carry out a spell- and grammar-check
- apply formatting to individual characters within words

Creating artistic text

Creating artistic text is easy from the Toolbox. First carry out the following action:

In versions before 7, the procedure is different: you have to select the Artistic Text tool.

Carry out step 1 on the right. Then click this button:

in the flyout which launches.

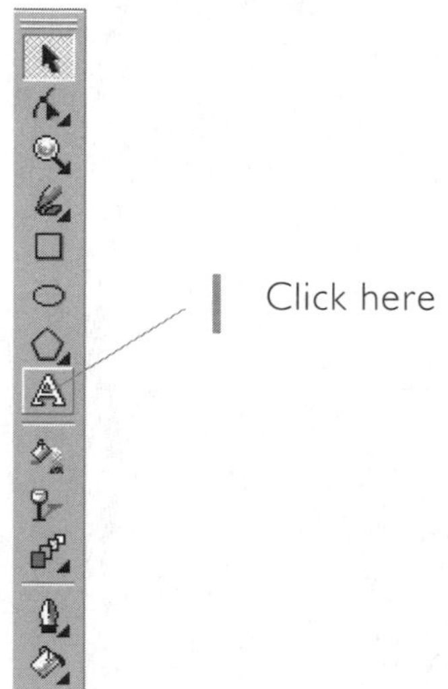

Click here

Now left-click in your document where you want the text to appear and start typing. When you need a new line, press Enter. When you've finished typing in text, click the Pick tool in the Toolbox.

When you create text in this way, CorelDRAW applies default formatting characteristics (for instance, a standard typeface).

You can easily change these later.

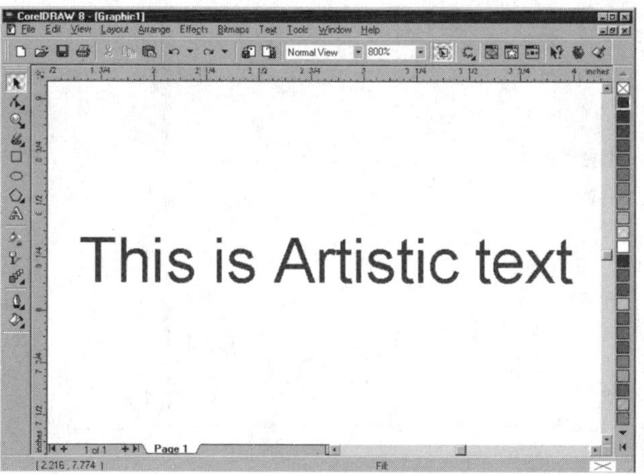

A zoomed view of artistic text

Creating paragraph text

In versions 4-6, the procedure is different: you have to select the Paragraph Text tool.

Carry out step 1 on the right. Then click this button:

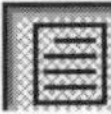

in the flyout which launches.

In version 3 (as in 8), there is no separate Paragraph Text tool. Instead, follow step 1. Click this button:

in the Text flyout. Now carry out the procedures on the right.

Don't press Enter to start a new line. Only press Enter if you want to start a new paragraph.

Creating paragraph text is almost as easy as artistic text. First turn to the Toolbox and do the following:

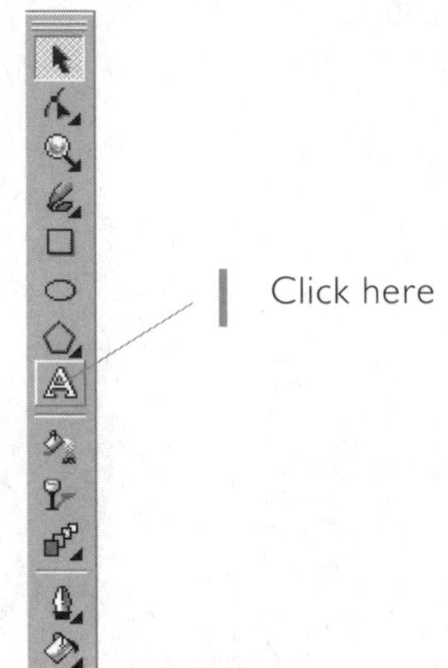

Now left-click in your document where you want the text to appear. Hold down the mouse button and drag out a frame. Release the button.

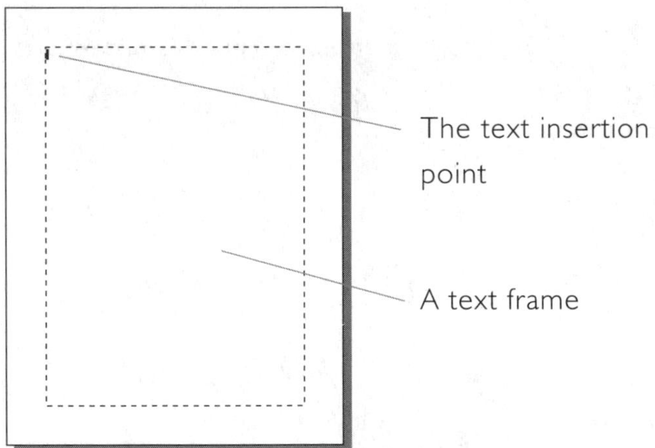

Start typing straight away. When you've finished typing in text, click the Pick tool in the Toolbox.

Changing the typeface

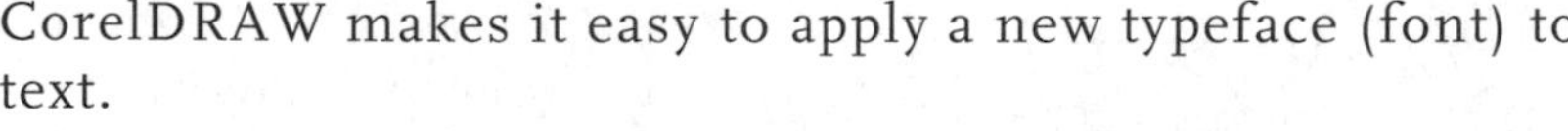

CorelDRAW makes it easy to apply a new typeface (font) to text.

REMEMBER

Users of versions 3-6 should refer to pages 59 and 60 for how to activate the Text tool.

First, activate the Text tool. Use standard Windows techniques to select the text whose formatting you want to amend (with both artistic and paragraph text, you can select individual characters, words or whole paragraphs).

Next, pull down the Text menu and choose Format Text. Follow the steps below.

REMEMBER

Users of versions 3-6 should choose Character in the Text menu. The dialog which launches is rather different (e.g. there are no individual tabs, so step 1 is not required).

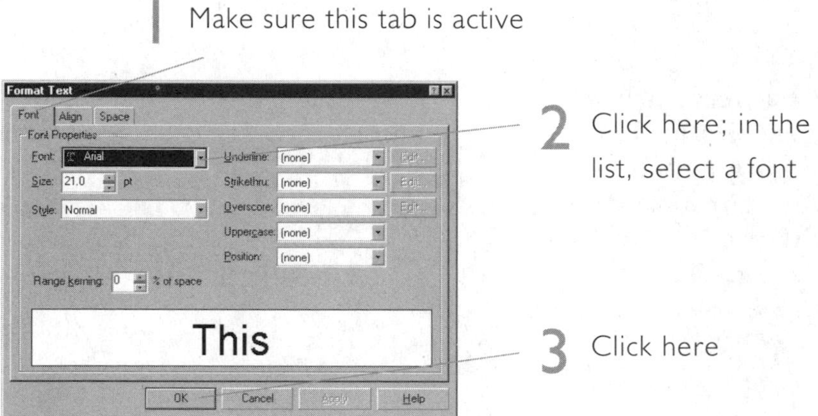

REMEMBER

By default, a standard typeface is imposed on text (depending on the fonts installed on your system).

Using the Text toolbar Versions 6-8 only

Many of the text operations described in this chapter can be undertaken with the use of the Text toolbar.

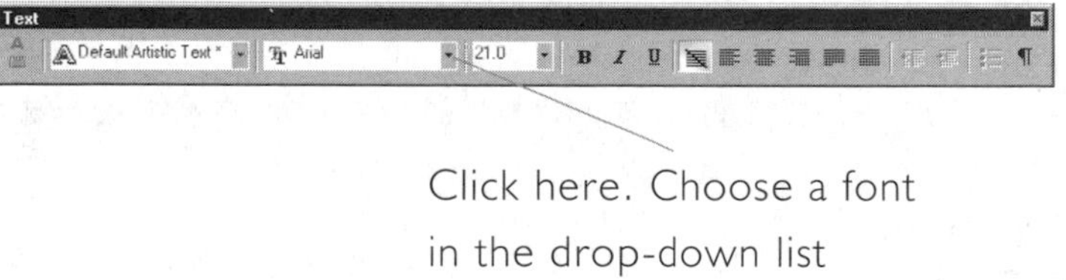

If you're unsure about a toolbar function, move the mouse pointer over it; a HELP bubble launches – e.g.:

Non-printing Characters

Changing the type size

Users of versions 3-6 should refer to pages 59 and 60 for how to activate the Text tool.

Users of versions 3-6 should choose Character in the Text menu. The dialog which launches is rather different (e.g. there are no individual tabs, so step 1 is not required).

Users of versions 7 and 8 can increase paragraph text size in a unique way.

Activate the Pick tool in the Toolbox. Click the paragraph text frame. Move the mouse pointer over a corner handle. Hold down Alt and drag in or out; the frame *and* the text are resized.

Printed text is usually measured in points. When you want to make text bigger or smaller, you change the point size. You can do this in increments of 0.001 pt. (except for versions 3-5, where the maximum increment is 0.1 pt.).

First, activate the Text tool. Use standard Windows techniques to select the text whose formatting you want to amend (with both artistic and paragraph text, you can select individual characters, words or whole paragraphs).

Next, pull down the Text menu and choose Format Text. Follow the steps below.

1 Make sure this tab is active

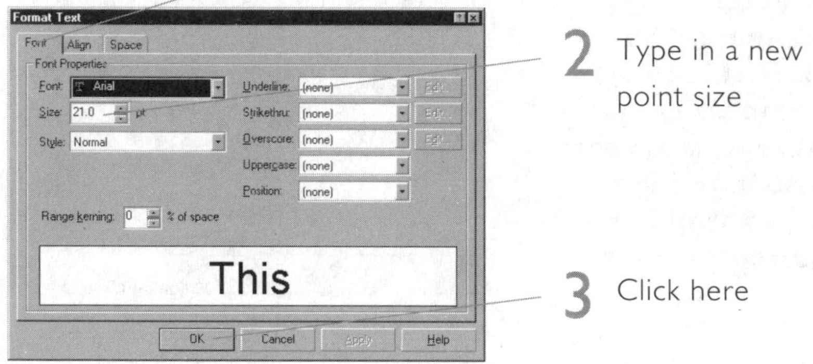

2 Type in a new point size

3 Click here

Using the Text toolbar Versions 6-8 only

You can also alter point sizes with the use of the Text toolbar. Do the following:

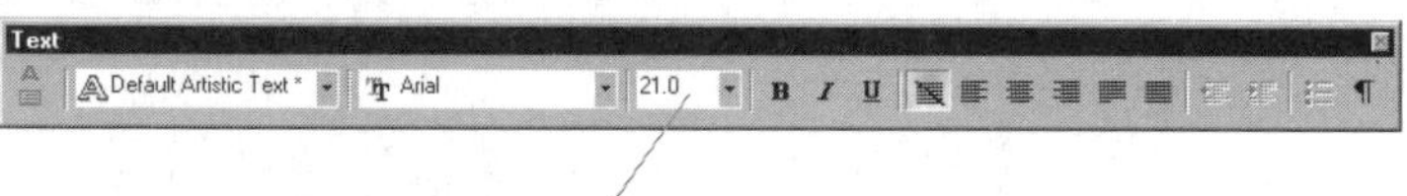

Type in the new point size here

Press Enter to implement the change.

Applying text effects

Users of versions 3-6 should refer to pages 59 and 60 for how to activate the Text tool.

Users of versions 3-6 should choose Character in the Text menu. The dialog which launches is rather different (e.g. step 1 is not required).

In version 7, the Format Text dialog is slightly different. For example, the subscript/superscript and small caps/all caps functions are achieved by clicking buttons.

Re step 2 – some fonts don't support italicisation and/or emboldening.

You can apply a variety of additional effects in CorelDRAW. You can:

- **embolden**, *italicise*, underline or ~~strikethru~~ ('strikeout' in versions before 8) text
- make text $_{\text{subscript}}$ or ^{superscript}
- change text to ALL CAPS or SMALL CAPS

First, activate the Text tool. Use standard Windows techniques to select the text whose formatting you want to amend (with both artistic and paragraph text, you can select individual characters, words or whole paragraphs).

Next, pull down the Text menu and choose Format Text. Follow the relevant steps below.

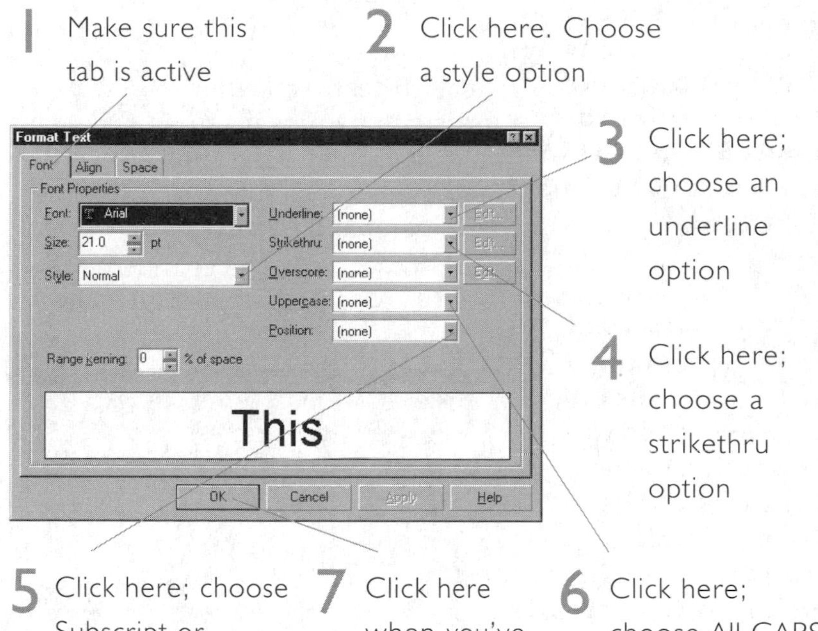

The above is the version of the Format Text dialog which launches over paragraph (as opposed to artistic) text.

Aligning text

Version 7 and 8 users can also set vertical alignment for paragraph text.

Select the text. Type Ctrl+T. Click the Frames and Columns tab. Click an option in the Vertical justification field. Click OK.

Users of versions 3-6 should refer to pages 59 and 60 for how to activate the Text tool.

Users of versions 3-6 should choose Character in the Text menu. The dialog which launches is rather different (e.g. step 1 is not required).

CorelDRAW lets you apply the following alignments to text:

Left

Artistic text aligns to the right of the insertion point; paragraph text is flush with the left frame margin

Center

Artistic text centres itself around the insertion point; paragraph text aligns between the left/right frame edge.

Right

Artistic text aligns to the left of the insertion point; paragraph text is flush with the right frame margin.

Full Justify

Text is right- and left-justified.

Force Justify

Text is stretched to achieve right *and* left justification.

To align text, activate the Text tool. Select the text whose formatting you want to amend (with both artistic and paragraph text, selecting *individual* characters or words is the same as selecting the whole paragraph). Pull down the Text menu and choose Format Text. Follow the steps below:

1 Ensure this tab is active

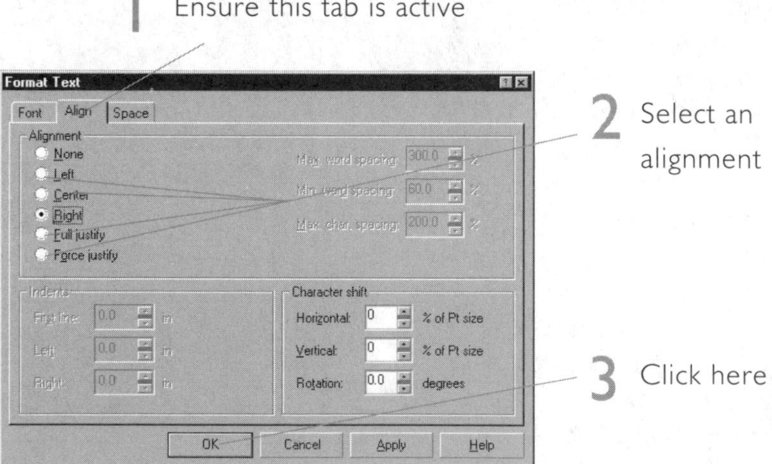

2 Select an alignment

3 Click here

Users of versions 3-6 should refer to pages 59 and 60 for how to activate the Text tool.

Using the Text Toolbar Versions 6-8 only

You can also align text with the help of the Text Toolbar. Activate the Text tool. Select the text whose formatting you want to amend. Click the appropriate button in the Text Toolbar:

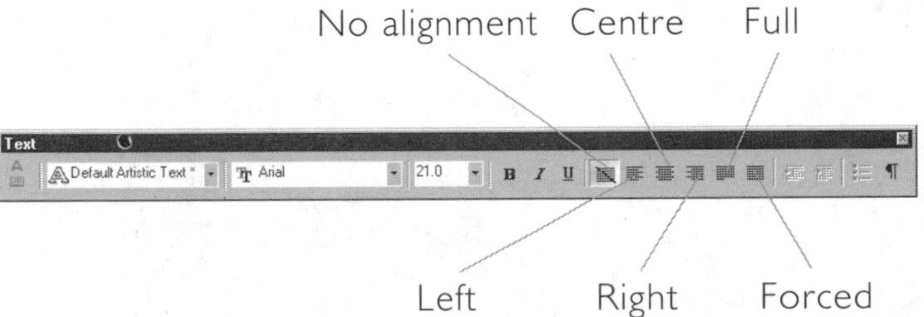

Alignment in action

The next illustration provides examples of the several types of alignment as applied to paragraph text.

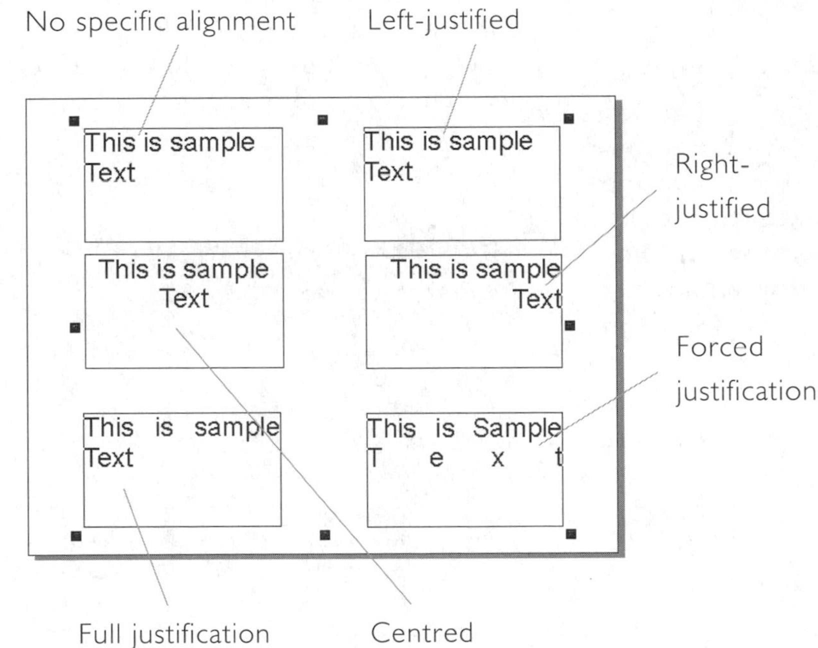

The paragraph text frames display as boxes here because they have been selected with the Pick Tool.

Adjusting spacing

In typography, line spacing is known as leading (pronounced 'ledding').

You can carry out three principal kinds of spacing adjustment on text in CorelDRAW. You can amend the spacing between:

- characters
- words
- lines

Character and word-spacing adjustments are measured as percentages of the size of one space character in the relevant font. By default, however, CorelDRAW sets the spacing between lines as a percentage of the character height. You can, though, choose to use different units: you can define line spacing in points, or as a percentage of the point size.

Users of versions 3-6 should refer to pages 59 and 60 for how to activate the Text tool.

Amending character, word or line spacing

Activate the Text tool. Select the text whose spacing you want to alter (with artistic and paragraph text, selecting *individual* characters or words is the same as selecting the whole paragraph). Pull down the Text menu and choose Format Text. Follow the steps below, as appropriate.

Users of versions 3-6 should choose Character in the Text menu. The dialog which launches is slightly different.

Re step 1 – in version 7, activate the *Spacing* tab.

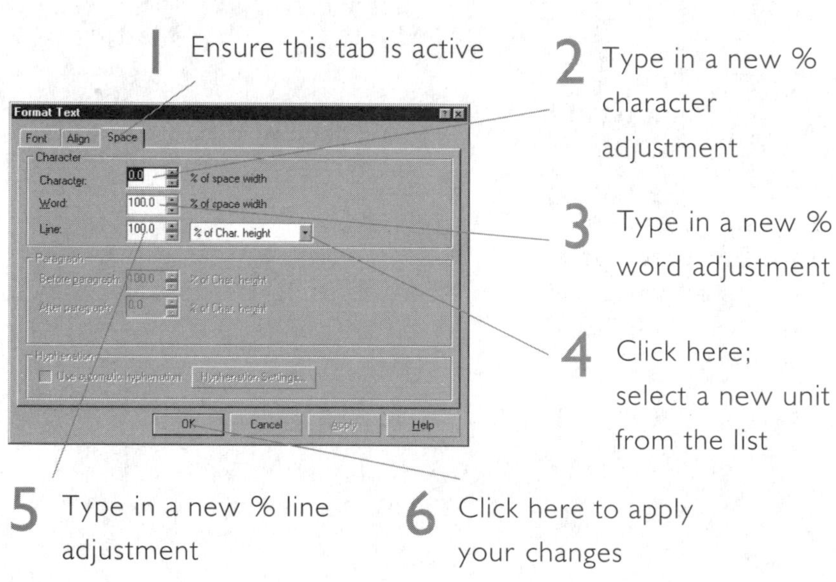

Shifting and rotating text

Users of versions 3-6 should refer to pages 59 and 60 for how to activate the Text tool.

Users of versions 3-6 should choose Character in the Text menu. The dialog which launches is slightly different.

Re step 1 – users of version 7 should activate the Spacing tab instead, and version 8 users the Space tab.

You can enter minus rotations e.g. -45°. Doing so produces clockwise, as opposed to anticlockwise, rotation.

CorelDRAW lets you adjust the position of text relative to the baseline, the lowest point reached by characters (excluding lower strokes) such as 'a'. You can:

- amend text horizontally in relation to the baseline
- amend text vertically in relation to the baseline
- rotate text in relation to the baseline

(Horizontal and vertical shift are measured in points, text rotation in degrees.)

Activate the Text tool. Select the characters or words you want to alter. Pull down the Text menu and choose Format Text. Do the following, as appropriate:

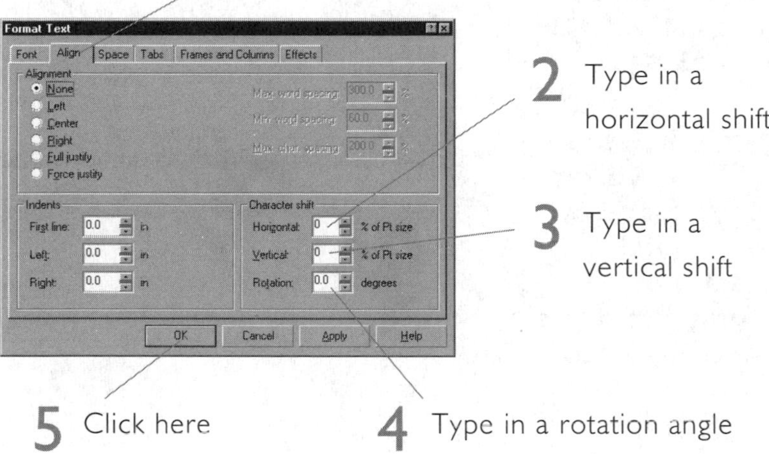

1 Ensure this tab is active

2 Type in a horizontal shift

3 Type in a vertical shift

4 Type in a rotation angle

5 Click here

Examples:

T he first character has been shifted horizontally

T he first character has been shifted vertically

T he first character has been rotated

Shift and rotation in action

The dedicated text editor

Versions 3 and 4 have a cut-down version of the text editor; to launch it, press Ctrl+T. (Ignore step 1 below, since text formatting options are immediately available).

Users of versions 3-6 should refer to pages 59 and 60 for how to activate the Text tool.

Re step 1 – in versions 5 and 6, click Character or Paragraph to access formatting options.

Text displays here. The editor isn't WYSIWYG ('What You See Is What You Get'). For example, point size increases don't display accurately.

With CorelDRAW, as we've seen, you can edit text in situ. Often, this is desirable. By selecting the Text tool (or, for users of versions 4-7, the Artistic Text or Paragraph Text tool) and clicking the relevant text, you can begin adding to it or changing it immediately. However, there are times when it's convenient to use a separate text editor.

One reason for this is that using the editor is quicker: you don't have to wait for the screen to redraw each time you make a correction or addition.

In versions 7 and 8, the editor provides access to the Format Text dialog we've been using in this chapter. And it also has its own mini Text toolbar which you can use to set a new typeface/type size or change the text style or alignment.

To launch the editor, first select the relevant text (either with the Pick tool or the Text tool). Press Ctrl+Shift+T.

The editor's toolbar

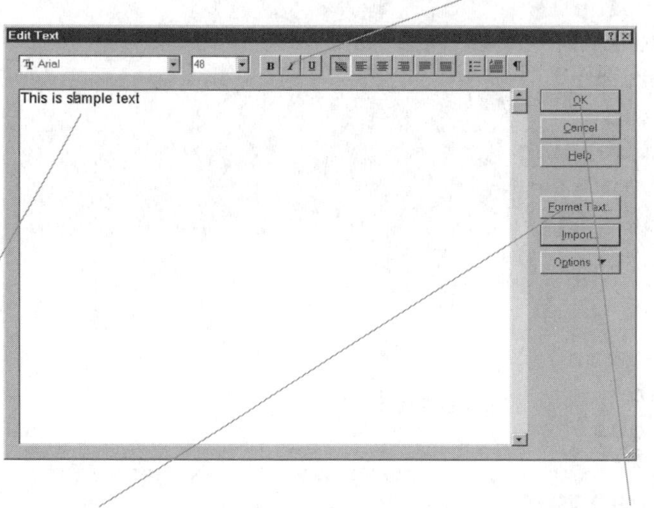

This dialog is slightly different in versions 5 and 6

1 Click here to launch the Format Text dialog (for how to use this, see earlier topics in this chapter)

2 Click here

Text shortcuts New in version 8

Using these shortcuts can save you a lot of time and effort.

CorelDRAW now allows you to:

- increase/decrease type sizes incrementally
- set the level of the increment for both increases and decreases
- increase/decrease type sizes relative to the next highest or lowest point size listed in the Font List

Incrementing type sizes

Select the text you want to change. Ensure Number Lock is enabled (by clicking the Num Lock key). Now do the following:

— Hold down one Ctrl key and press 8 on the numerical keypad to the right of your keyboard. Repeat as often as necessary

CorelDRAW adds one point to the existing text size.

Decrementing type sizes

Select the text you want to change. Ensure Number Lock is enabled (by clicking the Num Lock key). Now do the following:

— Hold down one Ctrl key and press 2 on the numerical keypad to the right of your keyboard. Repeat as often as necessary

CorelDRAW subtracts one point from the existing text size.

Specifying the increment/decrement

Press Ctrl+J; the Options dialog launches. Do the following:

— In the list of categories on the left, click Text. In the Keyboard Text Increment box, enter a new increment (in whole points). Click OK

Increasing type sizes relative to the Font List

Select the text you want to change. Ensure Number Lock is enabled (by clicking the Num Lock key). Now do the following:

— Hold down one Ctrl key and press 6 on the numerical keypad to the right of your keyboard. Repeat as often as necessary

CorelDRAW applies the next point size in the Font List:

The Text toolbar with the Font List displayed

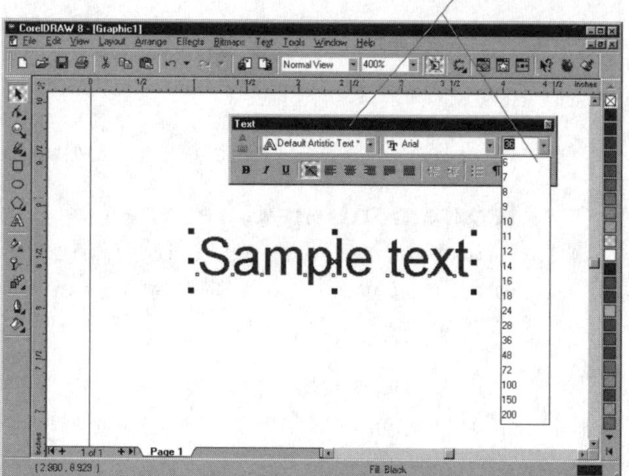

Here, Ctrl+6 increases the type size to 48 (the next highest)

Decreasing type sizes relative to the Font List

Select the text you want to change. Ensure Number Lock is enabled (by clicking the Num Lock key). Now do the following:

— Hold down one Ctrl key and press 4 on the numerical keypad to the right of your keyboard. Repeat as often as necessary

CorelDRAW applies the next lowest point size in the Font List (in the above example, 28).

Chapter Five

Advanced Text Work

CorelDRAW has a variety of advanced text features. In this chapter, you'll learn how to set tabs and indents; work with text columns; flow text between paragraph frames; carry out kerning; format single characters; flow text around shapes; create and apply text styles; proofread text; and (in version 8) make text three-dimensional.

Covers

Using tabs New in version 4

You can only apply tabs to paragraph, not artistic text.

Users of versions 4-6 should activate the Paragraph Text tool – see pages 59 and 60.

Users of versions 4-6 should choose Paragraph in the Text menu. The dialog which launches is rather different.

It's a good idea to use indents, rather than tabs, to align even the 1st lines of paragraphs. This is because tabs have to be physically inserted for each paragraph, whereas indents can be applied with a single command.

One feature of paragraph, as opposed to artistic text is the ability to impose tabs and indents. Tabs and indents are related features in that they both control the extent to which the first lines of paragraphs align with the left margin. Indents, however, go much further than this. You can also use them to control the alignment of subsequent lines with the left margin, and the overall alignment with the right margin.

Imposing tabs – the dialog route

First, activate the Text tool in the Toolbox (see page 60 for how to do this). Click anywhere in the paragraph for which you want to define tabs (or select more than one paragraph). Pull down the Text menu and click Format Text. Now carry out step 1 below. To impose tabs at regular intervals, follow step 2. To add a single tab, perform step 3 (in version 7, the Format Text dialog is slightly different):

1 Ensure this tab is active

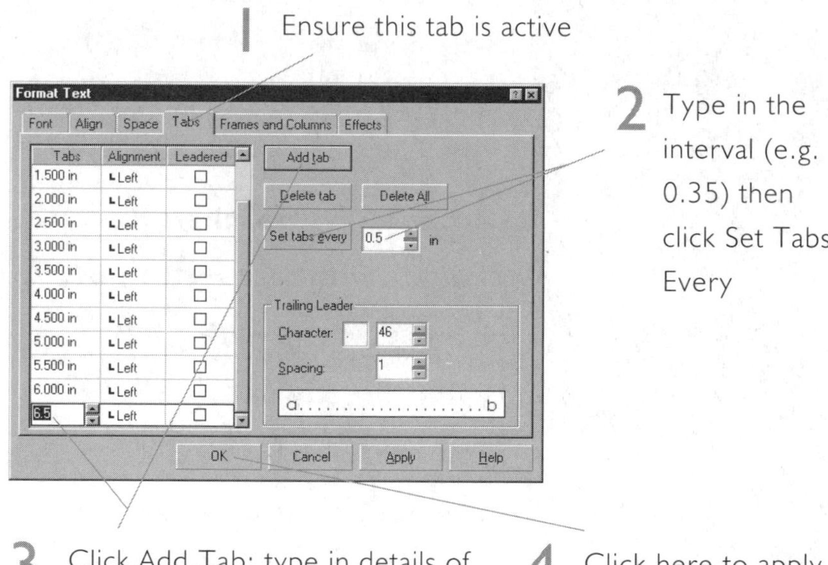

2 Type in the interval (e.g. 0.35) then click Set Tabs Every

3 Click Add Tab; type in details of the new tab. Press Enter

4 Click here to apply the tab settings

To make text conform to the tabs you've imposed, place the cursor at the start of the relevant paragraph. Press Tab as often as required.

Imposing tabs with the Paragraph Text ruler New in version 5

A quicker and more convenient way to set tabs is to use a special version of the ruler which appears over paragraph text:

Normally, tab marks don't display, but users of version 6 onwards can make them visible – and also other features e.g. paragraph marks:

Pull down the Text menu and click Show Non-Printing Characters.

In versions 5-7, the Paragraph Text ruler looks slightly different.

In version 5, you can only carry out option 3.

Tab/indent ruler

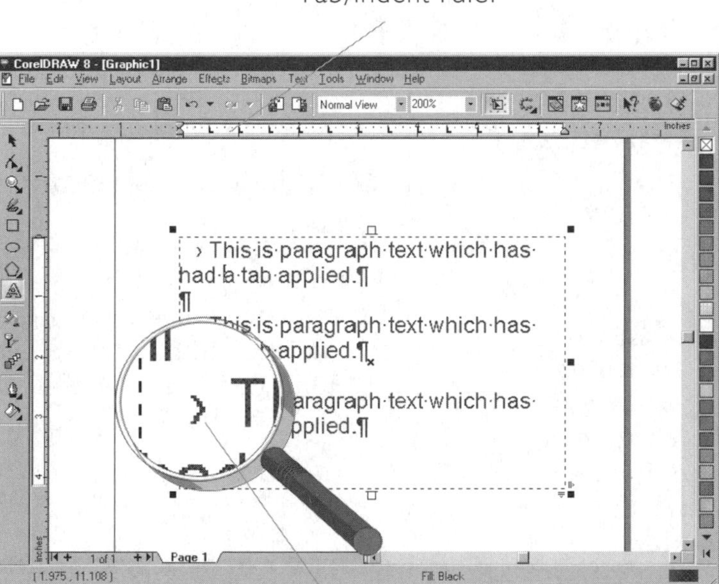

Magnified view of tab mark

You can use the ruler in the following ways:

1. To add a new tab, simply click the ruler where you want the tab to appear.
2. To remove a tab, left-click it. Hold down the mouse button and drag it off the ruler. When you release the button, it disappears.
3. To move an existing tab to a new position, left-click it. Hold down the mouse button and drag it to its new location. Release the button to confirm the move.

Using indents New in version 4

You can only indent paragraph, not artistic text.

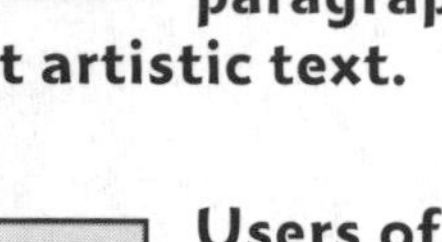

Users of versions 4-6 should activate the Paragraph Text tool – see pages 59 and 60.

Users of versions 4-6 should choose Paragraph in the Text menu. The dialog which launches is rather different.

Re step 1 – version 5 and 6 users should activate the Indents tab instead, while version 7 users should initiate the Tabs and Indents tab.

For reasons set out on page 72, indents are the preferred solution for aligning paragraph text. They're easier to apply, and more convenient, than tabs.

You can indent:

- the first line of one or more paragraphs
- all lines (excluding the first) of one or more paragraphs (CorelDRAW calls this a Left or Rest of Lines indent)
- one or more paragraphs from the right frame margin

You can apply these in any permutations.

Applying indents via a dialog

First, activate the Text tool in the Toolbox (see page 60 for how to do so). Click anywhere in the paragraph for which you want to define indents (or select more than one paragraph). Pull down the Text menu and click Format Text. Now carry out the following steps, as appropriate:

1 Ensure this tab is active

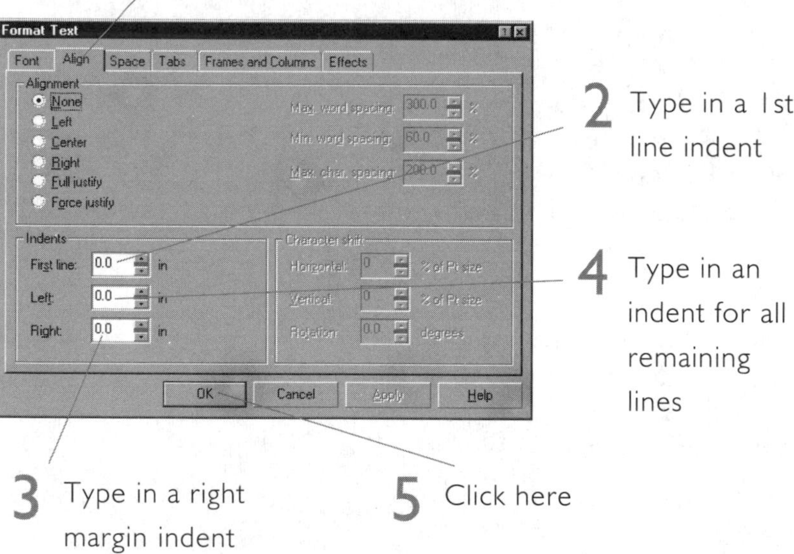

2 Type in a 1st line indent

3 Type in a right margin indent

4 Type in an indent for all remaining lines

5 Click here

Applying indents via the ruler New in version 5

You can use the special ruler which appears over paragraph text to impose indents, too. The next illustration shows the ruler, together with sample indents:

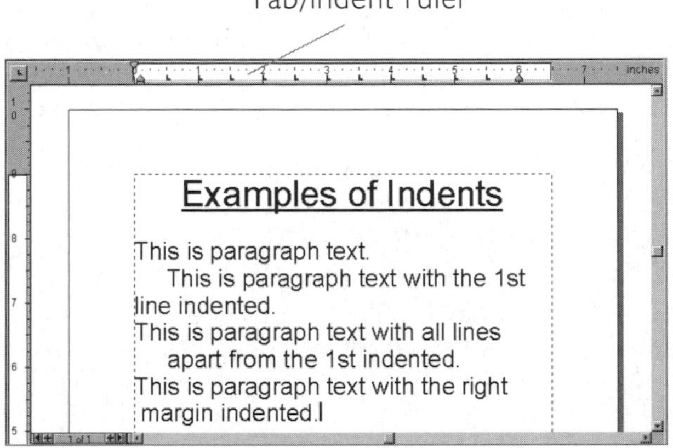

In version 6, the indent symbols in the ruler are rather different.

Users of versions 4-6 should activate the Paragraph Text tool – see pages 59 and 60.

First, activate the Text tool in the Toolbox. Click anywhere in the paragraph for which you want to define indents (or select more than one paragraph). Drag the First Line marker in the ruler to indent the first line. Drag the Rest of Lines indent marker to indent all subsequent lines. Drag the Right Indent marker to move the right frame margin inwards.

Version 7 and 8 users – if you drag on this section of the Rest of Lines marker:

Here

CorelDRAW moves the left indent for *all* lines in the specified paragraph(s).

The next illustration shows magnified view of, the markers:

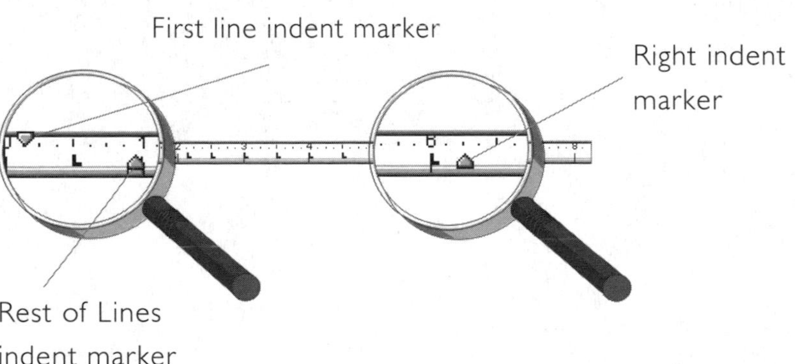

Applying columns to text New in version 4

Users of versions 4-6 should activate the Paragraph Text tool – see pages 59 and 60.

Users of versions 4, and 5 should do the following:

— click Frame in the Text menu, then complete the Frame Attributes dialog

Users of version 6 should do the following:

— click Columns in the Text menu, then complete the Columns dialog

Another feature which is unique to paragraph, as opposed to artistic text is the ability to have CorelDRAW format text in columns.

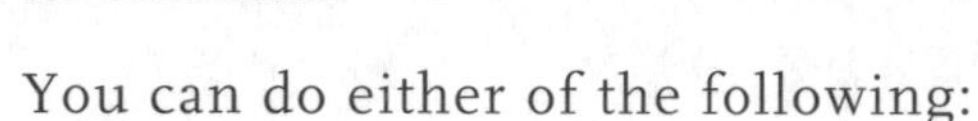

You can do either of the following:

- impose equal-sized columns (in which case you simply tell CorelDRAW how many you require)
- specify columns of varying width.

By default, CorelDRAW assumes you want the former.

Imposing columns

First, select the paragraph text frame, either with the Pick tool or the Text tool. Then pull down the Text menu and click Format Text. Now do the following:

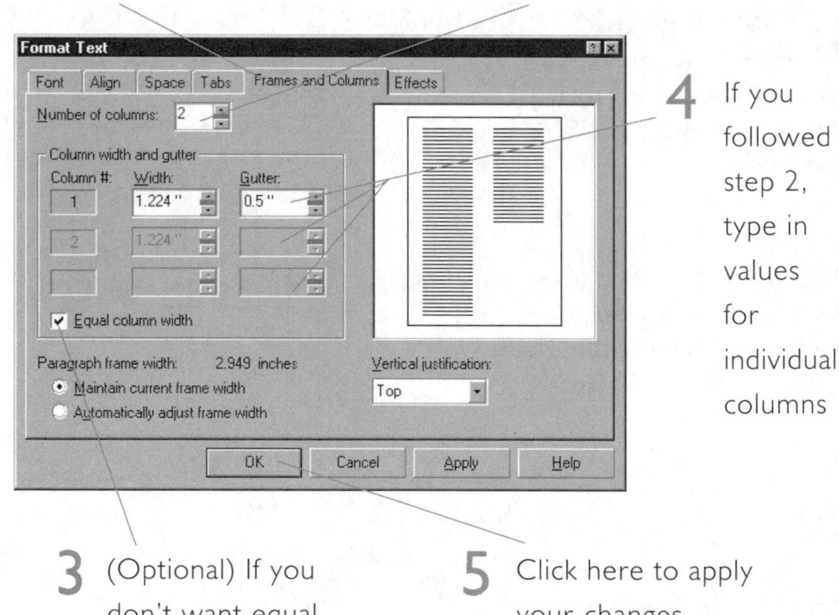

Linking frames New in version 4

In versions before 8, linked frames display slightly differently.

In earlier chapters, we mentioned that paragraph text is contained within frames. Frames are boxes which add useful structure to the text they contain. However, they also permit one further operation: you can have text flow from one frame to another. CorelDRAW achieves this by 'linking' frames.

The flow is dynamic. In other words, if you change the size of one frame (or resize the text), the contents of the second update automatically.

Linking frames

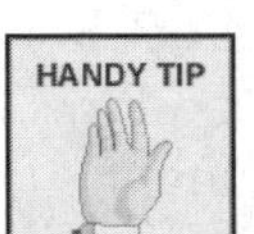

You can also use this procedure to link a text frame with another on a different page. Simply use the Page Forward or Page Backward controls in the Page Counter (see page 10) to move to the new page before you define or fill the second frame.

Activate the Pick tool and click the frame which has surplus text. Click the arrow – see the next illustration.

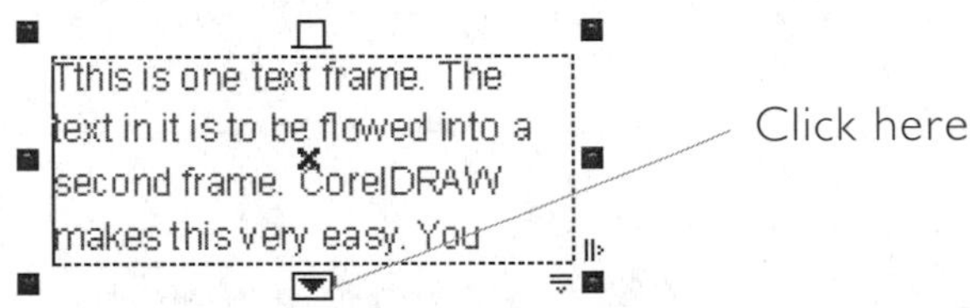

The cursor changes into a representation of a page. Left-click and hold down the mouse button. Drag to define an additional frame which you want to receive some or all of the overflow (or click inside an empty frame you've already created). When you release the button, CorelDRAW flows the text into the second frame.

You can now define a further frame, and repeat the process...

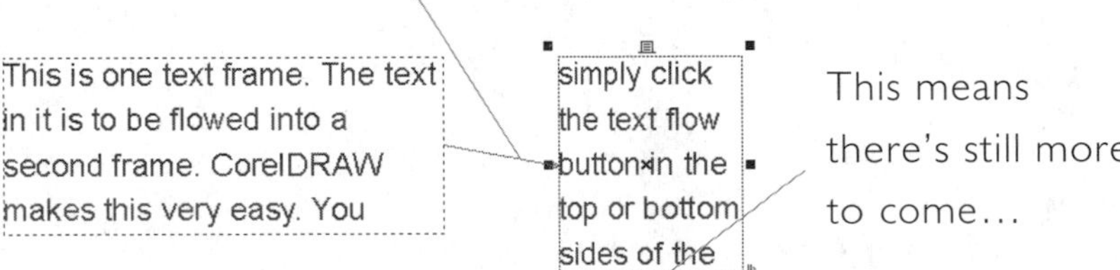

Editing individual characters

Version 7 and 8 users can add drop caps to paragraph text.

Click the Text tool. Select one or more paragraphs. Press Ctrl+T. In the Format Text dialog, click the Effects tab. Select Drop cap (version 8 users – in the Effect Type field).

Choose a drop cap type. In the Dropped lines field, type in the number of lines you want the drop cap to descend. In the Distance from text box, type in a horizontal separation. Finally, click OK.

In versions 3,4 and 5, there is no Shape flyout.

Instead, simply click the Shape tool icon in the Toolbox.

In Chapter 3, we looked at how to use the Shape tool to edit nodes as a way of redrawing curves and lines. An added benefit, however, is the ability to edit one or more text characters. You can:

- adjust letter spacing (i.e. carry out kerning)
- apply formatting (e.g. change the typeface/type size, apply a text style)

Kerning text

Kerning is the reduction of space between specific pairs of letters to compensate for the inherent awkwardness of their shapes. In the next illustration, the 'A' and 'v' are too far apart to be aesthetically pleasing. The answer is to move the 'A' nearer to the 'v'.

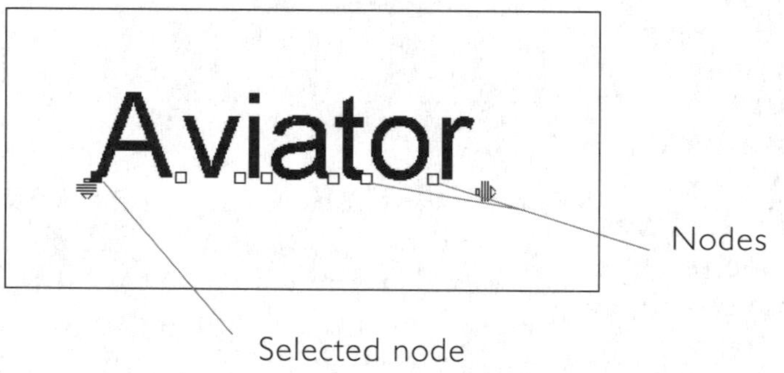

First, activate the Shape tool by carrying out steps 1 and 2.

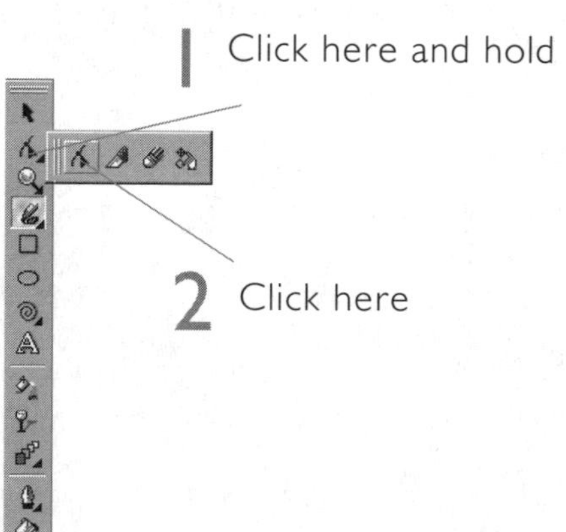

To select more than one node (and therefore more than one character), hold down one Shift key as you click them.

To kern an individual character in artistic text, click the text; to kern an individual character in paragraph text, click anywhere in the frame. Then, in either case, click the node to the left of the character you want to edit; CorelDRAW fills it to show it's selected. (See the first illustration on page 78.) Drag the node to the left or right to kern the character.

Kerning has taken place

Formatting individual characters

To change the formatting of an individual character in artistic text, click the text; to change the formatting of an individual character in paragraph text, click anywhere in the frame. Then, in either case, click the node to the left of the character you want to edit; CorelDRAW fills it to show it's selected.

Now follow any of the text formatting procedures discussed in Chapter 4 (bear in mind that some of them – e.g. alignment – affect the *whole* of the word or paragraph in which one or more nodes have been selected).

In the next illustration, the initial letter of 'Aviator' has had a new typeface and type size imposed on it.

Working with text styles

Earlier versions of CorelDRAW have different style allocations.

In versions 4 and 5, the procedure is slightly different.

In step 1, click Save As Style. Omit Step 2.

Additionally, the Save Style As dialog looks like this:

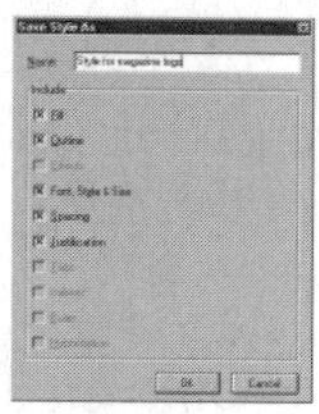

Carry out step 3. In 4, select the formatting areas you want to save. Finally, perform step 5.

Styles are collections of associated formatting commands which can be applied to text with a single mouse click, thereby saving a lot of time and effort. They also ensure a consistent look and feel within documents.

CorelDRAW 8 comes with one pre-defined artistic text style.

Creating a text style

First, create an artistic text string or a paragraph text frame. Apply all the relevant formatting attributes (e.g. font, type size, spacing etc.) to the text. Then right-click over the text; a special menu appears. Follow the steps below:

1 Click here

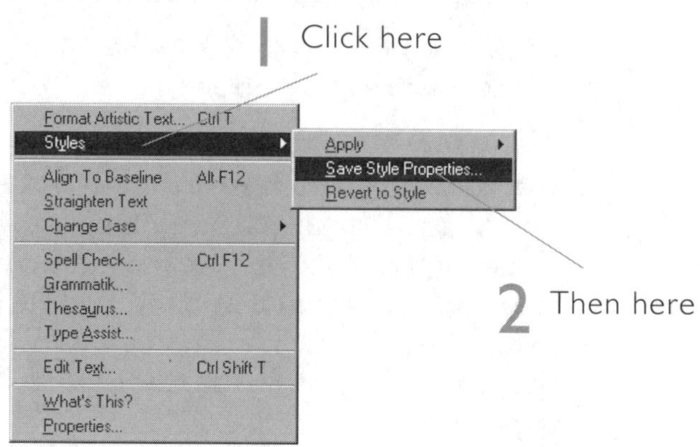

2 Then here

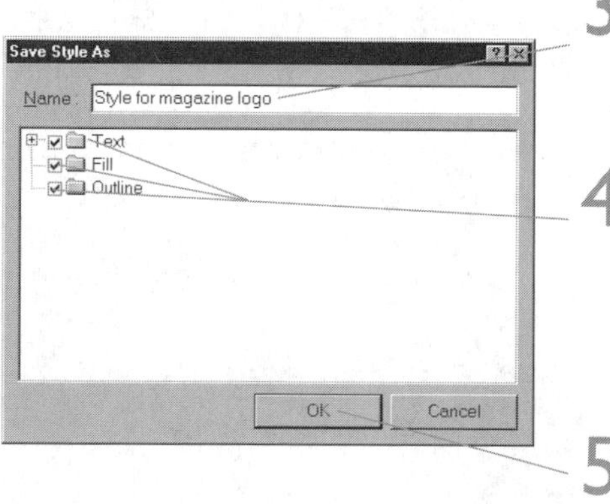

3 Type in a name for the new style

4 Click on any of these if you want to exclude them from the new style

5 Click here to save the style

Users of versions 3-6 should refer to pages 59 and 60 for how to activate the Text tool.

Applying styles

Once you've created a style, applying it to text is very easy. The procedure for both artistic and paragraph text is the same.

First, with either the Pick tool or the Text tool, select the text you want to apply the style to. Right-click over the text. Then do the following:

In versions 4 and 5, the procedure is slightly different. In step 1, click Apply Style. Omit Step 2. Finally, perform step 3.

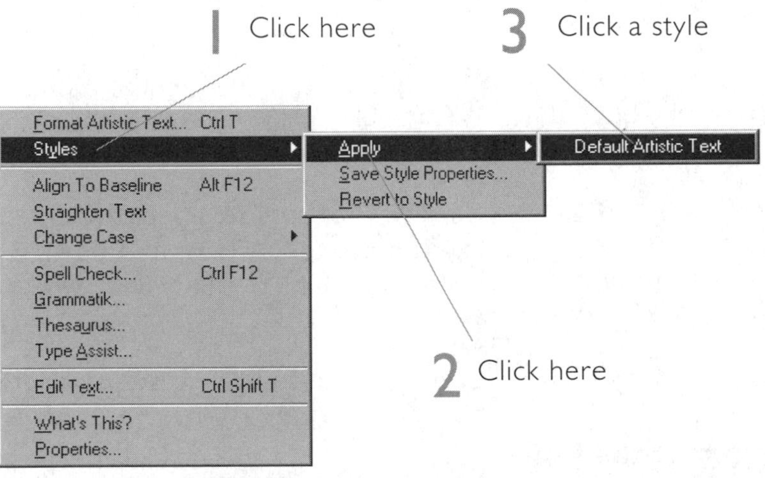

More styles New in version 8

If, in step 3, the style you want isn't listed, click More Styles and carry out the additional steps below:

Steps 4 and 5 are required if you've created more styles than can display in the earlier sub-menu.

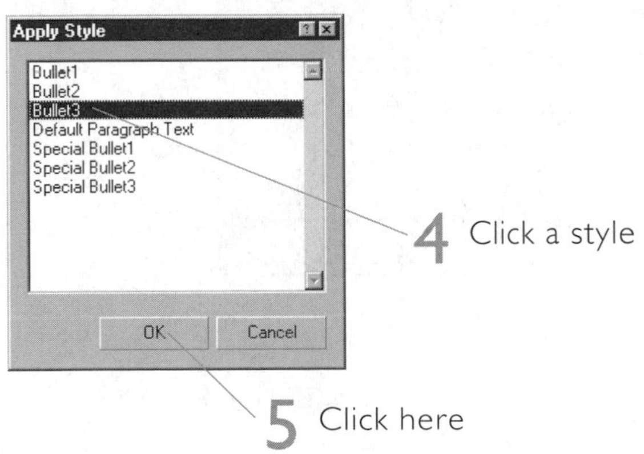

Fitting text to a path

The following are examples of Fit Text to Path roll-up controls in action:

Characters are slightly rotated

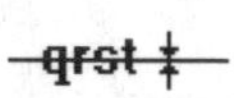

Text aligns above the baseline

Text aligns to the topmost side of the path

You can have artistic text conform to a path. In this sense, a path is any drawing object which has the requisite shape. For example, you can have CorelDRAW align text automatically along the perimeter of a rectangle, ellipse or polygon. When you do this, you can determine:

1. the text orientation relative to the path (the extent to which the characters are rotated)
2. the vertical position/alignment of the text (relative to the text baseline)
3. the horizontal alignment of the text (in the case of closed – filled – objects) i.e. you specify which side of the path text aligns with

Use the Pick tool to select the object with which you want to align the text. Then hold down Shift and select the text. In the Roll-Ups toolbar, click this button:

Carry out the following steps, as appropriate:

If the Roll-Ups toolbar isn't on-screen, click Toolbars in the View menu. In the Toolbars section of the Options dialog, click Roll-Ups. Click OK.

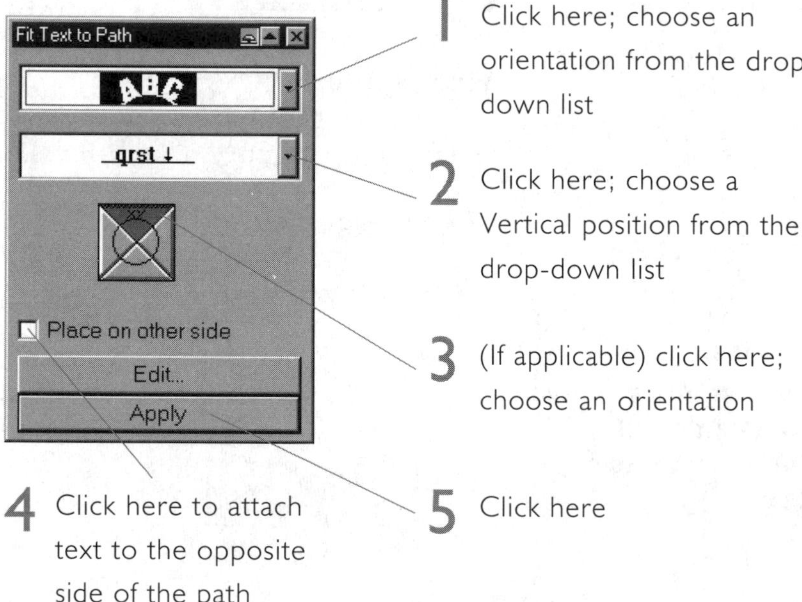

Typing directly onto paths New in version 7

In versions 7 and 8, you can type directly onto open or closed paths. This is a very useful technique because it saves time and effort.

There are, however, two caveats:

1. you can't insert text onto other text objects
2. if you need to vary the following:
   - the distance between the text and the object
   - the text placement on the object's path

   you need to follow the procedures listed on page 82 instead

Users of versions 3-6 should refer to pages 59 and 60 for how to activate the Text tool.

Typing onto paths

Activate the Text tool. Position the cursor near to the object along which you want the text aligned. This is the result:

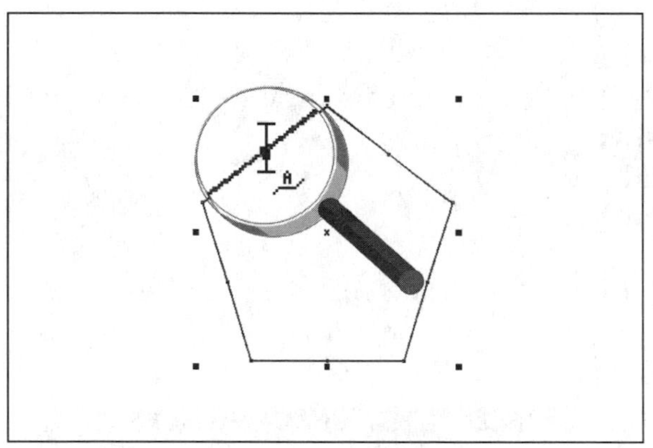

The cursor now shows as an insertion point

When the cursor changes to an insertion point (see above), click once and start typing.

Spell-checking text

Users of versions 3-5 should click Spell Checker in the Text menu. The dialog which appears is slightly different.

Users of version 6 should click Proofreading, Spelling in the Text menu. The dialog which appears is slightly different.

HANDY TIP

The Spell Checker maintains a special 'user' (or personal) dictionary (WT8OUK.UWL in version 8). If a correct word has been flagged and you want the Spell Checker to recognise it in future, click the Add (or Add Word) button, according to the version.

CorelDRAW lets you proofread text in a variety of ways. You can:

- carry out a spell-check
- run a grammar check (see page 86)
- run the Thesaurus to find synonyms (see page 87)

To spell-check artistic or paragraph text, select the text with the Pick tool or the Text tool. Press Ctrl+F12. Now carry out the following steps, as appropriate:

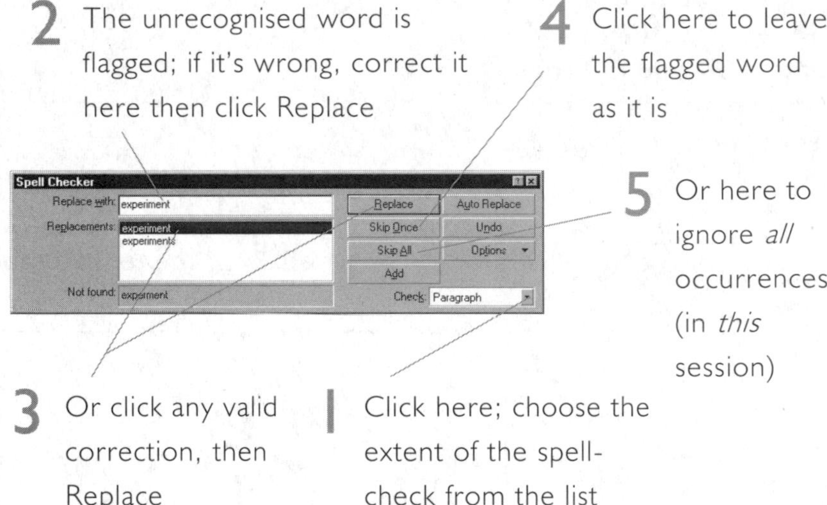

When the spell-check is complete, CorelDRAW launches this message. Do the following:

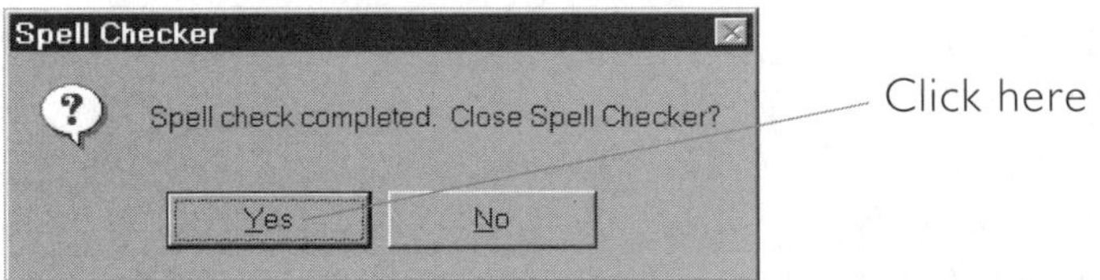

Automatic spell-checking New in version 7

You can also spell-check text on-the-fly, as you enter or amend text. CorelDRAW is automatically set up to do this. When automatic correction is in force, CorelDRAW flags any unrecognised words with a red underline.

The spell-checker also flags incorrect capitals, duplicated words, hyphenation errors, 'a/an' errors and other typographical mistakes.

Right-click the word, then carry out any of the following:

1 CorelDRAW provides alternatives; if one is correct, click it to have it replace the original word

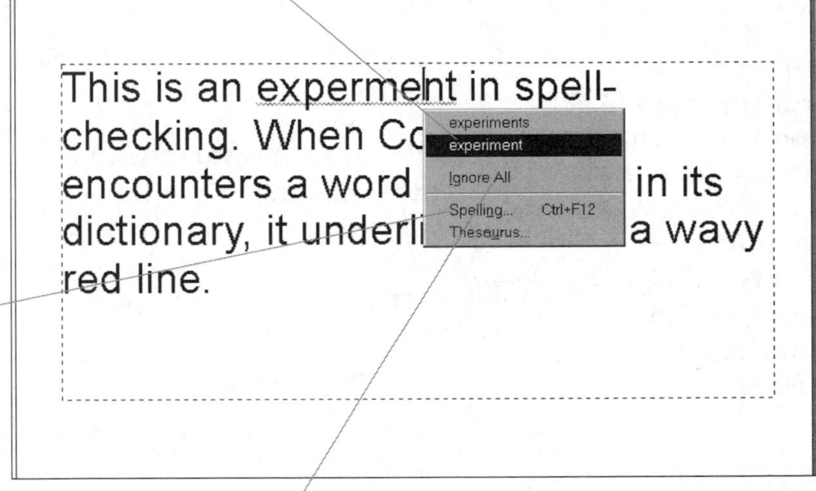

2 If you want the flagged word to stand, click here

To add the flagged word to your dictionary, click Spelling. In the Spell Checker dialog, click the Add button. Then click Yes to terminate the spell check.

Disabling on-the-fly checking

Sometimes, automatic spell-checking is intrusive. To turn it off, pull down the Tools menu and click Options. On the left of the dialog, click ⊞ next to Workspace and Text successively, then click Spelling. Deselect Perform automatic spell checking. Click OK.

Version 7 users should use a different procedure.

Press Ctrl+J. In the Options dialog, click the Spelling tab. Deselect Perform automatic spell checking. Click OK.

Grammar-checking text New in version 6

In version 6, there are no styles, just two overall categories: Quick and Full Proofreading.

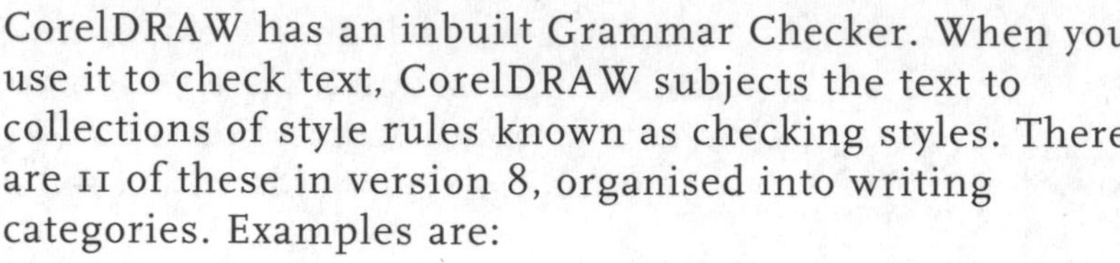

CorelDRAW has an inbuilt Grammar Checker. When you use it to check text, CorelDRAW subjects the text to collections of style rules known as checking styles. There are 11 of these in version 8, organised into writing categories. Examples are:

Spelling Plus	finds spelling errors and flags *simple* grammatical infringements
Quick Check	the default. Suitable for most documents
Fiction	accepts informal language
Formal Memo or Letter	for formal documents; rules are strictly adhered to

Users of version 6 should click Proofreading in the Text menu. In the sub-menu, click Quick Proofreading OR Full Proofreading. The dialog which launches is slightly different.

Running a grammar-check

Select the relevant text with the Pick or Text tools. Pull down the Text menu and click Writing Tools, Grammatik (Grammar Check in version 7). Now carry out the following steps, as appropriate:

If a correct word has been flagged as a misspelling and you want to add it to WT8OUK.UWL so that it's recognised in future, click Add.

2 The unrecognised expression is flagged; click a valid correction, then Replace

3 Click here to accept the flagged expression

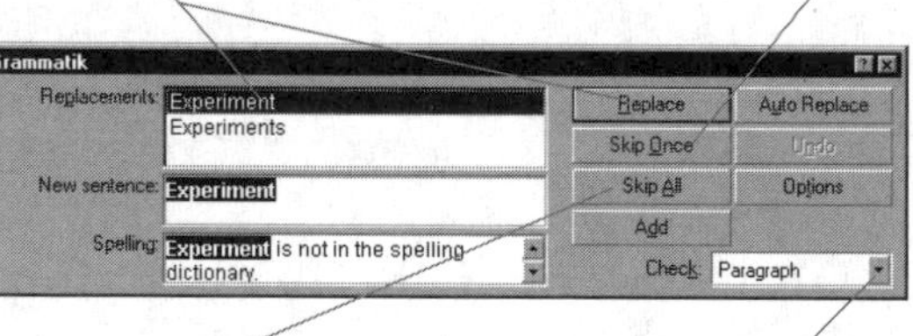

4 Or here to ignore *all* occurrences (in this session only)

1 Click here; choose the extent of the grammar-check from the list

When the check is complete, CorelDRAW launches a special message. Click Yes to return to your document.

Searching for synonyms

Users of versions 3-6 should refer to pages 59 and 60 for how to activate the Text tool.

Users of versions 3-6 should click Thesaurus in the Text menu. The dialog which appears is slightly different.

You can have CorelDRAW search for synonyms for a specified word. Once you've found the synonym you want to use, you can have it inserted into your document so that it automatically replaces the original word.

To find a synonym for a word in either artistic or paragraph text, select the word with the Text tool. Pull down the Text menu and do the following:

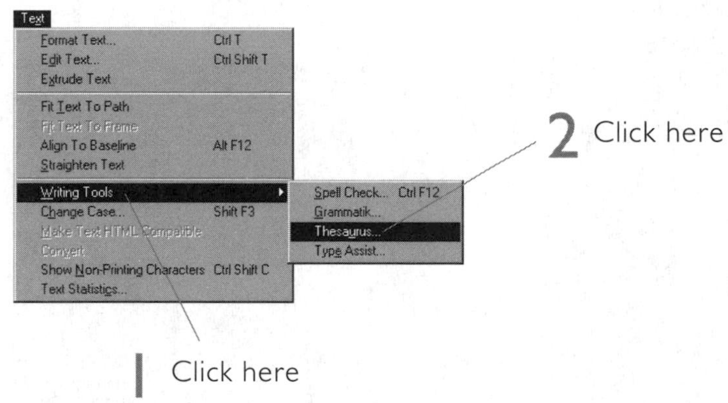

Now carry out the following steps, as appropriate:

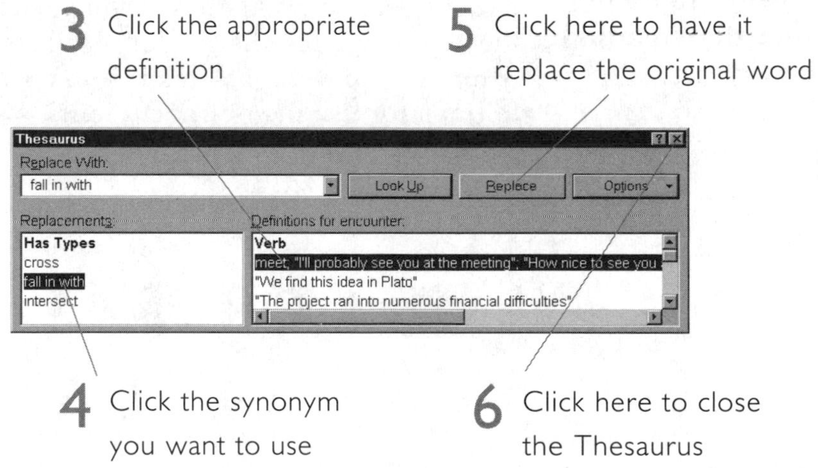

3D text – an overview New in version 8

Pages 88-100 describe features which relate to extruded text, a facility which is only available in version 8 of CorelDRAW.

Rendered bitmaps still *appear* to be three-dimensional, however.

With version 8 of CorelDRAW, you can make artistic text three-dimensional. Once you've done this, you can vary:

- the Viewport position (see below) and dimensions
- the depth of the extrusion
- the text rotation
- the camera settings
- the lens magnification

You can also:

— add a light source

— bevel the text edges

— apply pattern fills

When you convert text to 3D, you view it through a feature known as the 3D Viewport. This is a special way of looking at three-dimensional text, and is automatically opened as soon as you tell CorelDRAW you want to extrude text. In the 3D Viewport, you work in three dimensions; however, once you've achieved the effect you need, you launch the rendering process. Rendering takes your work and transforms it into a two-dimensional bitmap for use in your documents.

Extruded text, after rendering

Starting to extrude text

First, apply the relevant formatting to the artistic text you want to extrude. Select the text with the Pick tool. Pull down the Text menu and do the following:

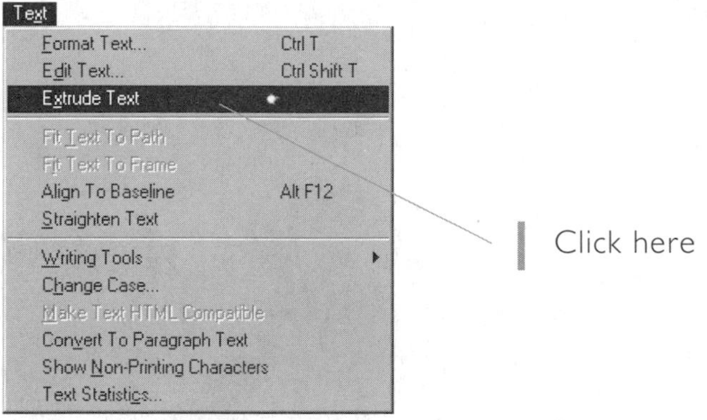

This is the result:

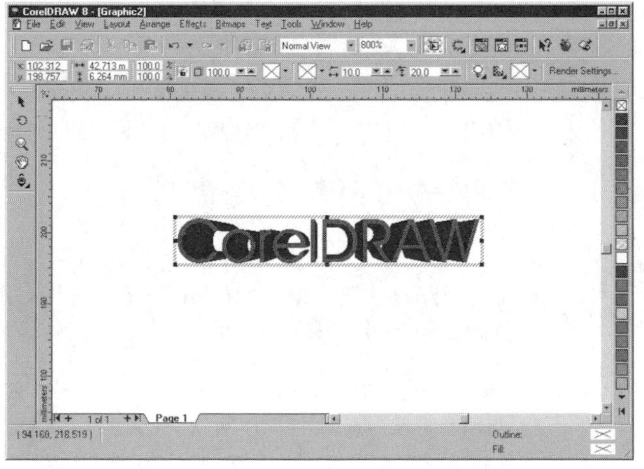

The 3D Viewport

The text is now ready to work with.

Repositioning the 3D Viewport

Repositioning the Viewport

Carry out the following action:

Now drag the Viewport to a new location

Resizing the Viewport

To resize the Viewport, position the mouse pointer over one of the corner selection handles. Alternatively, position it over one of the midpoint handles. In either case, the pointer changes to a double-headed arrow.

Drag the handle inwards to decrease the size of the Viewport, or outwards to increase it.

Specifying extrusion depth

CorelDRAW 8 makes varying the depth of 3D text extrusions easy.

Applying a new extrusion depth

While text is being viewed in the 3D Viewport, refer to the 3D Toolbox on the left of the screen and do the following:

Now refer to the Property Bar and carry out the following additional step:

If the Property Bar isn't currently on-screen, pull down the View menu and click Property Bar.

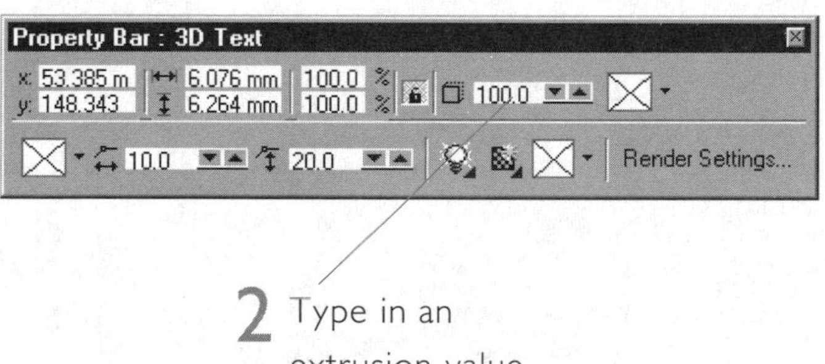

2 Type in an extrusion value

Text with an extrusion depth of 750

Rotating 3D text

You can easily and conveniently rotate three-dimensional text with the help of the mouse.

Rotating Viewport text

While text is being viewed in the 3D Viewport, refer to the 3D Toolbox on the left of the screen and do the following:

Click the Viewport text you want to rotate. Do the following:

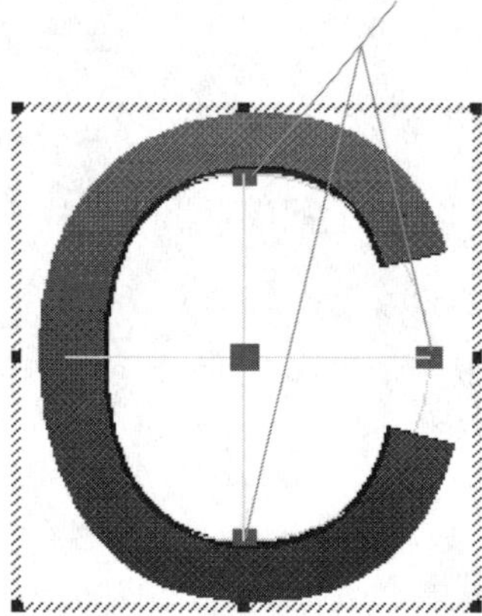

Specifying 3D camera zoom

The Viewport camera controls how you view 3D text. Getting the optimal view is important because:

1. it controls how you work with the text
2. it determines which portions of the text are visible

Setting camera magnification

To set the camera zoom level while text is being viewed in the 3D Viewport, refer to the 3D Toolbox on the left of the screen and do the following:

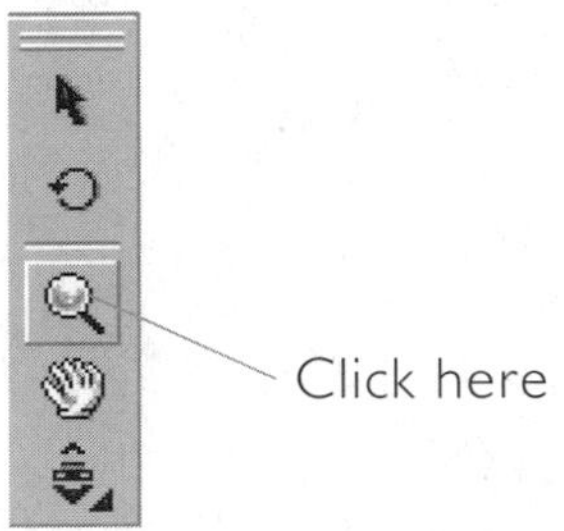

Now move the mouse pointer (a magnifying glass) over the Viewport text; click and hold the left mouse button. Do ONE of the following:

— move the mouse cursor *upwards* to increase the magnification

— move the mouse cursor *downwards* to decrease the magnification

Increased magnification

Decreased magnification

Repositioning the 3D camera

The text movement here is an illusion produced by rearranging the camera viewpoint.

You can reposition the camera in two ways:

- by dragging text in the Viewport; CorelDRAW calls this 'repositioning text on the xy plane'
- by making the camera approach – or distance itself from – the text; CorelDRAW calls this 'repositioning text on the z axis'

Repositioning text on the xy plane

Refer to the 3D Toolbox on the left of the screen and do the following:

Move the mouse pointer (it changes to a hand) within the Viewport; drag the text to a new position.

Repositioning text on the z axis

Refer to the 3D Toolbox on the left of the screen and do the following:

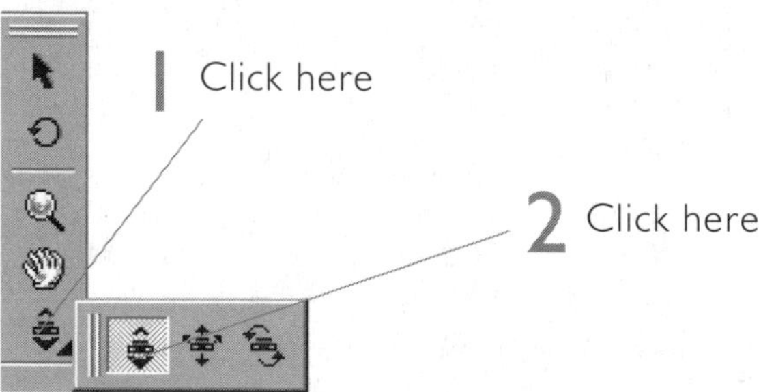

Move the mouse pointer within the Viewport; drag up to move towards the text, or down to move away.

Light sources – an overview

By default, extruded text is not lit. However, you can rectify this, if you want.

Adding a light source to 3D text has the following benefits:

1. the text looks more realistic (if the lighting has been applied effectively)

2. varying the quantity and attributes of lights has a considerable effect on the text

3. you can choose from two types of light source:

   — ambient

   — point

However, you need to bear in mind the following caveats:

— although you can add as many light sources to 3D text as you want, it's easy to overdo lighting effects

— as a result of the above, it's preferable to add no more than two or three light sources to given text

— the more light sources you use, the longer your text takes to render

Rendering is the final stage in the production of 3D text.

Light sources

Ambient light is a smooth, unchanging light which has no obvious source and produces no shadow. Its effect is consistent i.e. it has no position and radiates uniformly.

Point light, on the other hand, has – as the name implies – a specific point of origin. This can be varied; when you do so, the effect on the extruded text is considerable.

Adding light sources

If the Property Bar isn't currently on-screen, pull down the View menu and click Property Bar.

Adding ambient light

While text is being viewed in the 3D Viewport, refer to the Property Bar and do the following:

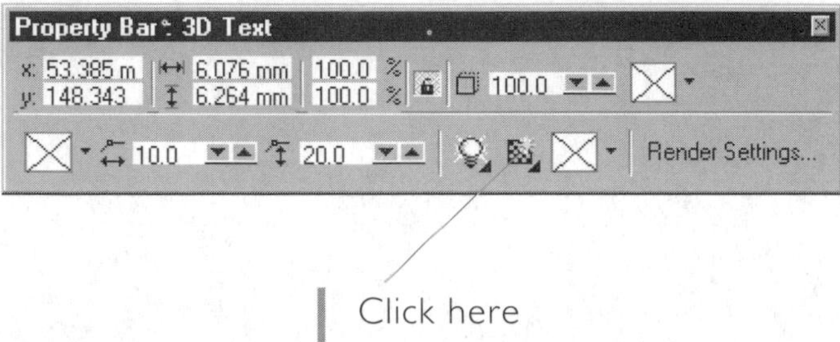

Now carry out the following additional steps

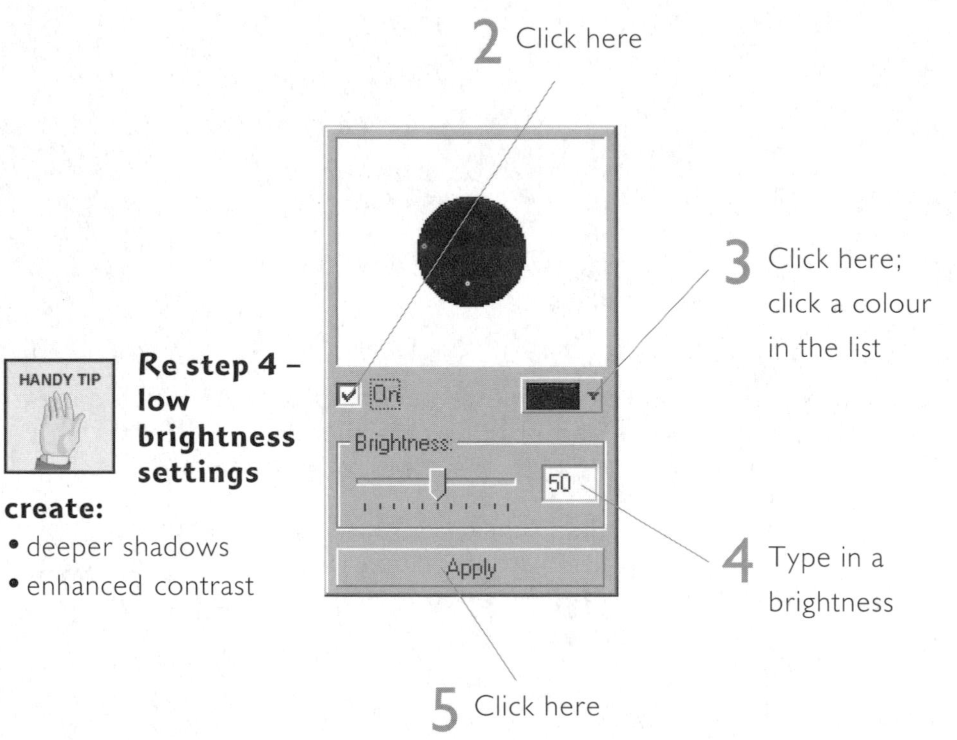

Re step 4 – low brightness settings create:

- deeper shadows
- enhanced contrast

Finally, click anywhere in the Work area.

Adding point light

While text is being viewed in the 3D Viewport, refer to the Property Bar and do the following:

If the Property Bar isn't currently on-screen, pull down the View menu and click Property Bar.

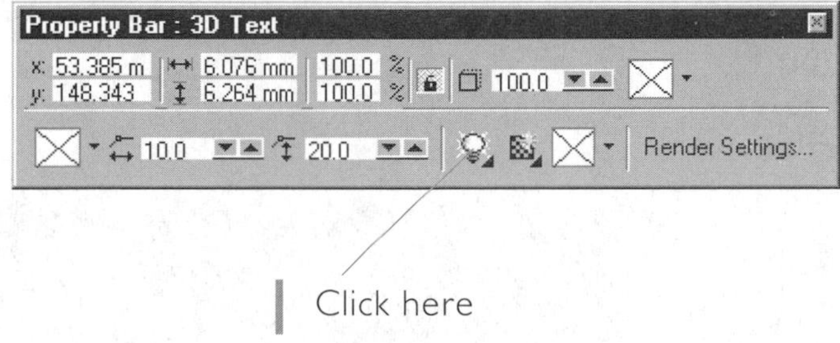

Now carry out the following additional steps

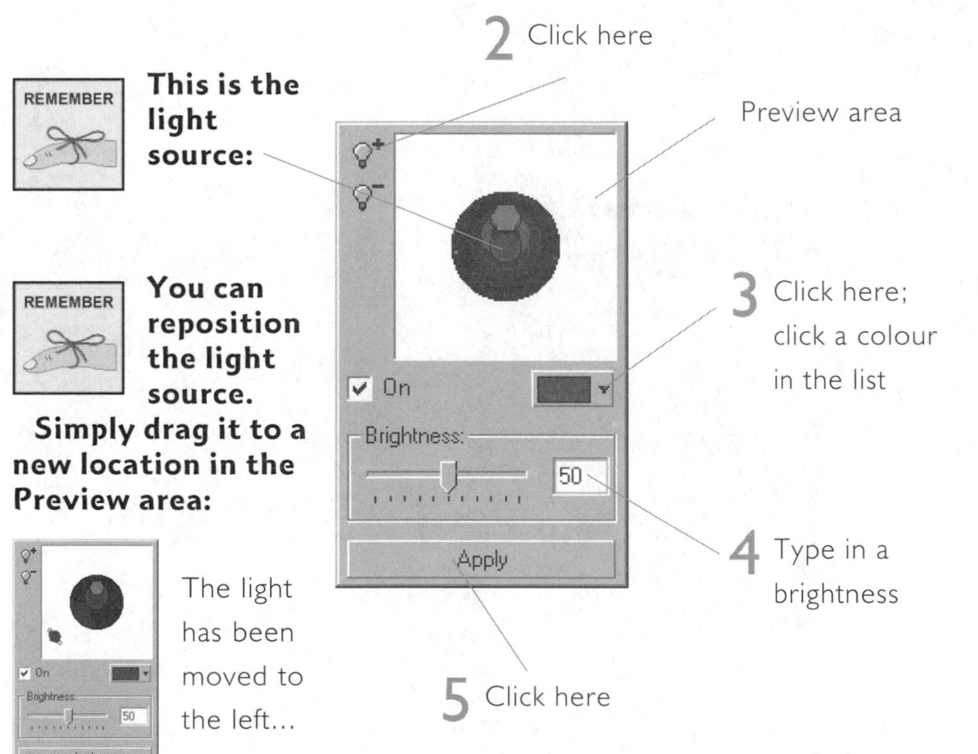

This is the light source:

You can reposition the light source. Simply drag it to a new location in the Preview area:

The light has been moved to the left...

Finally, click anywhere in the Work area.

Applying bevels to 3D text

If the Property Bar isn't currently on-screen, pull down the View menu and click Property Bar.

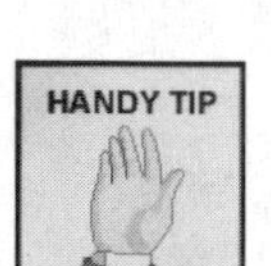

You can also vary the width and/or height of the bevel.

Enter a revised width in this field in the Property Bar:

Enter a revised height in this field in the Property Bar:

When you apply a bevel to text, you control how its edges are cut. You can apply bevels from the text front or back.

Applying a front bevel

While text is being viewed in the 3D Viewport, refer to the Property Bar and do the following:

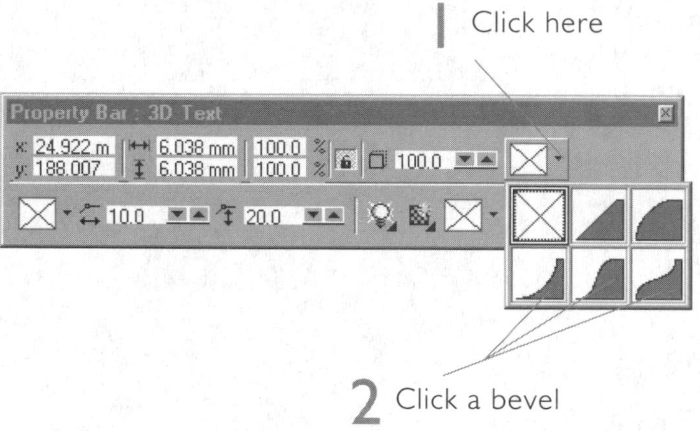

Finally, click anywhere in the Work area.

Applying a back bevel

While text is being viewed in the 3D Viewport, refer to the Property Bar and do the following:

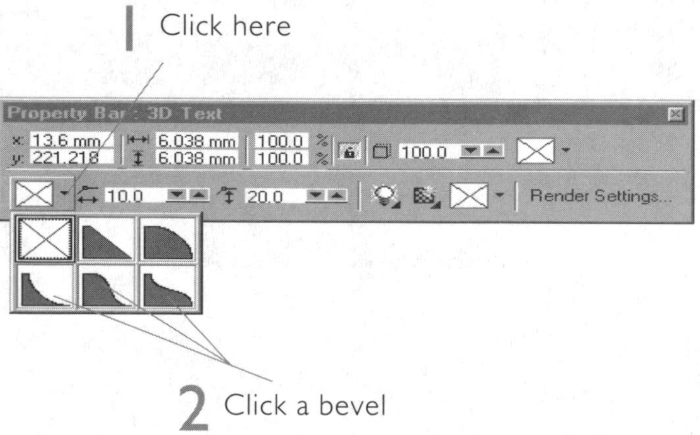

Finally, click anywhere in the Work area.

Applying pattern fills to 3D text

Filling extruded text with any of the patterns supplied with CorelDRAW 8 makes them look more natural. However, you should bear in mind the following restrictions:

1. applying pattern fills dramatically increases the size of the host file
2. as a result, 3D text which has had a fill imposed takes longer to render and print
3. because of 1. and 2. above, you should apply pattern fills sparingly

Applying a fill

While text is being viewed in the 3D Viewport, refer to the Property Bar and do the following:

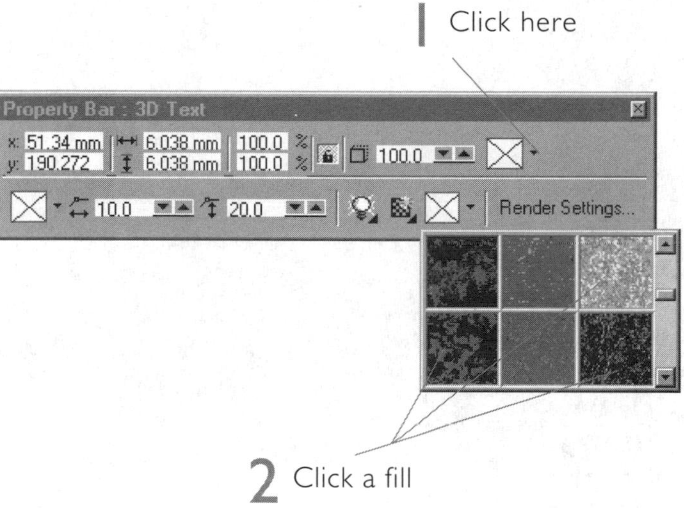

Finally, click anywhere in the Work area.

Rendering 3D text

Rendering is the final stage in the creation of extruded text. Prior to the rendering process, you can control:

- the unit of measurement
- the resolution (in d.p.i. – dots per inch)
- the image size
- the quality of the rendering process

Preparing to render

While text is being viewed in the 3D Viewport, click this button in the Property Bar:

Render Settings...

Carry out the following steps, as appropriate:

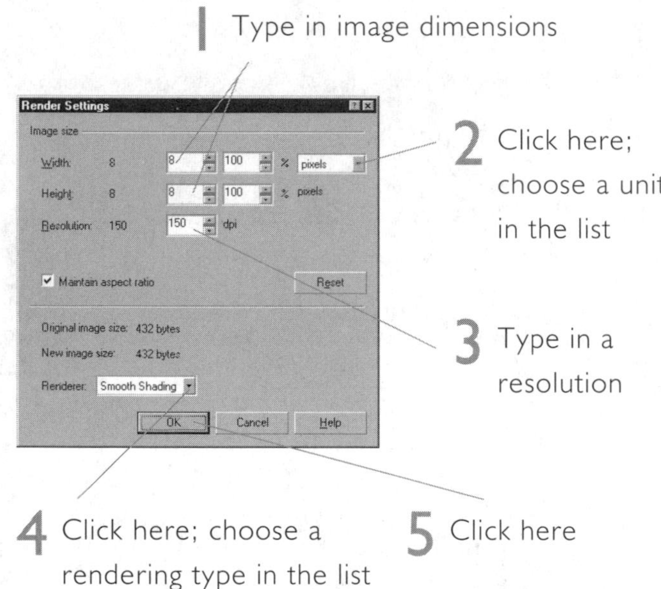

1 Type in image dimensions

2 Click here; choose a unit in the list

3 Type in a resolution

4 Click here; choose a rendering type in the list

5 Click here

If, after rendering, the 3D text isn't completely suitable, double-click the resulting bitmap. This launches the 3D Viewport; carry out any further editing required in line with earlier topics.

Initiating the rendering process

When you've finished customising your extruded text, simply click outside the 3D Viewport.

Chapter Six

The Outline Tool

This chapter shows you how to apply and customise object outlines. You'll learn how to apply pre-defined outlines; specify various outline settings (width, colour and style); add arrows to line ends; create your own arrow designs; customise line endings; use CorelDRAW's calligraphic pen; and preset outline defaults for objects you create in all future CorelDRAW sessions.

Covers

An overview

Every object you create in CorelDRAW automatically has a default outline. You can change this, if you want. Outline features you can change include:

- line colour
- line thickness (hairline to thick)
- line shape (slanted or symmetrical)
- line endings (of open – unfilled – objects)
- corner endings (of closed – filled – objects)

Technically, when you change an object's outline you amend the visible line which follows the object's perimeter. You don't need to concern yourself overly with what is generally, in practice, a fine distinction. However, you should bear in mind one result: if you apply a blank outline to an object (sometimes a worthwhile option), because it isn't visible CorelDRAW regards the object as not having an outline.

You can implement the various outline changes in the following ways:

— by using the Outline Tool and its fly-out

— by using the Outline Pen dialog

— by using the Pen roll-up

The available outline settings vary somewhat according to which version of CorelDRAW you're using – the differences are discussed in subsequent topics.

General guidelines

The Outline Tool provides access to several pre-defined outline settings, and is therefore a convenient short-cut. The Pen roll-up, like all roll-ups, can sit on screen more or less permanently, and is thus preferable if you're carrying out a lot of outline adjustments. However, the Outline Pen dialog is the main channel for working with outlines, if only because it provides the most features and precision.

Working with preset outlines

In versions before 8, the Outline fly-out is slightly different. For example, in the fly-out in versions 3-5, there are additional outline buttons. For instance, in version 5, the following button:

imposes a greyscale outline.

In all versions before 7, too, there are buttons which impose standard black and white outlines; in versions 5-6, they look like this:

White outline

Black outline

In versions 3 and 4. they're simply white and black squares, respectively.

The Outline Tool produces a useful fly-out. If you need to apply outlines to one or more objects quickly and conveniently, and the *precise* thickness of the outline isn't of primary importance, use the Outline fly-out.

First, select the object(s) you want to outline. (If you're about to create a new object and want to set its outline on-the-fly, see page 116 first). Turn to the Toolbox and carry out step 1 below. Then click one of the additional options detailed in the illustration below:

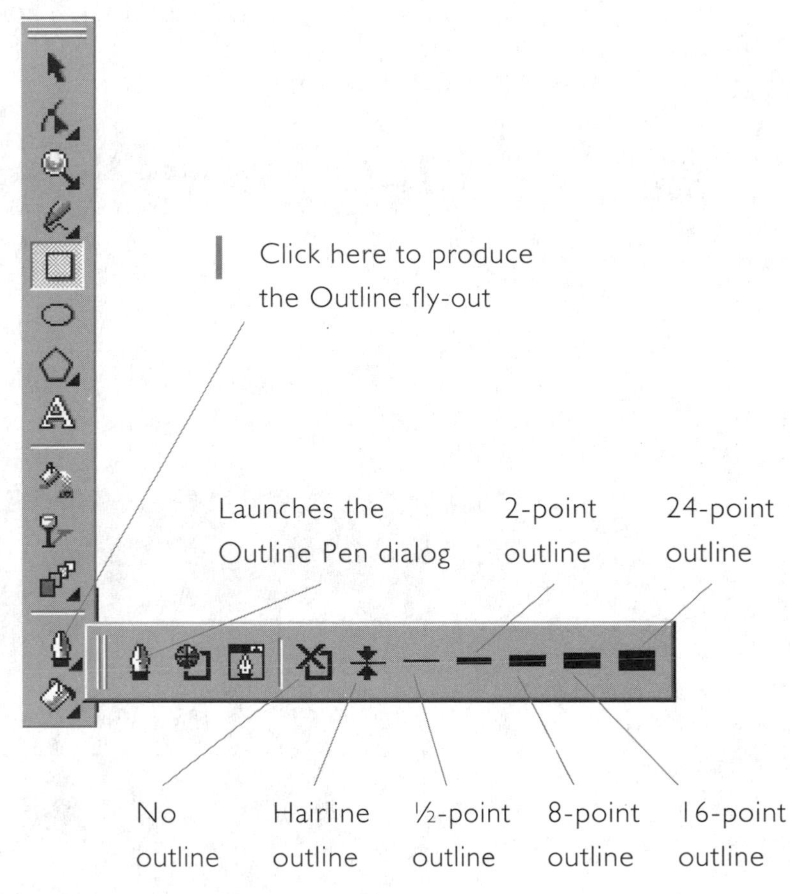

Setting outline widths

There are two principal routes to the establishment of *precise* outline widths: the Outline Pen dialog, and the Pen roll-up.

Using the Outline Pen dialog

You can specify a specific outline width from within the Outline Pen dialog. You can also specify which unit you want the width measured in.

First, select the object(s) you want to outline. Launch the Outline Pen dialog. To do this, launch the Outline fly-out (see page 103 for how to do this). Then do the following:

In versions before 8, the Outline fly-out is slightly different.

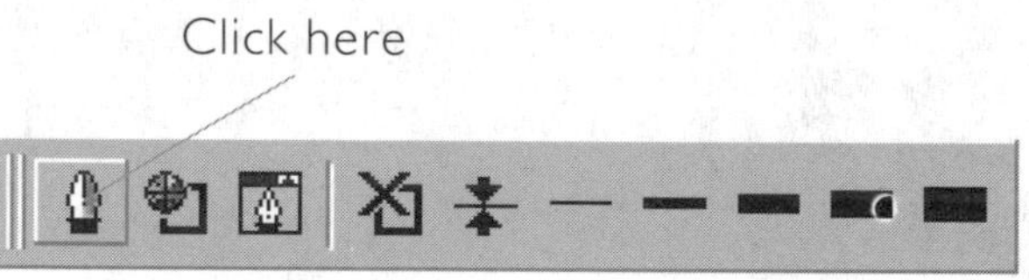

Now carry out the following steps:

1 (Optional) Click here and choose a new unit from the list

In versions before 8, this dialog is slightly different.

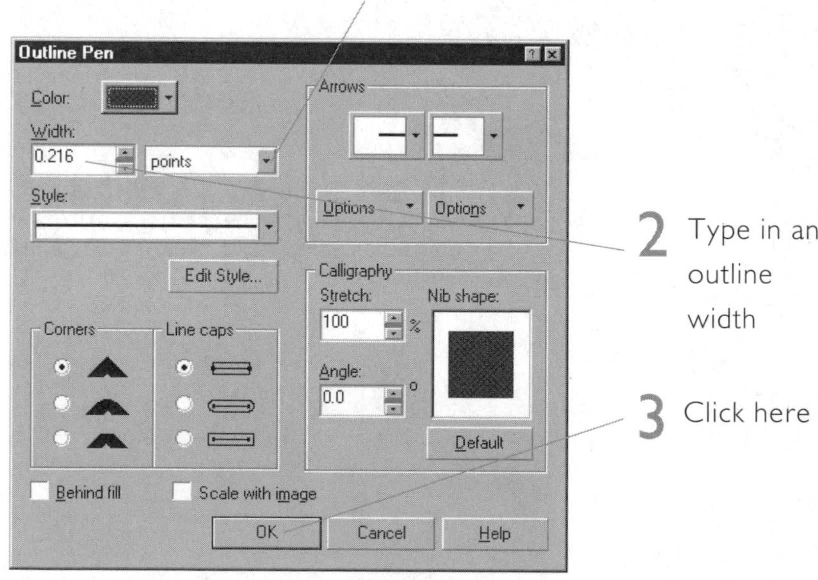

Using the Pen roll-up

The Pen roll-up has convenience on its side: you can keep it on-screen for as long as necessary without it getting in your way, which makes its use perfect if you want to work with a number of outlines. However, it doesn't offer the same precision as the Outline Pen dialog when it comes to setting outline width: you can only apply set increments.

In versions before 8, the Outline fly-out is slightly different.

In versions 3 and 4, the Pen Roll-Up button in the fly-out looks like this:

Re step 1 – in versions 3-6, click the Update From button instead.

If you need more precision when setting outline widths, you can reach the Outline Pen dialog directly from within the Pen roll-up. Simply click Edit.

First, select the object(s) you want to outline. Launch the Outline fly-out (see page 103 for how to do this). Now carry out the following procedure:

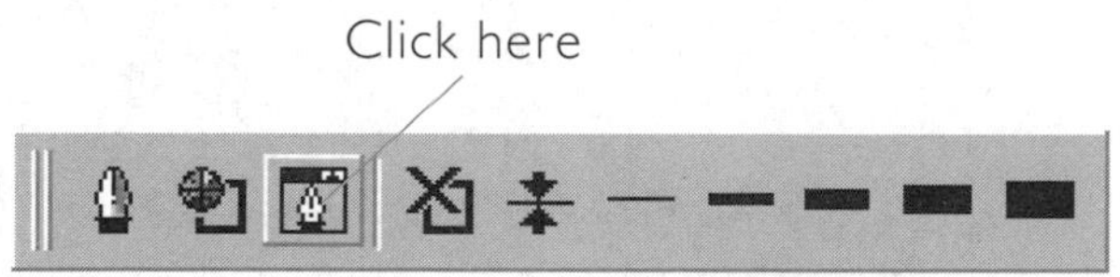

Carry out step 1 below if you want to copy an existing object's outline and apply it to the object(s) you selected above. OR follow step 2 if you want to impose your own settings. Finally, perform step 3 in either case:

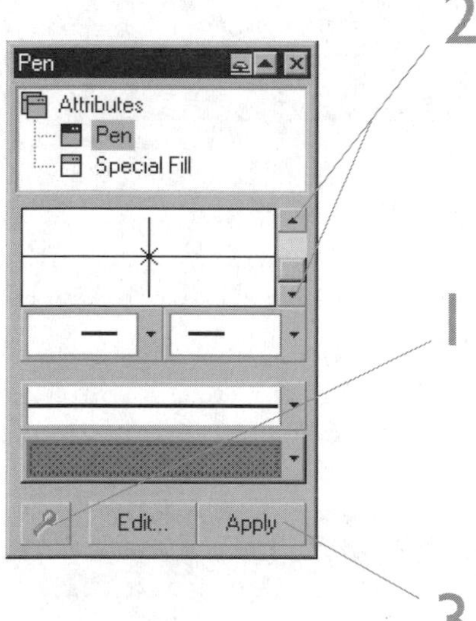

2 Click on the higher arrow to increase the outline width, or on the lower to decrease it. Repeat as often as necessary

1 Click here. The cursor turns into an arrow. Move it over the outline whose width you want to copy and left-click once

3 Click here

Setting outline colours

You can apply colours to outlines in a variety of ways. We'll be looking at the following methods:

- using the Outline Pen dialog
- using the Pen roll-up
- using the on-screen colour palette

Using the Outline Pen dialog

First select the object(s) whose outlines you want to colour. Then launch the Outline Pen dialog. Now carry out the following steps:

In versions before 8, this dialog is slightly different.

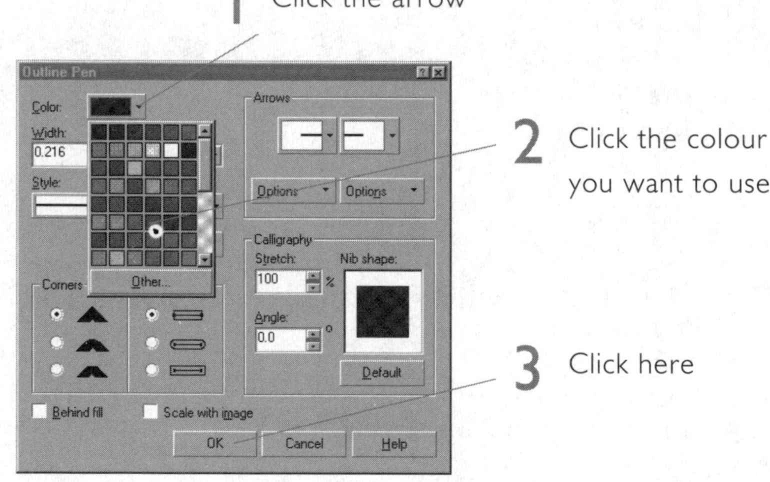

In versions before 8, the Outline fly-out is slightly different.

Using the Pen roll-up

First select the object(s) whose outlines you want to colour. Then launch the Pen fly-out by carrying out the following procedures:

In versions 3 and 4, the Pen Roll-Up button in the fly-out looks like this:

By default, the Colour Palette in version 8 displays on the right of the screen; in all earlier versions, however, the default location is on the bottom.

To reposition the Palette in versions 6-8, click it outside the colour swatches, then drag it to another screen edge.

In the roll-up, do the following:

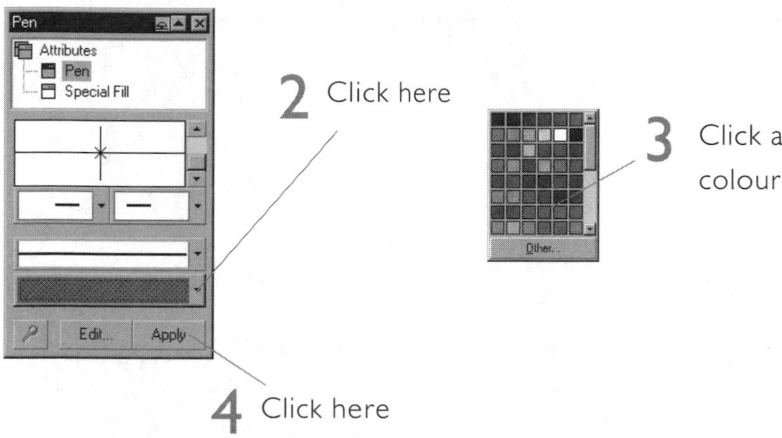

Using the Colour Palette

First select one or more objects whose outlines you want to colour. Then refer to the on-screen palette – see page 9 if you're not sure of its location, and see the Handy Tip if it isn't currently on screen.

If the Colour Palette isn't currently visible, users of versions 5-8 should pull down the View menu and click Color Palette. In the sub-menu, choose the palette you want to use.

Users of versions 3-4 should click Show Color Palettes and Color Palettes respectively in the Display menu. In the sub-menu, choose the palette you want to use.

Carry out the following procedure:

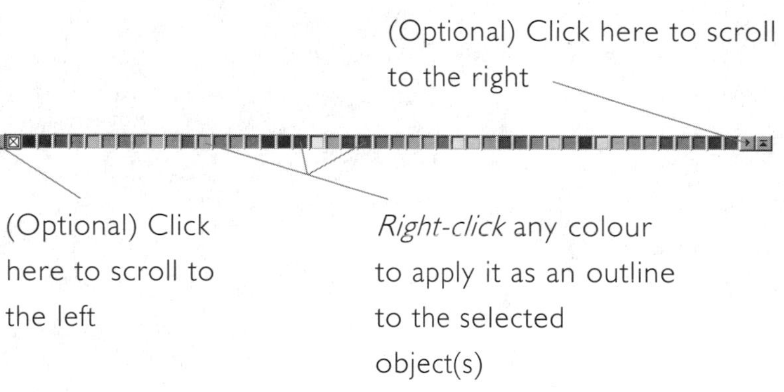

Setting outline styles

CorelDRAW provides a variety of pre-defined line styles (including a solid line) which you can apply as outlines. The numerous options include:

- dotted lines
- dashed lines
- lines with combinations of dots, dashes and spaces, in varying sizes and permutations

You can impose these styles in the following ways:

— by using the Outline Pen dialog

— by using the Pen roll-up

Using the Outline Pen dialog

First select the object(s) whose outlines you want to re-style. Then launch the Outline Pen dialog. Now carry out the following steps:

In versions before 8, this dialog is slightly different.

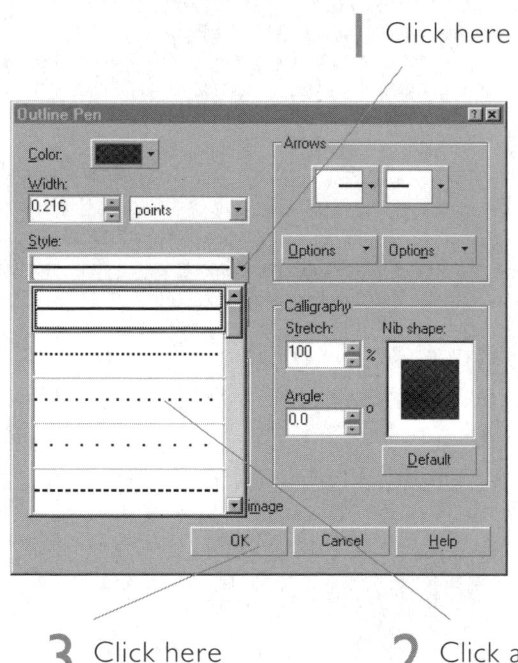

1 Click here

2 Click a line style

3 Click here

Using the Pen roll-up

First select the object(s) whose outlines you want to re-style. Then launch the Pen roll-up and carry out the following procedure:

In versions before 8, the Pen roll-up is slightly different.

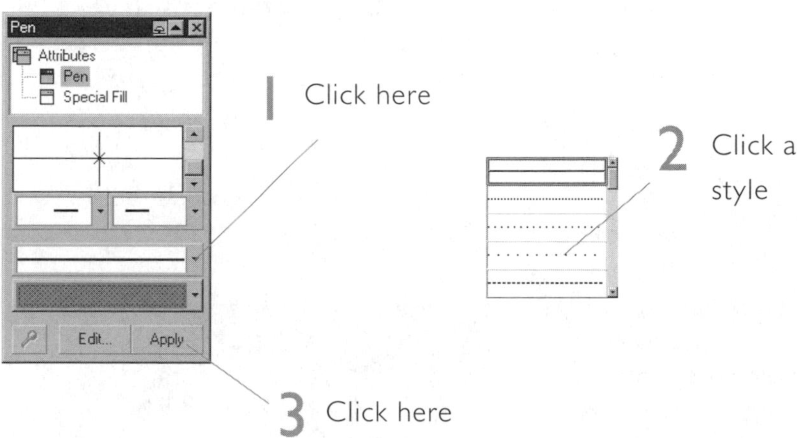

Example:

A polygon, outlined with one of the almost 30 line styles

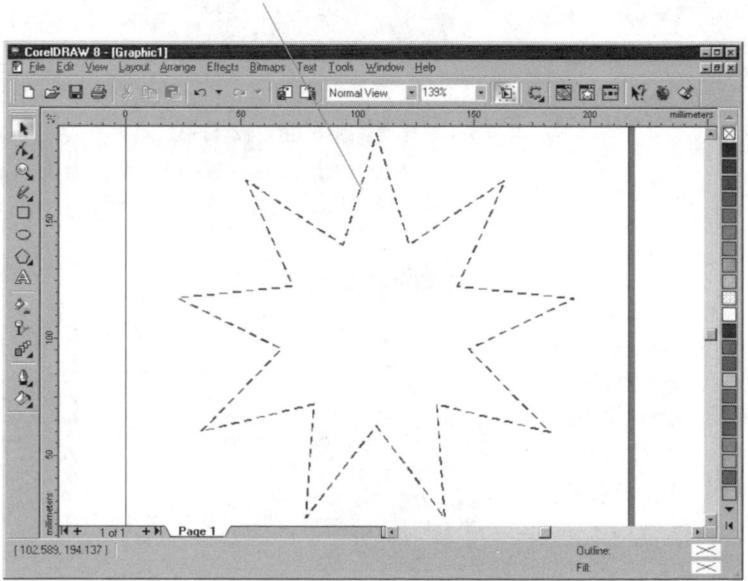

Applying outline arrows

You can add arrows to the ends of lines and open curves (CorelDRAW lets you choose from a wide selection of arrow designs) by means of the Outline Pen dialog or the Pen roll-up.

Using the Outline dialog

First select the line or curve whose ends you want to apply arrows to. Launch the Outline Pen dialog. Now carry out the following, as appropriate:

The left arrow selector defines the arrow for the *start* of your line/curve; the right-hand selector defines the *end* arrow.

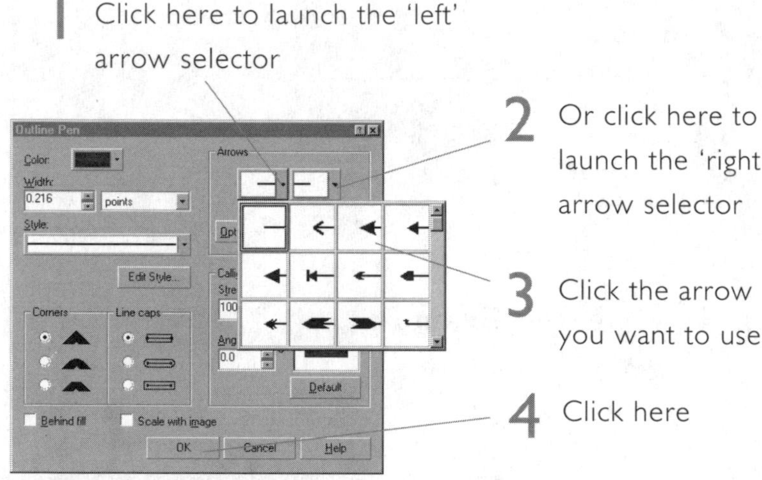

In versions before 8, this dialog is slightly different.

Using the Pen roll-up

First select the line or curve whose ends you want to apply arrows to. Launch the Pen roll-up; carry out the following:

In versions before 8, the Pen roll-up is slightly different.

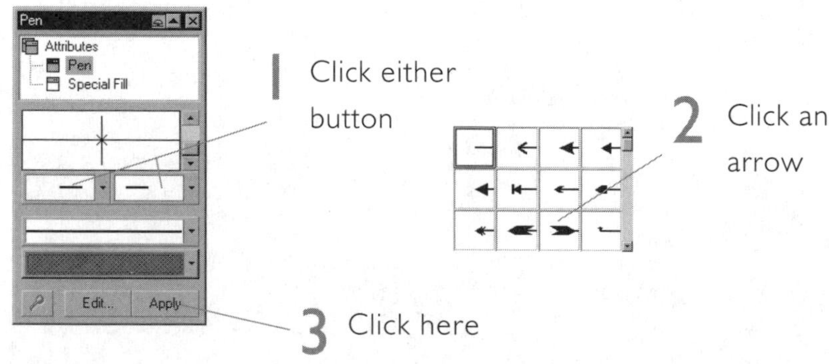

Editing arrows

When you apply arrows to line or curve ends, you're not limited to the arrows CorelDRAW supplies. You can, if you want, edit these to produce your own designs.

When you want to create your own arrow design, it's helpful to base it on the existing design which is nearest to what you want.

In versions before 8, this dialog is slightly different.

Launching the arrow editor

Use the Outline Pen dialog to select an arrow (see page 110). Then carry out the following steps, as appropriate:

An arrow has been allocated...

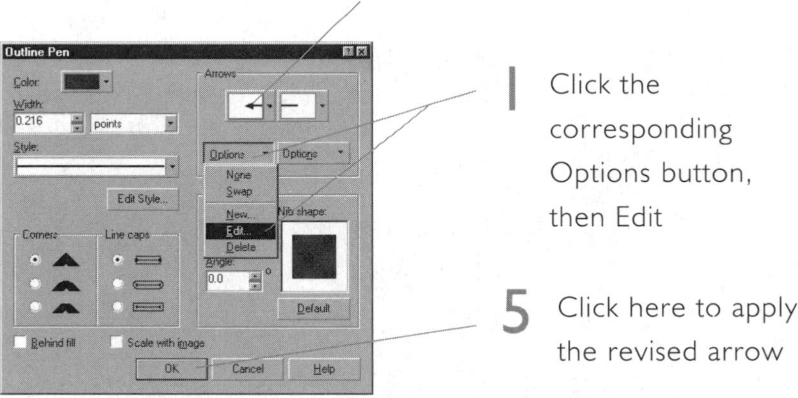

1 Click the corresponding Options button, then Edit

5 Click here to apply the revised arrow

In versions before 8, this dialog is slightly different.

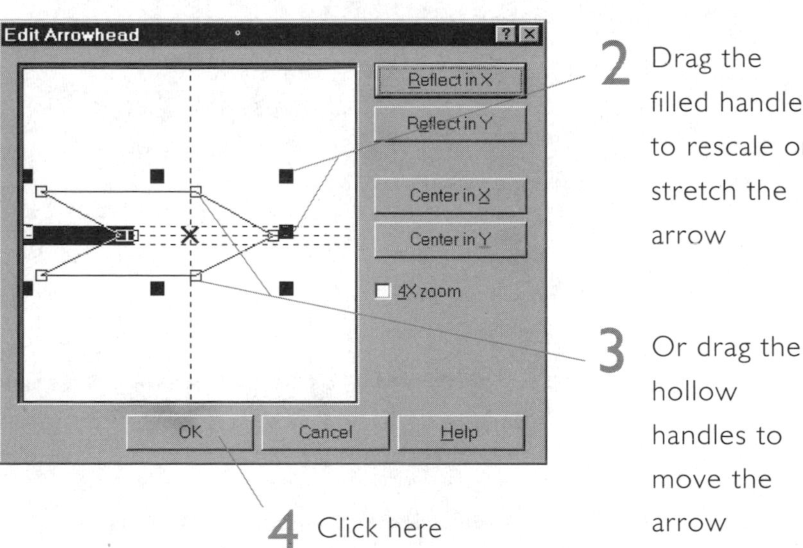

2 Drag the filled handles to rescale or stretch the arrow

3 Or drag the hollow handles to move the arrow

4 Click here

Configuring polygon corners

CorelDRAW lets you apply rounded corners to polygons. The effects of doing this can be quite subtle, but they are easy to implement.

Corners can be:

- pointed (the default)
- rounded
- blunt

Applying a specific corner type

First, select the polygon(s) whose corners you want to customise. Launch the Outline Pen dialog. Then do the following:

In versions before 8, this dialog is slightly different.

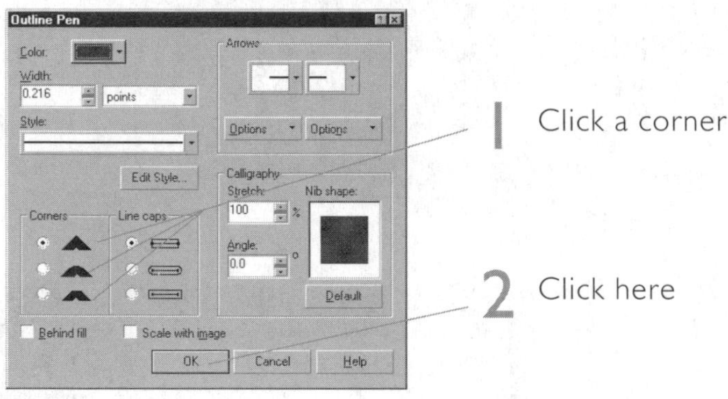

Examples:

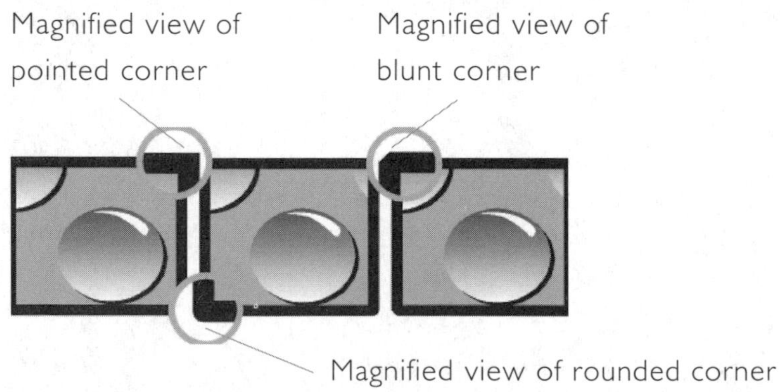

Configuring line caps

Another way in which you can customise lines is to specify how their ends are capped. There are three settings you can choose from:

- truncated
- round
- square

Capping lines

First, select the line(s) whose cap you want to customise. Launch the Outline Pen dialog. Then do the following:

In versions before 8, this dialog is slightly different.

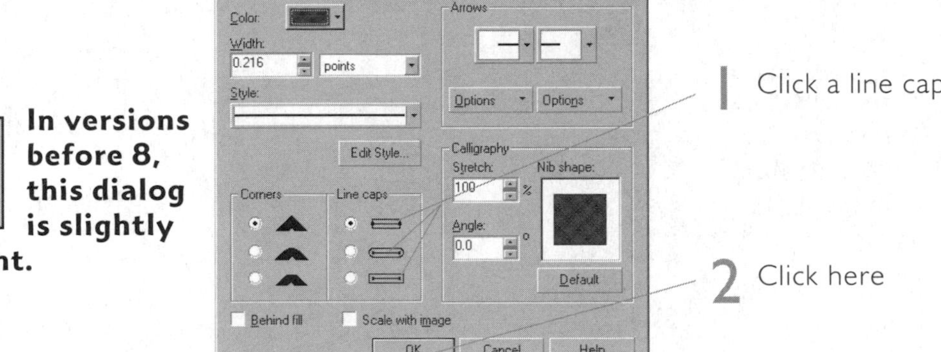

Examples:

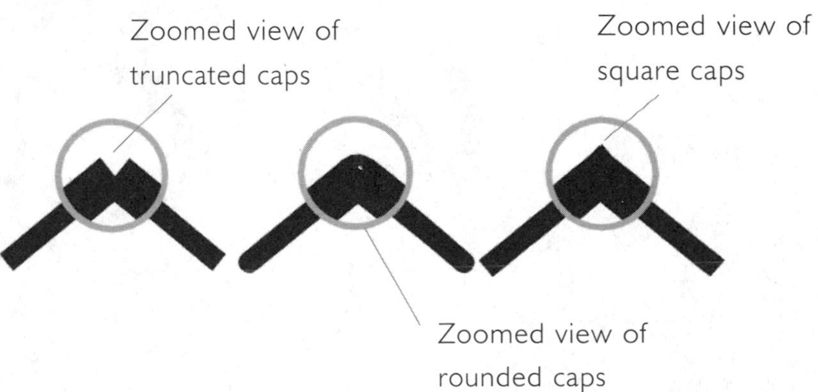

Applying calligraphic outlines

You can apply calligraphic effects to outlines. You do this by varying:

- the corner shape
- the nib stretch
- the nib angle

Applying a calligraphic outline

First, select the object(s) on which you want to impose a calligraphic outline. Launch the Outline Pen dialog. Then do the following:

In versions before 8, this dialog is slightly different.

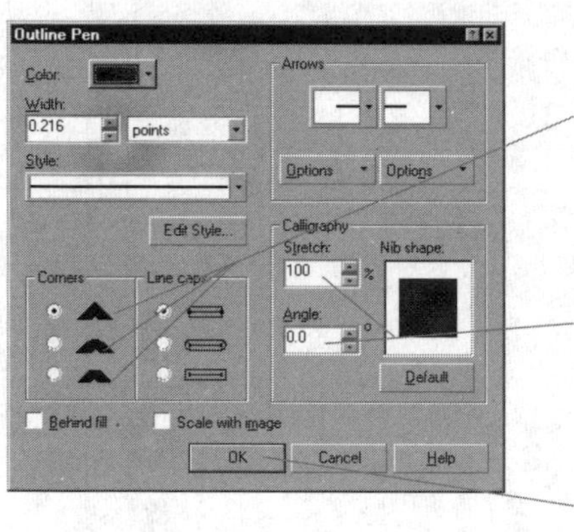

1 Select a corner style (to determine the basic nib shape)

2 Type in Stretch and Angle values

3 Click here

Examples:

Default

Very low stretch/ medium angle

Low stretch/ minus angle

Further outline options

There are two additional outline options which are only accessible from within the Outline Pen dialog. Both can have a substantial impact on the efficiency of your outlines.

The Behind Fill option is specially useful for work with text outlines.

The Behind Fill option

Click this to have your outline placed behind an object's fill. This helps to adjust an outline which is too emphatic by making only half its thickness visible.

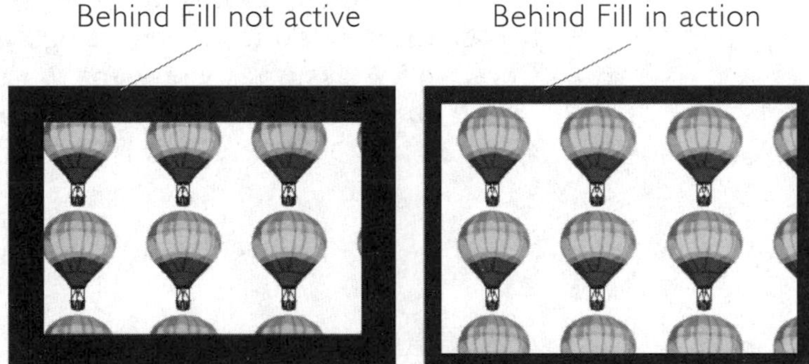

The Scale With Image option

This option ensures that outlines you apply are scaled proportionately when you resize an object.

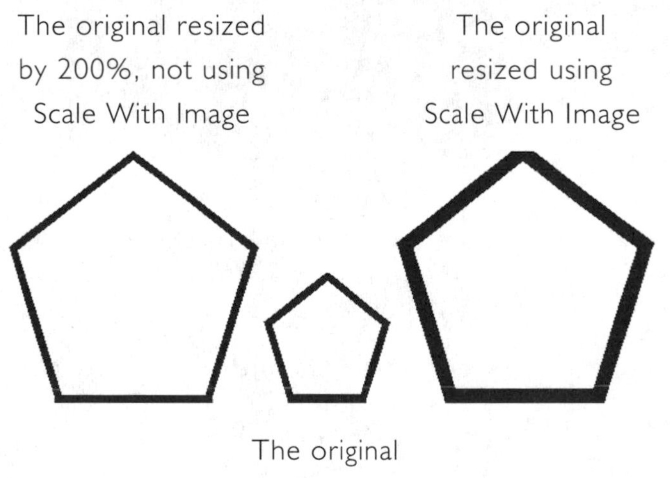

Setting outline defaults

By default, CorelDRAW applies the following outline defaults whenever you create a new graphic object:

- Width – around 0.2 points
- Colour – black
- No arrows, corners, line caps or calligraphic effects are in force.

If you implement any of the processes we've discussed in this chapter *without pre-selecting an existing object,* CorelDRAW assumes you want to set revised default values for *all* future outlines (except text unless you specify this – see the HANDY TIP). This is a useful device: it can save you a lot of time and effort.

To set revised outline defaults, do the following:

Re step 1 – select Artistic Text and/ or Paragraph Text if you want your new outline defaults to apply to these object types.

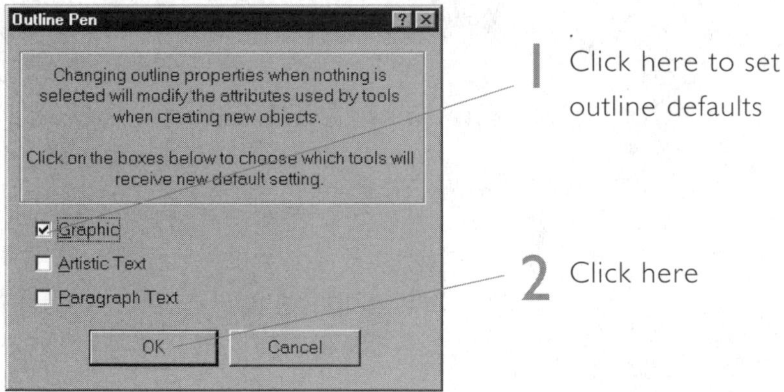

1 Click here to set outline defaults

2 Click here

CorelDRAW now launches the Outline Pen dialog. Use this in the normal way to set the appropriate outline defaults, then click OK.

Henceforth, the outlines of any objects you create (in this and subsequent CorelDRAW sessions) will automatically attract these default values.

Chapter Seven

The Fill Tool

In this chapter, you'll learn how to fill CorelDRAW objects. You'll learn to use the five fill types. We'll also discuss how to copy fills between objects, easily and conveniently, and how to preset fill defaults for objects you create in all future editing sessions. Additionally, you'll learn how to apply (and tile) fills *interactively,* with the mouse.

Covers

An overview

Fills are probably one of CorelDRAW's most popular and useful features. Any closed object in CorelDRAW can be filled.

You can apply any of the following fill types:

- uniform fills
- pattern fills
- fountain fills
- texture fills
- PostScript fills

Texture fills are unavailable in version 3.

HANDY TIP **In versions 3-5, the Special Fill roll-up is known as the Fill roll-up. (Henceforth, this chapter refers to it as the Special Fill roll-up).**

The permutations for each of these are almost infinite.

You can fill objects by using (variously):

— the Special Fill (or Fill) roll-up

— the various Fill dialogs

— the on-screen Colour Palette

The dialogs you can use offer the most precision, and change according to the function. For example, if you're imposing a fountain fill, you can work from the Fountain Fill dialog, while uniform fills can be manipulated from within the Uniform Fill dialog...

Earlier versions have more dialogs; these are discussed when we meet them.

General guidelines

Unlike outlines, there is no all-purpose dialog from which all fill settings can be implemented. Instead, CorelDRAW provides a series of independent dialogs. However, you can also use the Special Fill roll-up as a base from which to work with almost all the various CorelDRAW fills. If you need more precision, you can launch the appropriate dialog from within the roll-up.

To edit fills with greater precision, click the Edit button in the roll-up.

CorelDRAW lets you copy fills from one object to another very easily and painlessly... Use this technique to save yourself a lot of time and effort.

Another labour-saving technique is the ability to preset fill defaults. By using this, you can ensure that any objects you create, in the current and any subsequent CorelDRAW editing session, automatically inherit the fill you've stipulated.

The illustration below shows a light-hearted use of the fill techniques we'll go on to discuss in the rest of this chapter.

A uniform (conical) fill

A two-colour fill

A vector pattern fill

A full-colour fill

A texture (fractal) fill

Applying uniform fills

Uniform fills are solid, single-colour/shade fills. These are the easiest to impose, and arguably the most often used. You can apply uniform fills in two principal ways:

- by using the on-screen Colour Palette
- by using the Uniform Fill dialog

In versions before 8, the Fill fly-out is slightly different. For example, in versions 3-5, there are additional fill buttons. As an illustration, the following button :

imposes a greyscale fill in version 5.

In all versions before 7, too, there are buttons which impose standard black and white fills; in versions 5-6, they look like this:

 White fill

 Black fill

while – in versions 3 and 4 – they're simply white and black squares, respectively.

The Uniform Fill dialog provides the most complexity; use this to achieve greater fill precision.

In addition, you can use the Fill fly-out to *remove* fills directly. (We'll look at the use of the on-screen palette and the Uniform Fill dialog on page 121.)

Removing existing fills

First, select the closed object(s) whose fill you want to remove. (If you're about to create one or more new objects and want to ensure that they – and all objects you create subsequently – do not have a fill, see page 136 first.) Now turn to the Toolbox and carry out the following steps, as appropriate:

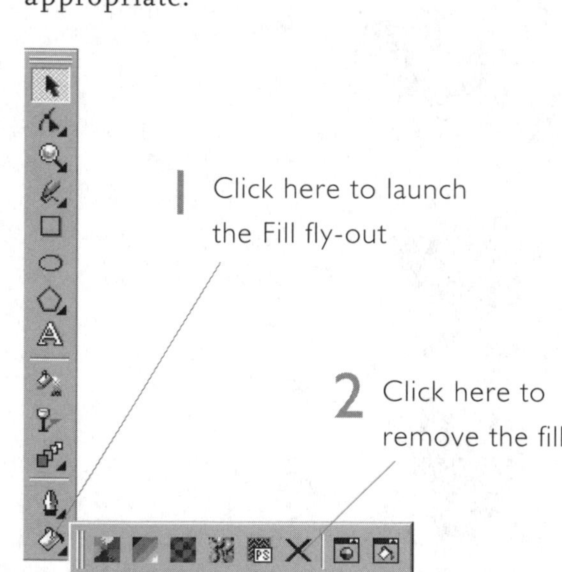

If the Colour Palette isn't currently visible, see the HANDY TIP on page 107 for how to make it display.

In versions before 8, the Fill fly-out is slightly different.

The Uniform Fill button resembles this:

The dialog which launches after step 1 varies considerably according to which version of CorelDRAW you're using.

In essence, select a colour model and/ or palette. Click a colour in the Colour display. Finally, click OK.

There are two ways to apply *customised* uniform fills:

Using the Colour Palette

First select the closed object(s) you want to fill. Then refer to the palette at the edge of the screen and do the following:

(Optional) Click here to scroll to the right

(Optional) Click here to scroll to the left

Left-click any colour to apply it as a fill

Using the Uniform Fill dialog

First, select the object(s) you want to fill. Launch the Fill fly-out (see page 120 for how to do this). Then do the following:

1 Click here

Now carry out the following steps:

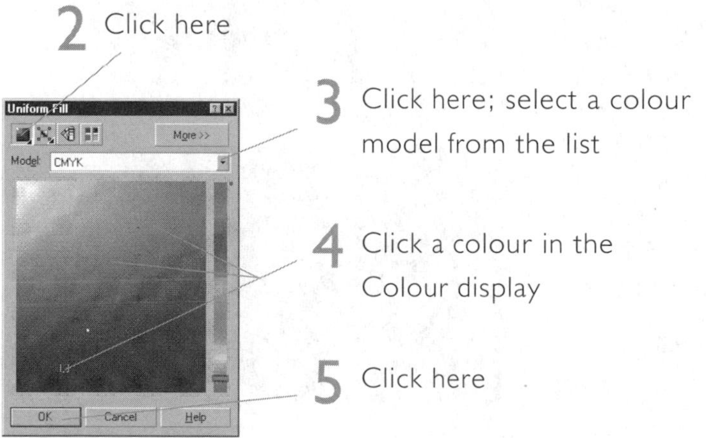

Pattern fills – an overview

Two-colour patterns are particularly simple designs (by default, black and white) which are easy and quick to use, though nonetheless effective.

Full-colour patterns are more complex, with greater colour detail.

Bitmaps are photograph-quality designs which can place heavy demands on your system in terms of memory use. However, they do provide excellent results.

Versions before 6 do not offer bitmap fills.

In some versions, full-colour fills are known as vector fills.

Pattern fills are special fills where one symmetrical design is repeated to occupy the available space (CorelDRAW calls this process 'tiling') without any perceptible seams. You can use three basic pattern types:

- Two-colour patterns
- Full-colour patterns
- Bitmaps

Examples:

A pre-defined two-colour pattern

A pre-defined full-colour pattern

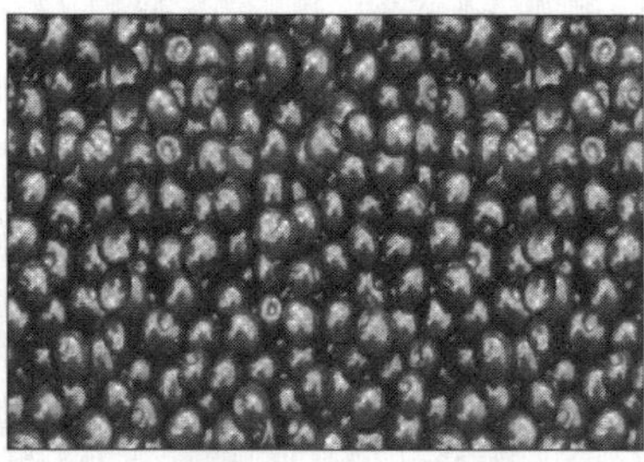

A pre-defined bitmap pattern

Using two-colour pattern fills

First, select the object(s) you want to fill. Launch the Fill fly-out. Then do the following:

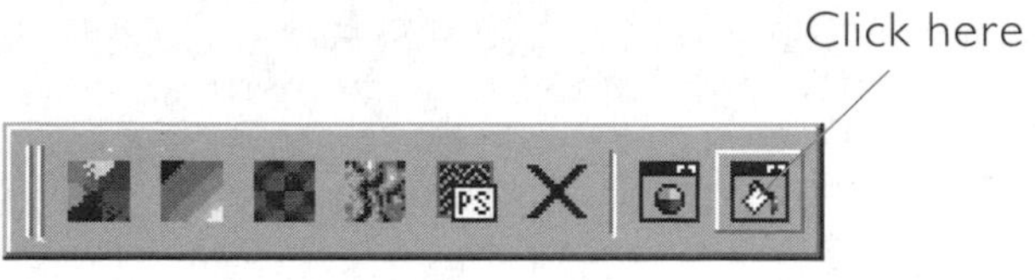

Now carry out the following steps:

In versions 3-6, the Special fill roll-up is slightly different.

For instance, this button:

(or one very much like it) specifically denotes 2-colour patterns. Therefore, step 2 on the right should be omitted.

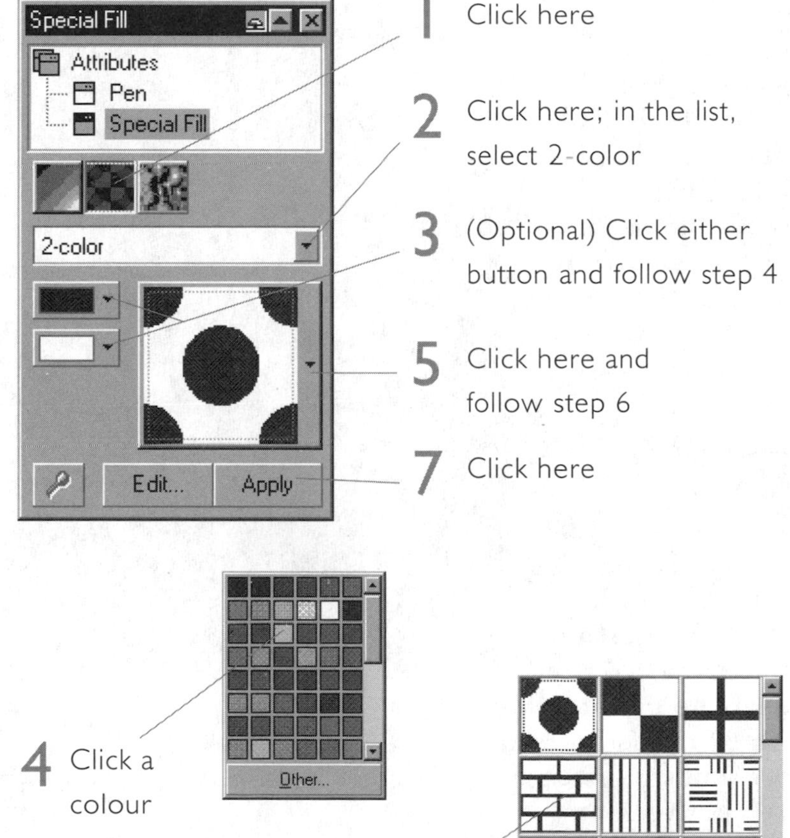

Versions 7 and 8 have one overall pattern dialog. Earlier versions, though, have individual dialogs for each pattern type.

In versions before 7, therefore, click:

(or a button very much like it) in the Fill fly-out. Then complete the resultant dialog as per the steps on the right.

If you want to apply start or end colours to the pattern, click either of the arrows to the right of the Front and Back fields *before* you carry out step 4. In the drop-down list, click a colour.

You can also apply 2-colour fills from within a special dialog.

First, select the object(s) you want to fill. Launch the Fill fly-out. Then do the following:

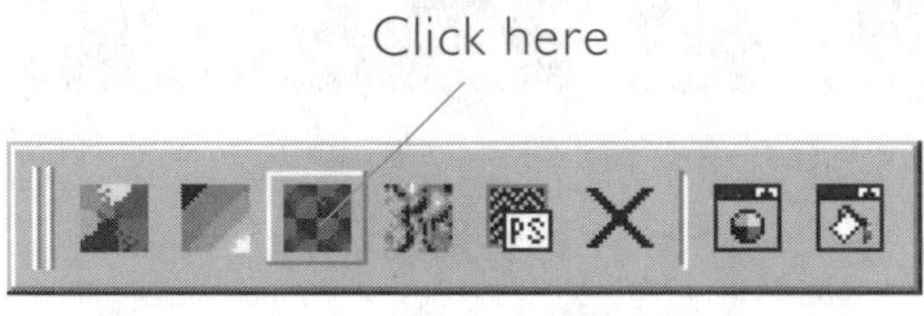

Now do the following:

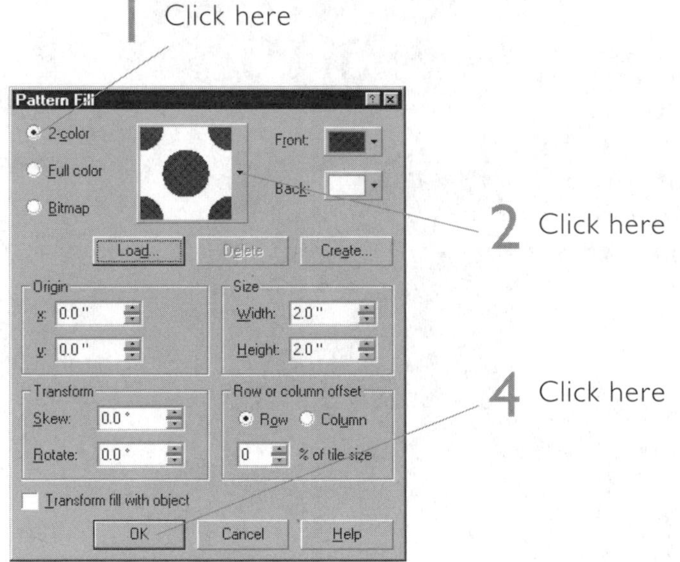

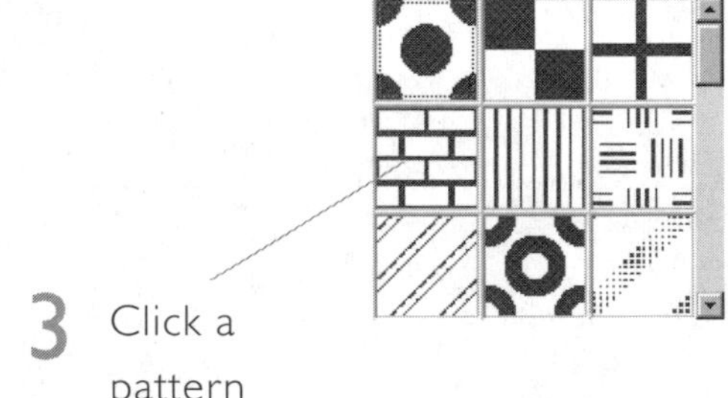

Using full-colour pattern fills

In versions before 7, the Special Fill roll-up is slightly different. Click this button:

in step 1. Then carry out the remaining steps (but omit step 2).

Versions 7 and 8 have one overall pattern dialog. Earlier versions, though, have individual dialogs for each pattern type.

In versions before 7, therefore, click:

(or a button very much like it) in the Fill fly-out. Then complete the resultant dialog as per the steps on the right.

Applying full-colour patterns (1)

First, select the object(s) you want to fill. Launch the Special Fill roll-up. (For how to do this, see page 120.) Now do the following:

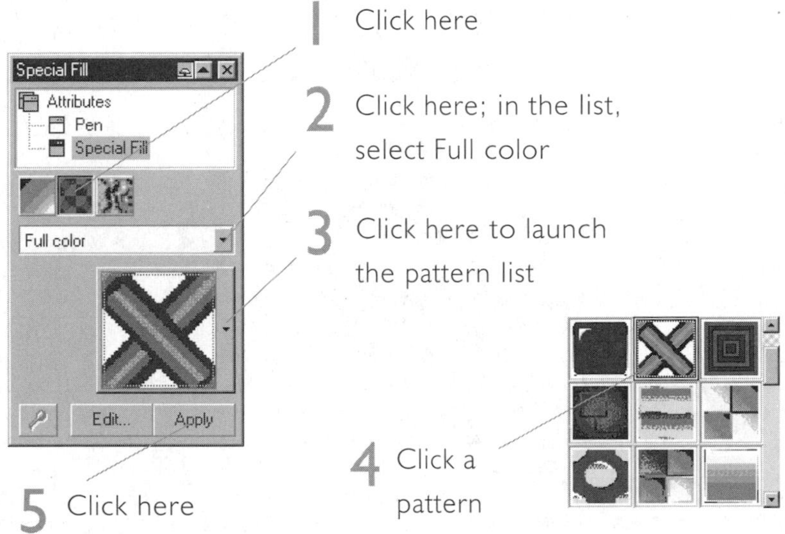

Applying full-colour patterns (2)

First, select the object(s) you want to fill. Launch the Pattern dialog (see page 124 for how to do this). Now do the following:

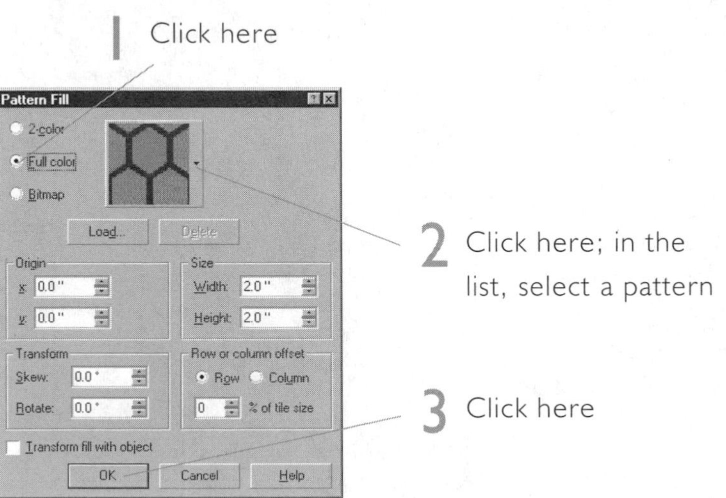

Using bitmap pattern fills

In versions before 7, the Special Fill roll-up is slightly different. Click this button:

in step 1. Then carry out the remaining steps.

Versions 7 and 8 have one overall pattern dialog. Earlier versions, though, have individual dialogs for each pattern type.

In versions before 7, therefore, click:

(or a button very much like it) in the Fill fly-out. Then complete the resultant dialog as per the steps on the right.

Applying bitmap patterns (1)

First, select the object(s) you want to fill. Launch the Special Fill roll-up. (For how to do this, see page 120.) Now do the following:

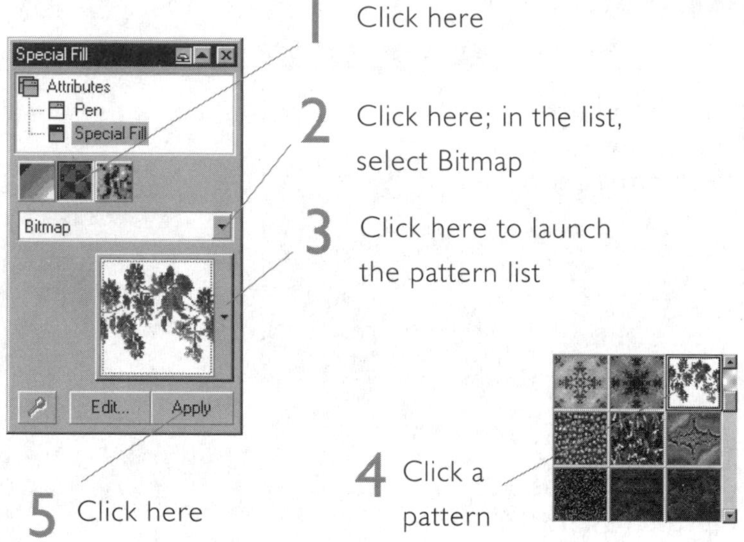

Applying bitmap patterns (2)

First, select the object(s) you want to fill. Launch the Pattern dialog. Now do the following:

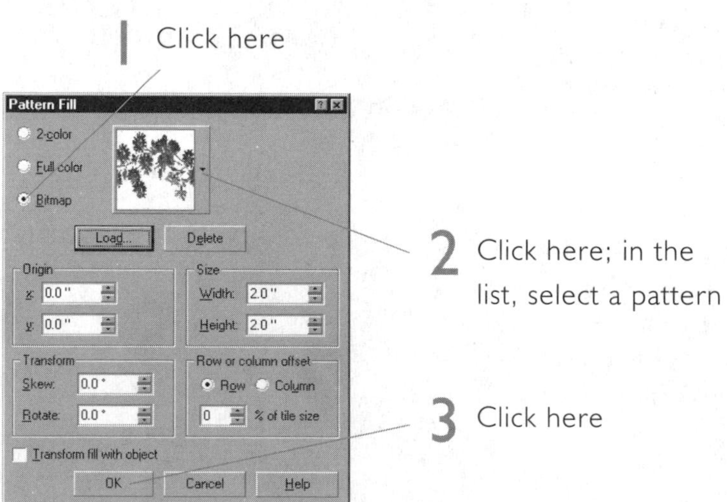

Using fountain fills

You should apply fountain fills with discretion: although spectacular, they can cause problems when printed out or when exported into bitmap formats.

Version 3 users only have access to Linear and Radial fountain fills.

Version 4 users, however, can also use Conical fills.

In versions before 7, the Special Fill roll-up is slightly different.

However, the Fountain Fill button remains substantially unaltered.

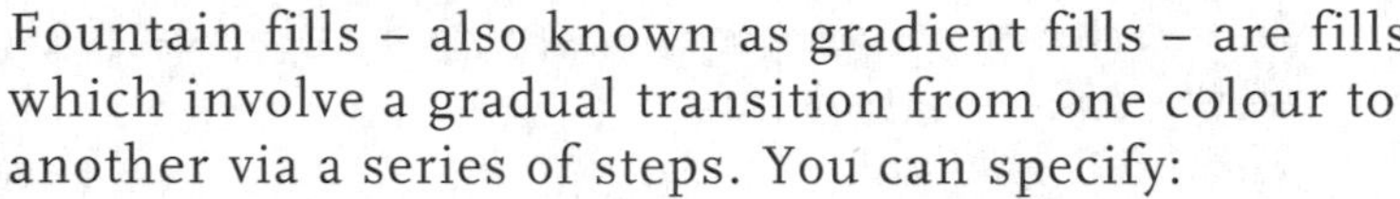

Fountain fills – also known as gradient fills – are fills which involve a gradual transition from one colour to another via a series of steps. You can specify:

- the two colours
- where the transition should start
- how gradual the transition should be (i.e. the number of steps)

There are four kinds of fountain fills:

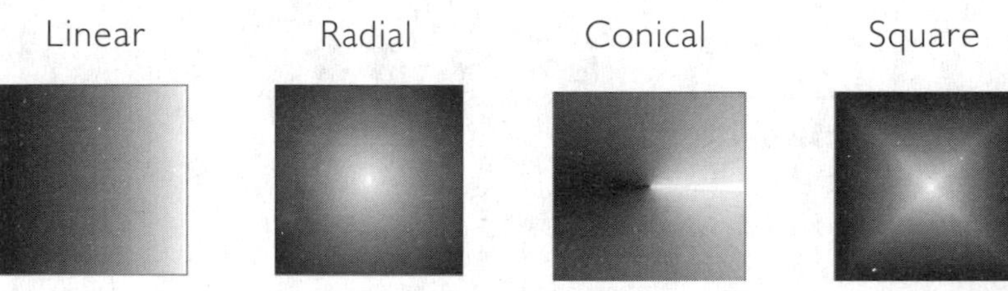

Applying fountain fills with the Special Fill roll-up

First, select the object(s) you want to fill. Launch the Special Fill roll-up. Now do the following:

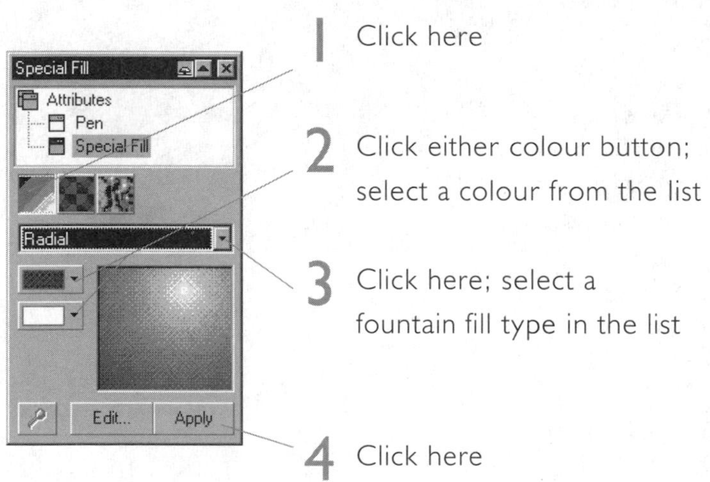

In versions before 7, the Fill fly-out is slightly different. However, the Fountain Fill button is substantially unaltered.

As a shortcut, instead of following steps 1-5, click the arrow button to the right of the Presets field and choose from a wide selection of pre-defined fountain fills.

Then follow step 6.

Re step 2 – by default, versions 7 and 8 use 256 steps to define fountain fills.

Allocations for the other versions are:

Version 3	Unspecified
Version 4	20
Version 5	20
Version 6	50

Applying fountain fills with the Fountain Fill dialog

First, select the object(s) you want to fill. Launch the Fill fly-out. (For how to do this, see page 120.) Then do the following:

Click here

Now carry out the following steps, as appropriate:

1. Click here; select a fountain fill type
2. (Optional) Click here, then type in the no. of steps

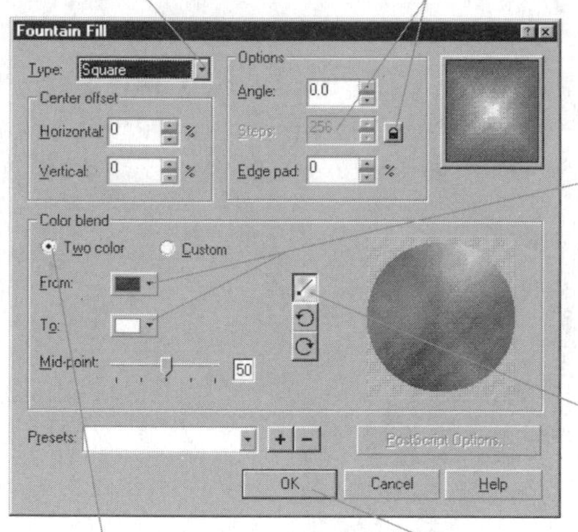

4. Click either colour button; select the colour you want from the list
5. Click here
3. Make sure this is selected
6. Click here to apply the fill

In versions before 7, the Fountain Fill dialog is rather different.

Using texture fills New in version 4

Texture fills are fractal-based, which means they mimic natural materials very realistically. In CorelDRAW 8, texture fills are organised into six texture libraries.

Earlier versions have fewer libraries.

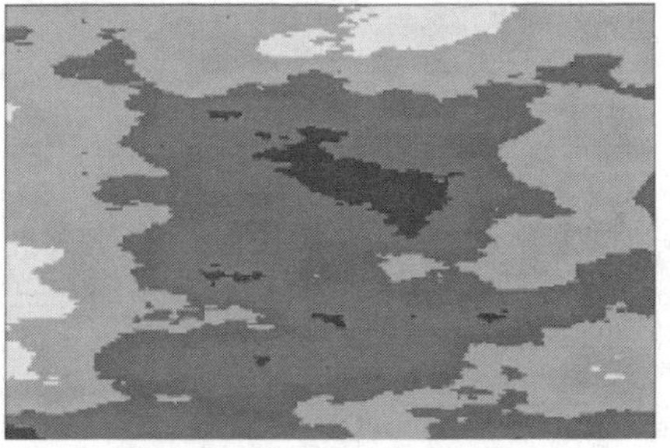

One of CorelDRAW's texture fills

You should apply texture fills with discretion. Though spectacular – not to say highly enjoyable! – they're very memory intensive. They also take up a lot of hard disk space, and can occasionally cause problems when printed.

One feature of texture fills is that they're almost infinitely customisable; each texture offers millions of control permutations.

Creating texture fills with the Special Fill roll-up

First, select the object(s) you want to fill. Launch the Special Fill roll-up. Now do the following:

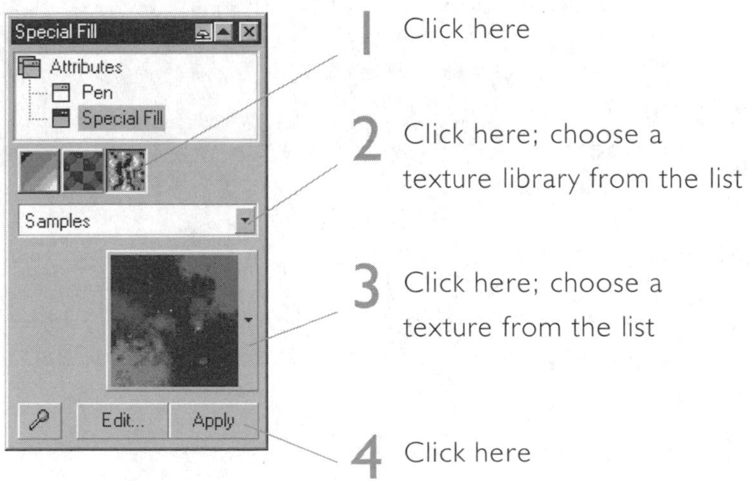

In versions before 8, the Special Fill roll-up is slightly different.

The Texture Fill button looks like this:

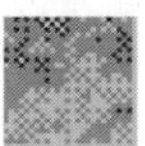

In versions before 8, the Fill fly-out is slightly different. However, the Texture Fill button remains unaltered. (It isn't present in version 3).

Creating texture fills with the Texture Fill dialog

First, select the object(s) you want to fill. Launch the Fill fly-out. (For how to do this, see page 120). Then do the following:

Now carry out the following steps, as appropriate:

If you change the texture settings, click the Preview button at any time to see what the new texture looks like before you carry out step 5.

The number and type of fields present in the lower half of the dialog depend on which texture you choose in step 2.

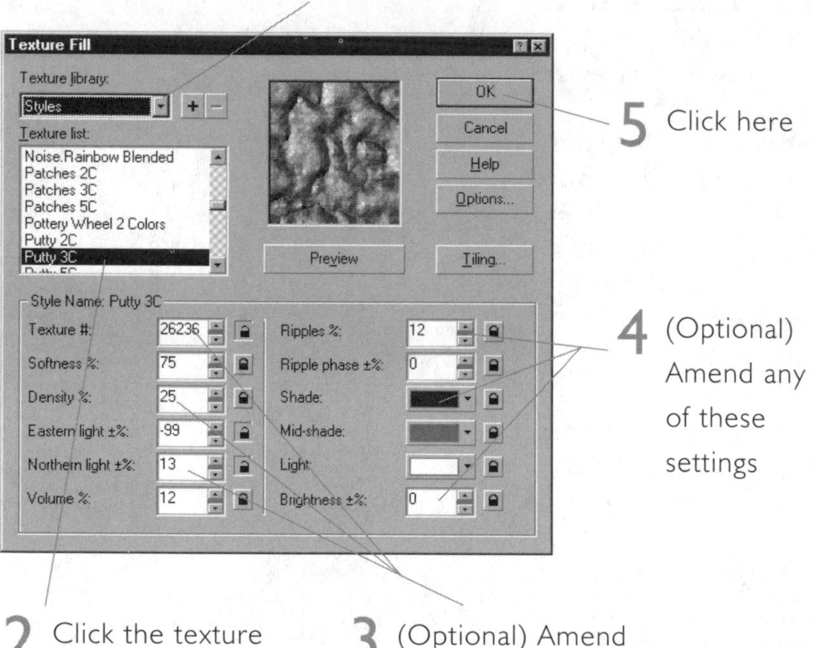

Using interactive fills New in version 7

Version 7 users should click this Toolbox button:

You can use a special tool to apply any of the fills we've discussed in this chapter *interactively*. This means that you can adjust any of the fill parameters on-screen, with the help of the mouse and Property Bar.

Creating a fill interactively

Select one or more objects. Then click this button:

in the Toolbox. Now carry out the following steps:

Re step 1 – the Property Bar changes according to which fill type is chosen.

1 Click here; in the list, select a fill type

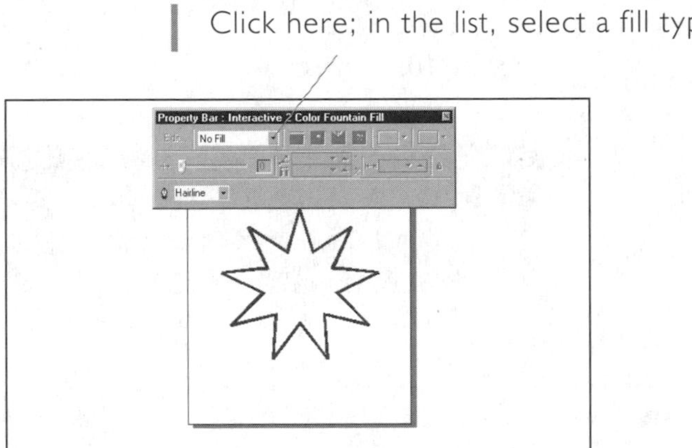

Complete more fields in the Property Bar, as appropriate. For instance, clicking any of these:

selects a specific fountain fill type.

2 Click in the object where you want the fill to start

3 Drag to where you want the fill to end

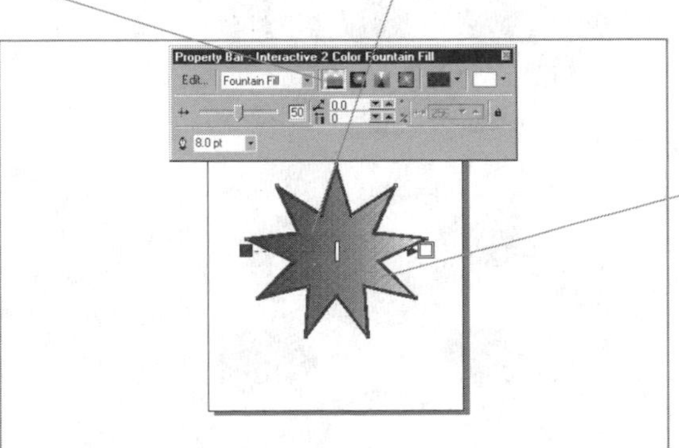

Re steps 2 and 3 – a basic fill is inserted automatically; use the interactive cursor to redefine it.

Tiling pattern fills

It's often desirable to control the dimensions of the tiles with which CorelDRAW constructs pattern fills. You should note the following:

— making pattern tiles smaller results in a denser pattern

— making pattern tiles larger results in a pattern which is easier to see, and often more effective

Tiling fills with the Property Bar

Re step 1 – note the following limitations:

Maximum tile width 15"
Minimum tile width 0.1"

Ensure the Pick tool is active in the Toolbox. Select the pattern fill whose tiling you want to redefine. Now activate the Interactive Fill tool in the Toolbox (see page 131).

Do the following:

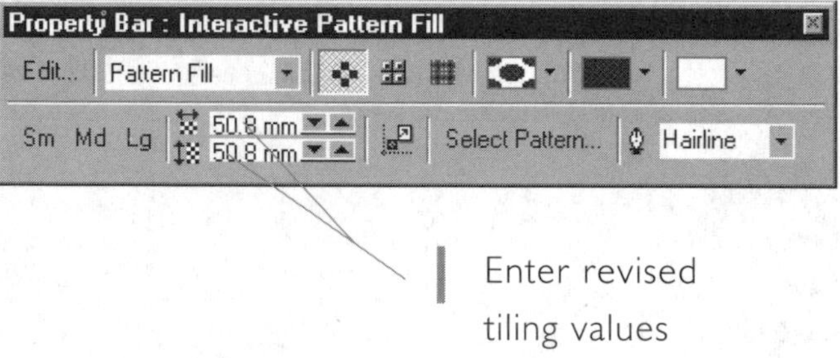

Enter revised tiling values

To tile pattern fills in versions 3-6, launch the relevant pattern dialog. Select Small, Medium or Large.

Alternatively, click the Tiling button. Complete the dialog which launches to specify tiling dimensions in detail. Click OK.

Finally (in both cases), click OK.

Press Enter to implement the tiling amendments.

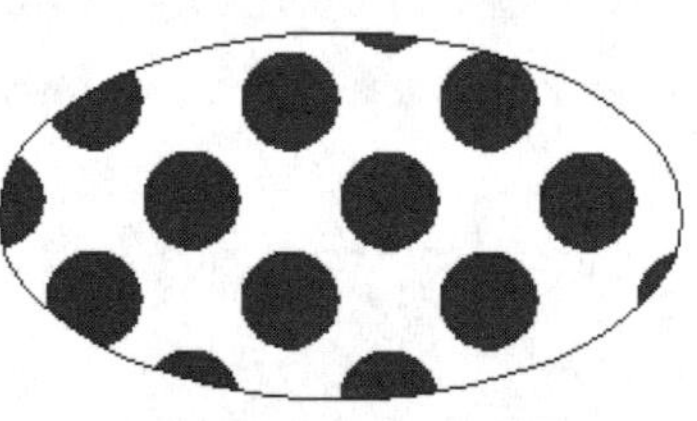

A pattern fill before alteration . . .

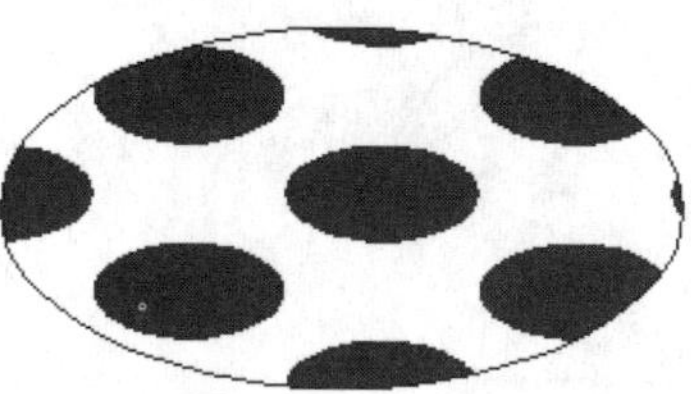

And after the pattern size has been increased

Tiling pattern fills interactively

You can only carry out interactive tiling in versions 7 and 8.

You can also use the Interactive Fill tool to specify tiling dimensions on-the-fly.

Specifying tiling interactively

Ensure the Pick tool is active in the Toolbox. Select the pattern fill whose tiling you want to redefine. Now activate the Interactive Fill tool in the Toolbox (see page 131).

Do the following:

Drag either of these to a new position

The tiling vector

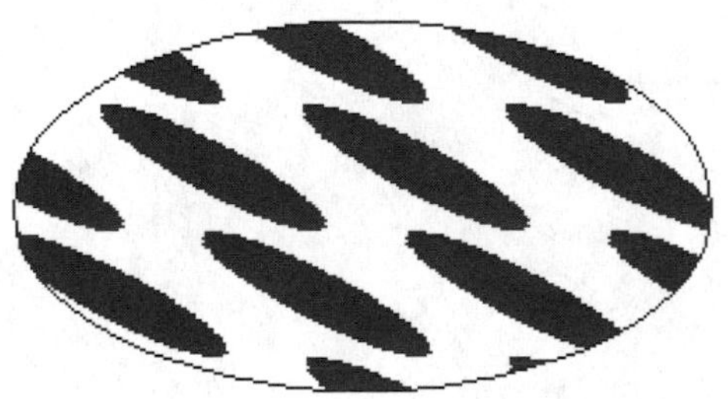

The result of dragging the top handle in the tiling vector to the left . . .

Using PostScript fills

You can also use PostScript fills if you have a GDI printer (e.g. an inkjet optimised for use with Microsoft Windows) installed.

If you have a PostScript printer installed, you have access to a range of additional fills. However, some PostScript fills are complex and require a lot of time to draw or print, so they should be used with discretion.

You can only apply PostScript fills from within a dedicated dialog.

A PostScript fill as it appears on screen

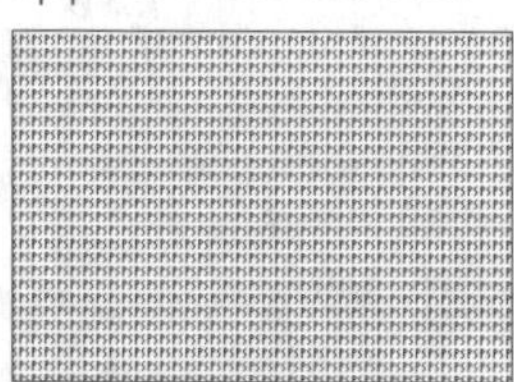

And the same fill as it prints

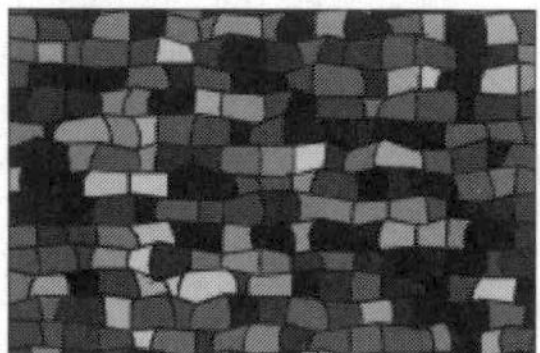

In version 6, click this button in the Fill fly-out:

In versions 3-5, click this button:

Creating PostScript fills with the PostScript Texture dialog

First, select the object(s) you want to fill. Launch the PostScript Texture dialog. To do this, launch the Fill fly-out. Then do the following:

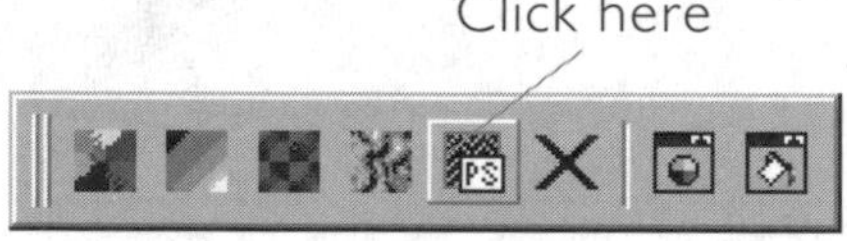

Now carry out the following steps:

PostScript fills do not display faithfully on screen. If you want to know what they look like before you apply them, make sure Preview Fill is selected (as here).

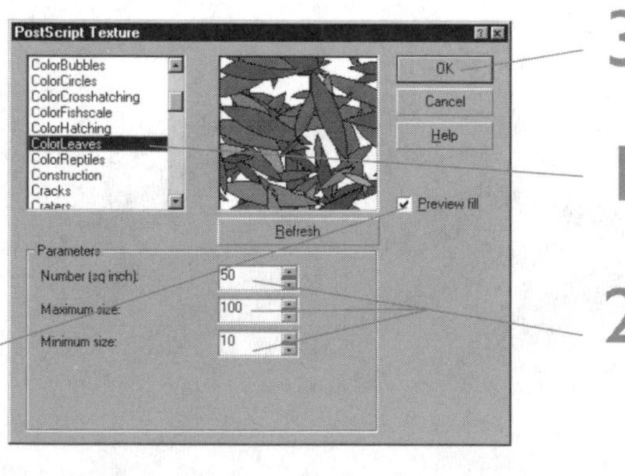

3 Click here

1 Click a fill

2 (Optional) Amend these settings, as required

Copying fills

There is a simple technique you can use to copy any kind of fill from one object to another. This saves time and energy: you don't have to go to the trouble of noting a fill's characteristics and then applying these laboriously to the second object.

First, select the empty object which you want to fill. Launch the Special Fill roll-up. Now do the following:

In versions before 7, the Special Fill roll-up is slightly different. Don't follow the procedure on the right. Instead, click the Update From button.

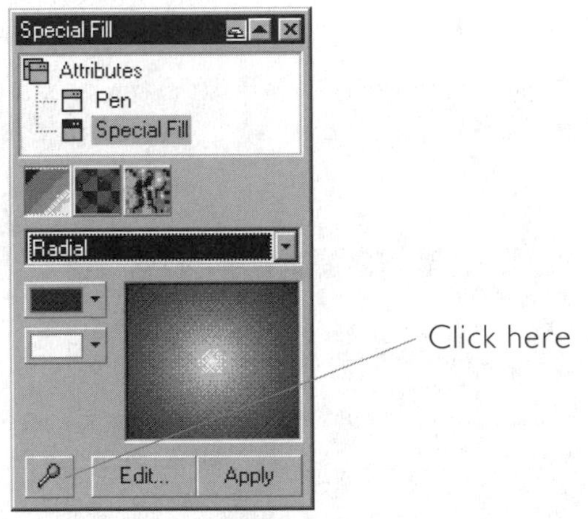

The cursor changes to a thick arrow. Move this over the object whose fill you want to copy and click. Finally, click Apply in the roll-up. CorelDRAW copies the fill across. The next illustration shows this process just before the fill is transferred across to the polygon.

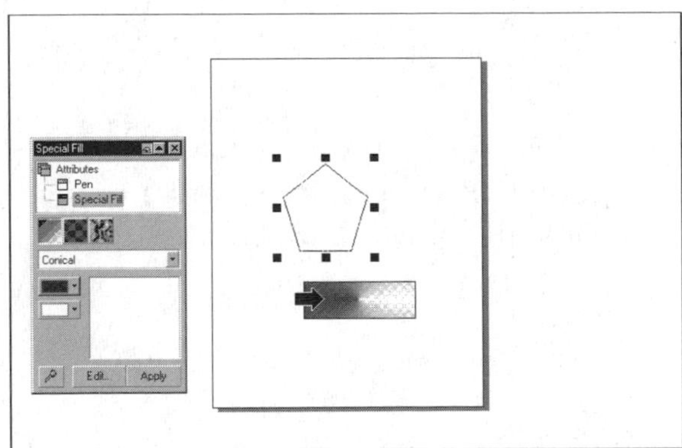

Setting fill defaults

By default, CorelDRAW applies no fill when you create new objects. However, you can change this if you want. You can have CorelDRAW automatically impose any fill you opt for as standard, with any object type.

If you try to implement any of the processes we've discussed in this chapter *without pre-selecting an existing object*, CorelDRAW assumes you want to set revised default values for *all* future fills (except text – see below). This is a useful device: it can save you a lot of time and effort.

Re step 1 – if you want to apply the fill defaults to artistic or paragraph text, click either or both of these:

To set revised fill defaults, make sure no objects are selected, then activate any tool in the Fill fly-out. Now do the following:

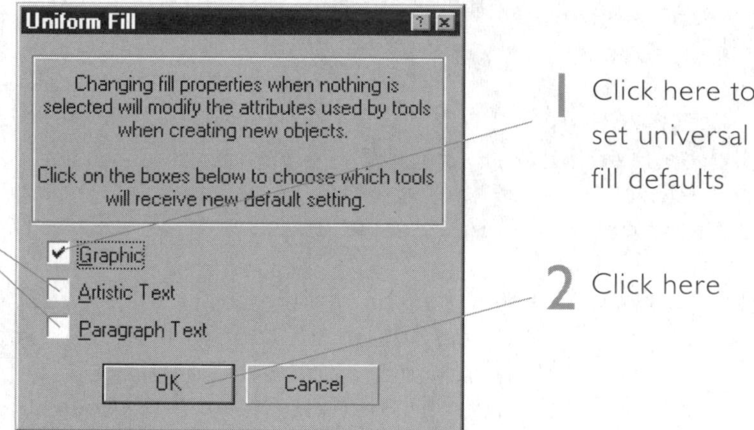

CorelDRAW now launches the appropriate fill dialog. Use this in the normal way to set the relevant fill defaults, then click OK.

Henceforth, any objects you create (in this and subsequent CorelDRAW sessions) will automatically adopt these default values.

Chapter Eight

The Interactive Tools

In this chapter, you'll learn how to use the new Interactive tools which allow you to perform complex reshaping and design operations on objects visually, with the mouse. You'll warp objects; apply interactive extrusions and blends; apply interactive envelopes; and then use free transformations. Finally, you'll create drop shadows interactively.

Covers

Interactivity – an overview

We've already looked at two aspects of the use of interactive tools:

- the Interactive Fill tool (see page 131)
- interactive pattern fill tiling (see page 133)

However, version 8 of CorelDRAW offers the following additional interactive tools:

— the Interactive Distortion tool

— the Interactive Extrude tool

— the Interactive Blend tool (also present in version 7)

— the Interactive Envelope tool

— the Free Transformation tools

— the Interactive Drop Shadow tool

In any of the interactive tools, you can use the Property Bar to specify additional settings which are not discussed separately.

For example, when you use the Interactive Drop Shadow tool, you can specify:

- shadow feathering
- shadow opacity
- horizontal/vertical shadow offsets
- shadow direction
- shadow colour

These allow you to reshape or reconfigue objects on-the-fly, with the mouse. As you do this, CorelDRAW displays a dashed version of the changes you're making, so you can preview what they'll look like once they're implemented.

Some of the new interactive tools relate to (and improve on) functions which already exist in CorelDRAW. For instance, you can rotate objects with the techniques discussed on page 53. However, if you do so with the Free Rotation tool discussed on page 143, the process is much more customisable – see the HANDY TIP.

Artistic text which has been shadowed

Distorting objects New in version 8

You can apply interactive distortions to objects, using the mouse.

You can distort any object, including artistic (but not paragraph) text.

Distorting on-the-fly

Do the following in the Toolbox:

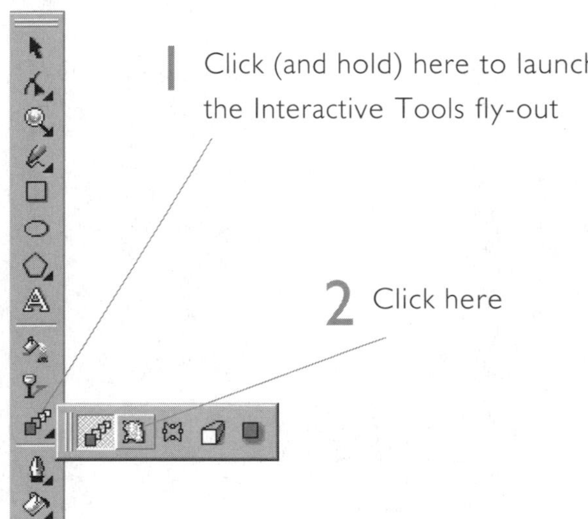

REMEMBER

Re step 3 – you can carry out three types of distortion:

— Push-Pull
— Zipper
— Twister

The best way to become familiar with the effects they produce is to use them.

Now perform the following operations:

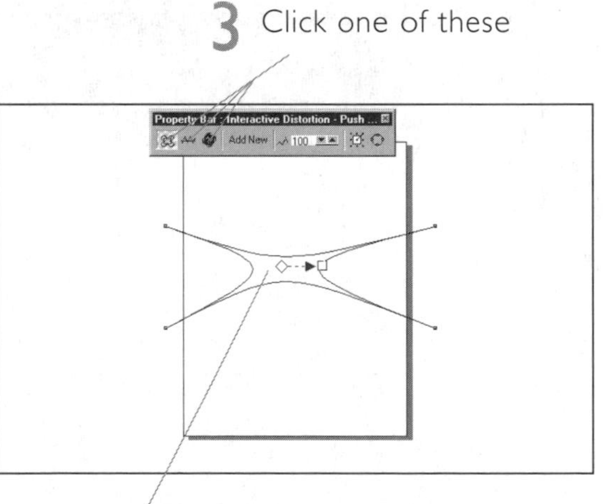

4 Drag appropriately to define the distortion

Here, a rectangle has been subjected to Push-Pull distortion

Don't be afraid to apply multiple distortion effects e.g. apply Push-Pull and Zipper to the same object . . .

Extruding objects New in version 8

You can apply interactive extrusions to objects, using the mouse.

Extruding on-the-fly

Do the following in the Toolbox:

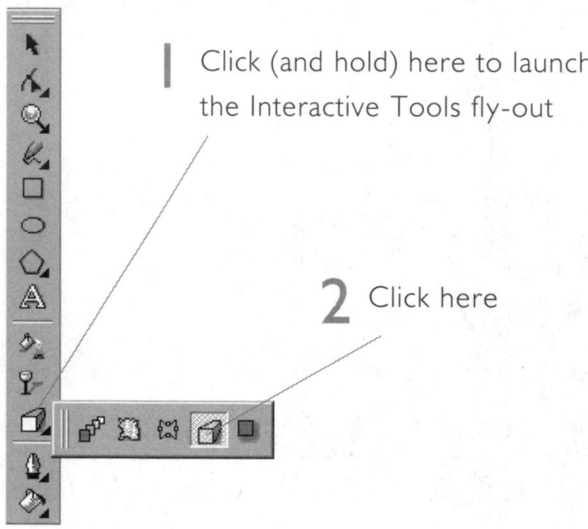

1. Click (and hold) here to launch the Interactive Tools fly-out
2. Click here

Now perform the following operation:

HANDY TIP

When the extrusion is complete, click the Pick tool in the Toolbox.

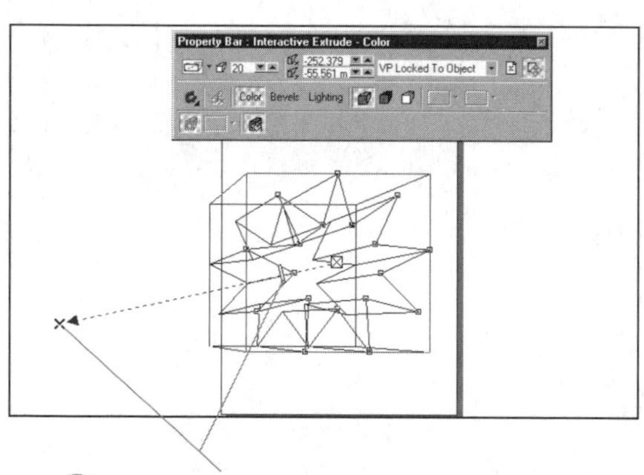

Here, a star is being extruded to the left

3. Drag either or both of these to apply the extrusion

Blending objects New in version 7

You can blend objects interactively, using the mouse.

Blending on-the-fly

Do the following in the Toolbox:

Re step 1 – as there is no Interactive fly-out in version 7, users should click this button in the Toolbox:

Additionally, omit step 2.

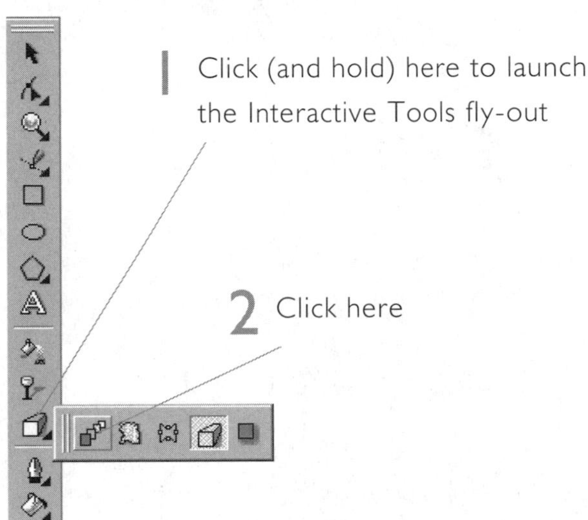

1 Click (and hold) here to launch the Interactive Tools fly-out

2 Click here

Now perform the following operation:

When the blend is complete, click the Pick tool in the Toolbox.

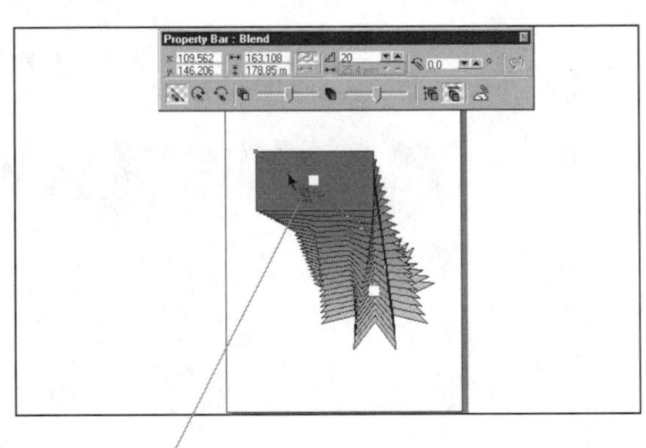

Here, a star is being blended interactively with a rectangle

3 Drag from one object to another to define the blend

Interactive envelopes New in version 8

You can reshape objects by applying an envelope and manipulating this interactively, using the mouse.

Step 1 positions an envelope (of exactly the same dimensions) around the selected object.

It also selects the Interactive Envelope tool in the Toolbox.

Using interactive envelopes

Select the object you want to reshape. Pull down the Effects menu and click Envelope. Do the following in the Envelope roll-up.

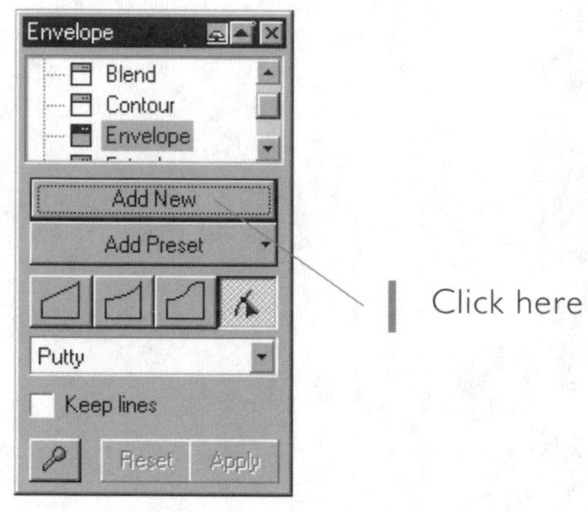

1 Click here

Re step 2 – you can carry out four types of envelope reshaping:

— Straight Line
— Single Arc
— Double Arc
— Unconstrained (the default)

The best way to become familiar with the effects they produce is to use them.

Now perform the following operations:

2 Click one of these

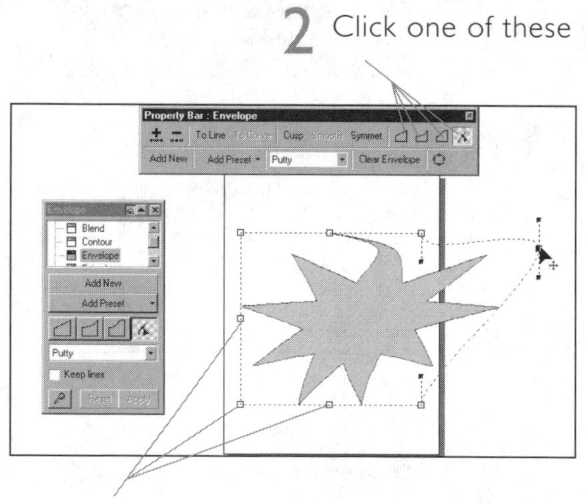

Here, a star has been reshaped by dragging its envelope to the right

3 Drag any node to reshape the object

When the reshaping is complete, click the Pick tool in the Toolbox.

Free transformations New in version 8

You can carry out four types of interactive transformation:

- Free Rotation
- Free Angle Reflection
- Free Scale
- Free Skew

See the tip below.

Here, a Free Rotation operation is being carried out. Below are details of the other tools:

- The Free Reflection tool mirrors objects
- The Free Scale tool scales objects along the horizontal/vertical axes
- The Free Skew tool slants an object's horizontal/vertical lines

To use these tools, make the appropriate selection in step 3. In step 4, click to define an anchor point, then drag appropriately.

You can apply a variety of interactive transformations.

Transforming on-the-fly

Do the following in the Toolbox:

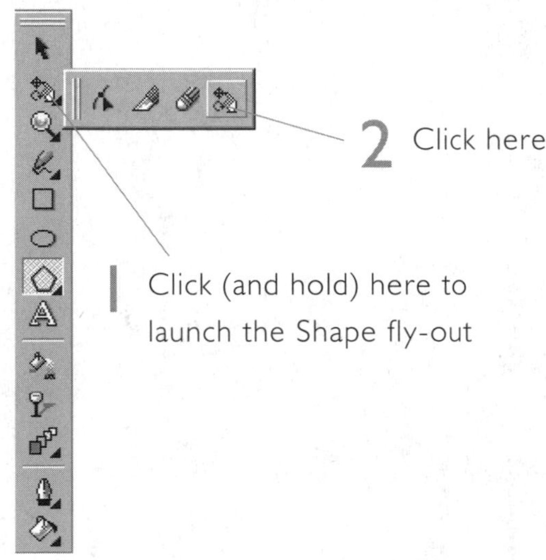

Now perform the following operations:

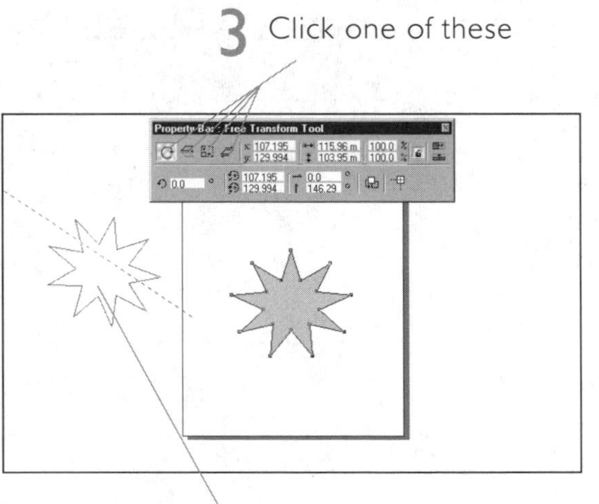

Interactive shadows New in version 8

You can apply drop shadows to objects, interactively.

Drop shadows make objects look more realistic.

You can shadow most object types in CorelDRAW 8 (including artistic and paragraph text) but you can't shadow extruded objects.

Shadowing on-the-fly

Do the following in the Toolbox:

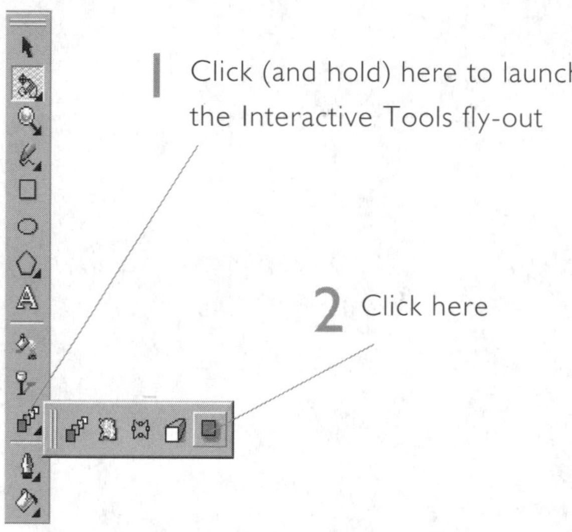

Now perform the following operations:

When the shadowing is complete, click the Pick tool in the Toolbox.

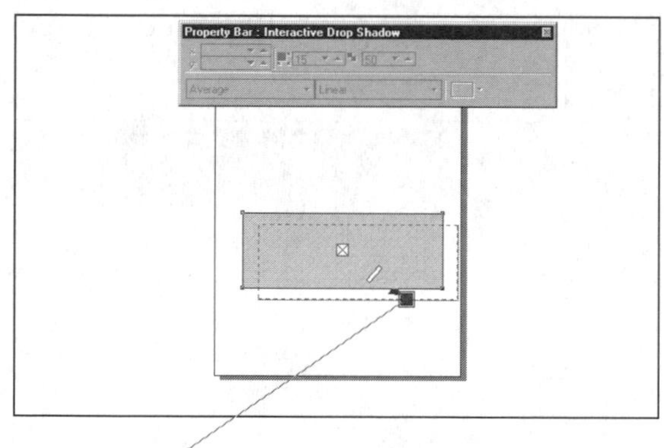

3 Drag the handle to define the drop shadow

Chapter Nine

Working with images

In this chapter, you'll learn how to import bitmap and vector images into CorelDRAW, via a dialog and the Scrapbook. You'll learn something about the various graphics formats, and also how to perform operations which are specific to bitmaps (including applying special effects). Finally, you'll make your image work easier and more convenient with colour styles, and export your work into third-party formats.

Covers

An overview

Be careful how you resize imported bitmaps: rescaling them can cause distortion. If you must resize bitmaps, do so in round numbers if possible – i.e. use increments or decrements of 50%, 100%, 150% etc.

In version 8, you can insert graphics directly into artistic or paragraph text. (When you do so, CorelDRAW treats them as text characters).

First, select the image you want to embed. Press Ctrl+X (this deletes the graphic and copies it to the Windows Clipboard). Select the Text tool in the Toolbox; click in the text where you want the graphic to appear. Press Shift+Insert.

CorelDRAW works with both bitmap and vector images. We touched on this briefly in Chapter 7; however, we now need to go into the subject in rather more detail.

Bitmap images

Bitmaps consist of pixels (dots) arranged in such a way that they form a graphic image. Because of the very nature of bitmaps, the question of 'resolution' – the sharpness of an image expressed in dpi (dots per inch) – is very important. Bitmaps look best if they're displayed at their correct resolution. CorelDRAW imports (i.e. translates into its own format) a wide variety of third-party bitmap formats.

Look at the illustration below.

This image – one of the many royalty free-images supplied by Corel Corporation in Kodak Photo CD format – was imported into CorelDRAW in a matter of seconds.

Once you've imported a bitmap into CorelDRAW, you can:

- colour black and white bitmaps
- crop bitmaps
- rescale bitmaps
- rotate or skew bitmaps
- apply special effects

Once you've finished working with bitmaps in CorelDRAW, you can export the finished result as another bitmap, or as a vector image. In this way, they can be utilised in other programs which are unable to import CorelDRAW's native .CDR or .CMX formats.

Vector images

CorelDRAW will also import vector graphics files in formats native to other programs. Vector images consist of, and are defined by, algebraic equations. One practical result of this is that they can be rescaled without any loss of definition. Another corollary is that they're not as complex as bitmaps: they contain less detail. Vector files can also include bitmap information.

In versions before 7, clip art is sometimes supplied in .CMX **(Corel Presentation Exchange) format.**

The illustration below is one of the images supplied with CorelDRAW. These images are supplied in .CDR format.

Vector images can also include bitmap information. For example, PostScript files often have an illustrative header (used for preview purposes) which is a bitmap.

Once you've imported a vector image into CorelDRAW, you can edit it in much the same way in which you edit objects you've created yourself. See Chapters 2 and 3 for more information.

When finished, vector images can also be exported, either as vector or bitmap files.

Brief notes on image formats

CorelDRAW will happily import/export a wide selection of bitmap and vector graphic formats. These are some of the main formats:

Many bitmap formats have compression as an option. This allows bitmaps – often very large – to be stored on disk in much smaller files.

Bitmap formats

PCX — An old standby. Originated with PC Paintbrush, a paint program. Used for years to transfer graphics data between Windows applications. Supports compression.

TIFF — Tagged Image File Format. Suffix: .TIF. If anything, even more widely used than PCX, across a whole range of platforms and applications. Supports numerous types and levels of compression.

BMP — Not as common as PCX and TIFF, but still popular. One drawback: sometimes, compression isn't available. It is, however, with CorelDRAW.

TGA — Targa. A high-end format, and also a bridge with so-called low-end computers (e.g. Amiga and Atari). Often used in PC and Mac paint and ray-tracing programs because of its high-resolution colour fidelity. Supports compression.

REMEMBER

Earlier versions of CorelDRAW support fewer bitmap and vector formats.

GIF — Graphics Interchange Format. Developed for the on-line transmission of graphics data across the CompuServe network. Just about any Windows program – and a lot more besides – will read GIF. Disadvantage: it can't handle more than 256 colours. One of the few graphics formats which can be used in HTML (HyperText Markup Language) documents on the World Wide Web. Compression is supported.

PCD — (Kodak) PhotoCD. Used primarily to store photographs on CD. Corel Corporation sells a vast range of images in this format.

JPEG — Joint Photographic Experts Group. Suffix: .JPG.

Used on the PC and Mac for the storage and display of photographs. One of the few graphics formats which can be used in HTML (HyperText Markup Language) documents on the World Wide Web. A very high level of compression is built into the format.

You can use standard Windows techniques to copy- and cut-and-paste graphics/objects into CorelDRAW documents. However, you can also:

- 'duplicate' objects. Select one or more objects; press Ctrl+D. CorelDRAW inserts an identical copy, but at a precise horizontal/vertical offset
- 'clone' objects (*does not apply to version 3*). Select one or more objects; pull down the Edit menu and click Clone. CorelDRAW inserts an identical copy. However, any changes you make to the original (the 'master') are automatically applied to the clones

Vector formats

CGM	Computer Graphics Metafile. Frequently used in the past, especially as a medium for clip-art transmission. Less frequently used nowadays.
EPS	Encapsulated PostScript. Perhaps the most widely used PostScript format. Actually, PostScript (a programming language in its own right) combines vector *and* bitmap data very successfully. Incorporates a low-resolution bitmap 'header' for preview purposes. If you want to export to a vector format and have a choice, you'd be well advised to use EPS.
WMF	Windows Metafile. Similar to CGM, but even more frequently used. Used for information exchange between just about all Windows programs. Often produces files which are much smaller than the equivalent bitmaps (though not because of compression – there isn't any). If you need a vector format and can't use EPS, use WMF wherever possible.
AI	A special implementation of the PostScript format, native to Adobe Illustrator. A frequently used standard.

Importing images

In versions before 7, the Import dialog is rather different.

For example, versions 3 and 4 lack a Preview facility (see below).

If you want to view an image *before* you import it, make sure Preview is ticked.

If, when you try to import an image, CorelDRAW fails to recognise it, you may not have installed the required filter during installation.

To rectify this, rerun Setup.

You can import both bitmap and vector images into CorelDRAW very easily and quickly.

First, pull down the File menu and click Import. Carry out the following steps:

2 Click here; in the list, click the drive/folder which hosts the graphic file

4 Click here

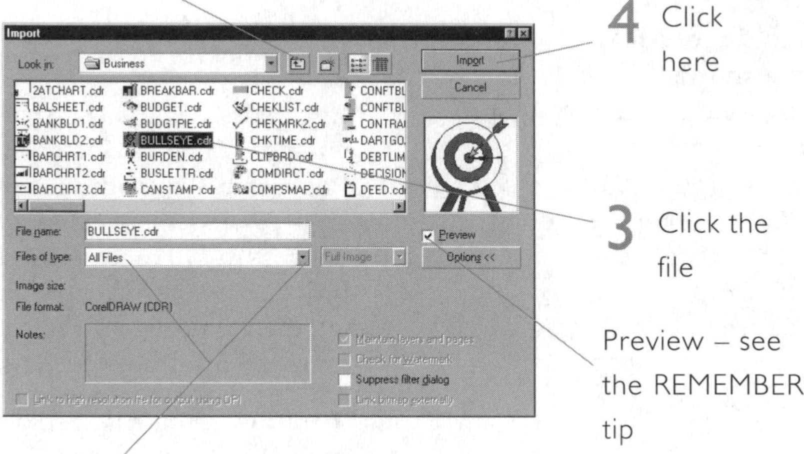

3 Click the file

Preview – see the REMEMBER tip

1 Make sure All Files is shown. If it isn't, click the arrow and select it from the list

The inserted image

Using the Scrapbook New in version 7

Version 7 users should click Clipart in the Tools menu, instead.

Version 8 users can connect to FTP sites.

With your Internet connection live, click Scrapbook, Ftp Sites in the View menu. Right-click in the Scrapbook; click Go To Site in the menu. In the dialog, type an address – e.g. ftp.corel.com**. Click OK.**

Follow steps 1-3 to download images.

To insert a photo, click Scrapbook, Photos in the View menu. (Version 7 users should click Photos in the Tools menu, instead).

Make sure the relevant CD is in the drive and follow steps 1-3.

You can also import images via the Scrapbook. The Scrapbook is a docker (*a roll-up*, in version 7) from which you can drag pictures into your CorelDRAW documents.

Adding images from the Scrapbook

Ensure the relevant CD is in the drive. Pull down the View menu and click Scrapbook, Clipart. Now do the following:

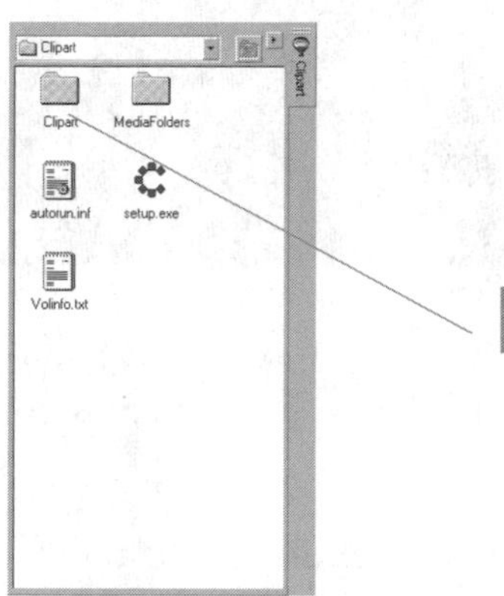

1 Double-click the relevant folder(s) until the Scrapbook displays image icons

2 Click an icon...

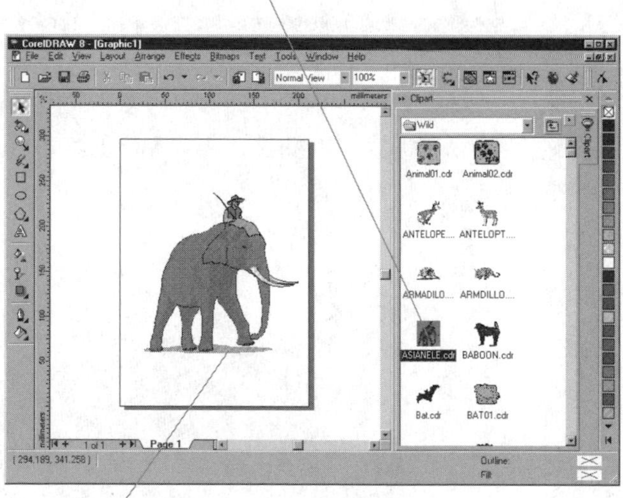

3 Drag the icon into your document and release the mouse button

Colouring a black and white bitmap

It's sometimes useful to work with monochrome bitmaps. Look at the next illustration:

This Corel PhotoCD has been converted to black-and-white. CorelDRAW lets you apply background/foreground colours.

First, select the bitmap. Then refer to the colour palette at the edge of the screen. Do the following:

(Optional) Click here to scroll right

(Optional) Click here to scroll to the left

Left-click any colour to apply it as a background; or *right-click* it to apply it as a foreground

The same image, with new foreground & background colours

Tracing bitmaps

If you find the tracing process doesn't work well, you need to run CorelTRACE (in later versions, OCR-TRACE), a separate Corel program.

As we've seen, CorelDRAW will happily import both bitmap and vector images. One feature of vector images is that they consist of objects which can be isolated and acted on. Bitmaps, on the other hand, don't, because pixels can't be classified in the same way. A dot is a dot is a dot...

One attribute a pixel can possess, however, is colour. This has the merit of making it possible to identify bitmap components. CorelDRAW calls this 'tracing'. When you tell CorelDRAW to trace part of a bitmap, it looks for pixels of the same colour and isolates them. You can then apply standard outline and fill techniques.

The Toolbox looks slightly different in earlier versions of CorelDRAW.
In versions 3-6, the Freehand tool looks like this:

Tracing will only work if you've pre-selected a bitmap. If you haven't, CorelDRAW assumes you want to draw a freehand line or curve.

Tracing a bitmap

First, select the bitmap you want to trace. Then refer to the Toolbox and carry out the following steps:

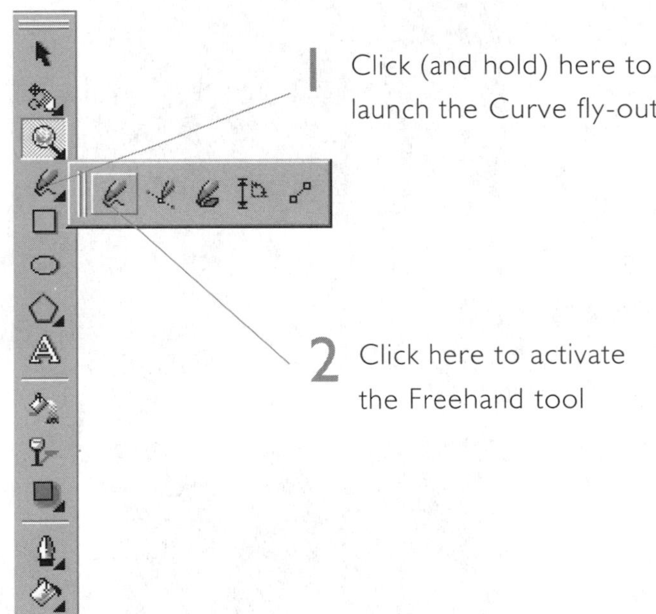

The cursor changes into an elongated cross. Move this over the section of the bitmap which you want to trace.

A magnified view of the transformed cursor

Now left-click once. CorelDRAW surrounds the nearest traceable area with a border.

A magnified view of the bitmap's traced section

Now apply the outline and/or fill you require. The result might look something like this:

A magnified view of the traced section, filled with a texture

Cropping bitmaps

One thing you can't do is mark out a section of a bitmap and then extract it as an image in its own right.

Cropping is the process of:

- trimming bitmap (not vector) images to make them fit into the required space
- removing parts which are surplus

CorelDRAW will perform both operations. However, there are certain limitations you should bear in mind before you crop bitmaps.

When you crop an image in CorelDRAW, what you perform is a kind of sleight of hand. CorelDRAW merely displays that part of the image which lies within the revised outline. The image data outside the outline is still there; it's simply hidden. This means that the overall file size won't change. Also you can restore the original image however many cropping operations have been performed.

Cropping a bitmap

First, turn to the Toolbox and activate the Shape tool.

The Toolbox looks slightly different in earlier versions of CorelDRAW.

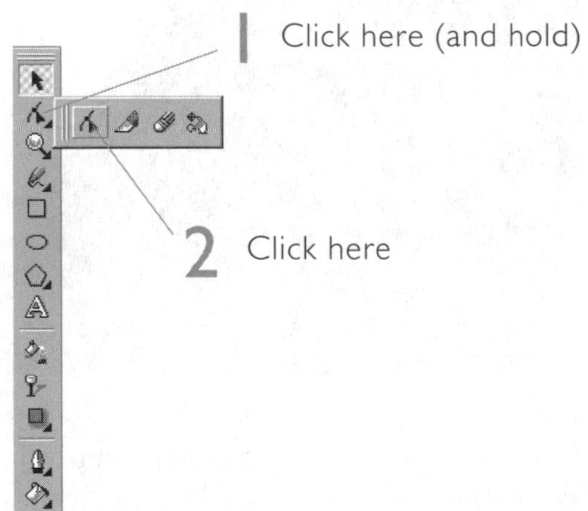

In versions 6-8, hold down Ctrl as you drag to ensure horizontal or vertical cropping.

Now select the bitmap you want to crop. Move the mouse pointer over any of the visible nodes. Click and hold down the left mouse button. Drag the node to reshape the bitmap. Release the mouse button when you've finished.

The illustrations on page 156 show cropping in action.

This is a bitmap before cropping (after it has been selected with the Shape tool):

A magnified view of a node

You can use the Shape tool to edit bitmaps in other ways, too. See pages 50-56 for more information.

And this is what it looks like afterwards:

The same image after being cropped

Restoring a cropped bitmap

To 'undo' the effects of cropping, delete all the nodes on the outline path. To do this, hold down one Shift key as you click on all of the nodes, then press Delete.

CorelDRAW recreates the original bitmap automatically.

Resizing & rotating/skewing images

Resizing

You can rescale both bitmap and vector images imported into CorelDRAW using standard Windows techniques. However, you should bear in mind that increasing or decreasing the size of bitmap images results in distortion, to varying degrees. To minimise this, you should do the following:

- try to achieve the correct resolution/size in the *originating* program, before you import the image into CorelDRAW
- only rescale within CorelDRAW (especially in the case of bitmaps) if you absolutely have to
- if you do have to, rescale – wherever possible – in increments or decrements which are whole numbers. Mathematically, this results in sharper images

Rotating/skewing

You can rotate or skew bitmaps in the same way that you can rotate or skew objects you create yourself. See pages 52 and 53 for how to do this.

Having said this, you should bear in mind the following tips:

- Large, complex bitmaps can require a lot of processing power and time to rotate or skew. To help mitigate against this, follow the relevant instructions on pages 17-18 to enter Draft view mode. This forces bitmaps to display less accurately, but saves time. (Printing is unaffected.)
- Alternatively, follow the instructions on pages 17-18 to enter Wireframe or (in the case of versions 7 and 8) Simple Wireframe view modes. In both Wireframe modes, objects display as outlines, and screen redrawing is even quicker. The disadvantage is that Wireframe mode reveals very little image detail. (Printing is unaffected.)

Bitmap special effects New in version 7

Users of versions 5-8 can apply a lens.

Create an object, then move it over the drawing you want to magnify. Press Alt+F3. In the Amount field in the Lens roll-up, type in a magnification level. Click Apply.

The lens feature is used throughout this book.

BEWARE

Applying special effects to bitmaps makes heavy demands on computing power, and can take some time to effect.

You can apply a large number of special effects to bitmaps within CorelDRAW. Examples include:

- 2D and 3D effects
- varieties of Blur, Noise and Sharpness
- Artistic and Colour Transformation effects
- an assortment of plug-ins (additional specialist programs)

Applying special effects

Select the bitmap(s). Pull down the Bitmaps menu and carry out the following steps:

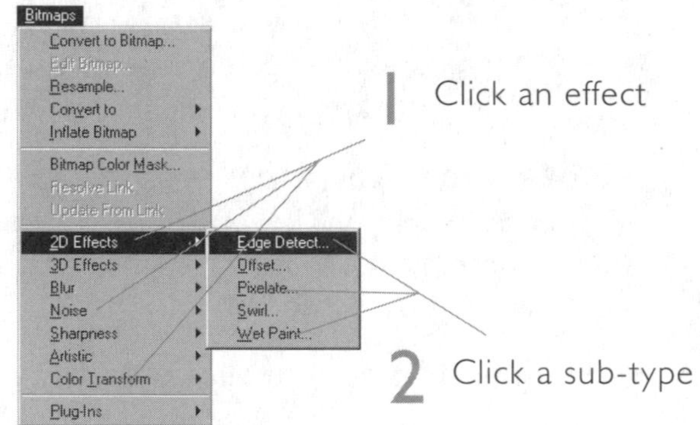

Often, CorelDRAW launches a further dialog. Complete this as appropriate, then click OK.

The 3D/ Page Curl special effect in action

Colour styles New in version 7

In version 7, the Color Styles docker appears as a roll-up:

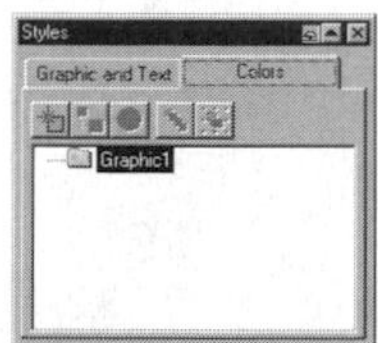

Click this button in the Colour Styles docker:

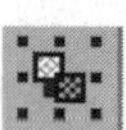

to have CorelDRAW create colour styles (based on 1 or more selected objects) automatically. Complete the dialog which launches, then click OK.

In Chapter 5, we looked at the use of text styles. CorelDRAW now lets you work with colour styles. You can create a colour style with the use of the Colour Palette, and then apply it to a drawing. Once a style has been applied, changing it also updates all objects on which the style has been imposed.

Creating a colour style

Pull down the Layout menu and click Color Styles. Now do the following:

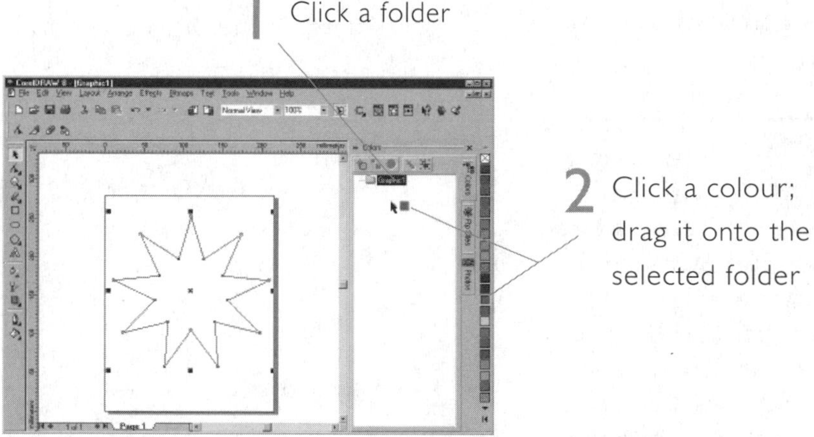

Applying a colour style

Select the object(s) you want to apply the style to. Pull down the Layout menu and click Color Styles. Now do the following:

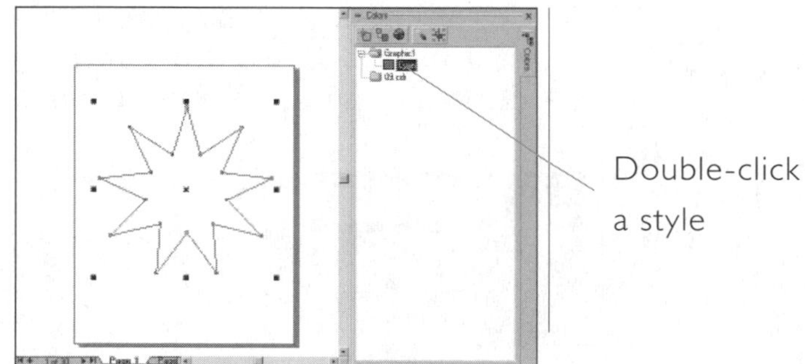

Exporting images

When you've finished working with an imported graphics image, the normal – and correct – response is to save it as a CorelDRAW file. However, it's sometimes necessary to 'export' your work in a format which can be read into other programs. The problem is that few applications will read .CDR files directly. Even those that will are usually limited to earlier version formats.

In versions 3-5, the Export dialog is slightly different.

To export your work back into graphics files, pull down the File menu and click Export. Carry out the following steps:

Before you export a graphic, you need to find out which formats are supported by the destination program. Consult the documentation which came with the program.

2 Click here; in the drop-down list, click a drive/folder combination

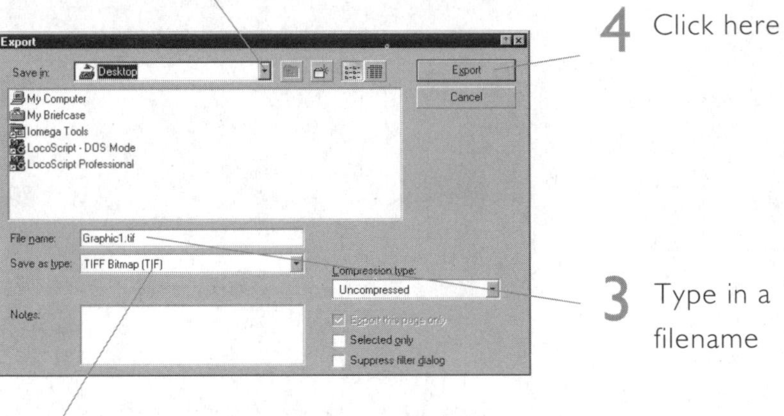

4 Click here

3 Type in a filename

1 Click here; in the list, click a format

Re step 1 – if the format you want to export to isn't in the list, you may not have installed the required filter during installation. To rectify this, rerun Setup.

Most graphics formats you choose in step 1 will give rise to a further dialog when you carry out step 4. These dialogs vary according to whether you've selected a bitmap or vector format, and also from format to format. Complete the dialog as appropriate, then click OK.

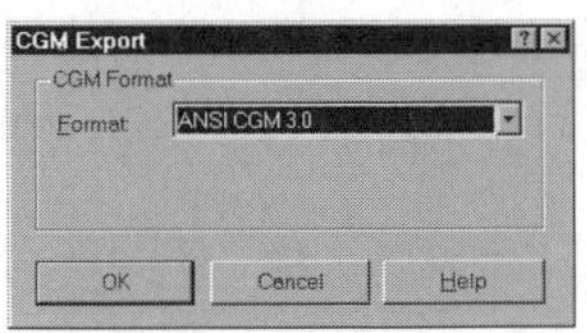

The CGM Export dialog

Chapter Ten

Page Layout

Before you can start to print out your work, you need to make sure that you've selected the correct page layout. This involves using the correct page size/orientation, and applying a style, if applicable. There are also other important issues which affect how you work with your document on screen.

Covers

An overview

CorelDRAW gives you a lot of control over page layout. For instance, you can:

- apply a pre-defined layout style
- specify the page size you want to use
- create your own custom page size, if none of the existing sizes or layouts are suitable
- specify the page orientation
- apply a background (paper) colour
- apply a background frame
- hide the on-screen page border
- work with facing pages
- set the start page (if you're working with facing pages)
- add and delete pages at will
- jump to a specific page

You can set most of these before or after you create a document.

Note that you can also adjust many of these settings – in particular, layout styles – from within the Print dialog (see chapter 11). This isn't altogether a duplication, however. Instead, think of it like this. The techniques discussed in this chapter set the *drawing* parameters, while those mentioned in chapter 11 set the parameters for the *printed* output, including the paper.

In Version 3, you can only have 1 page in each document.

CorelDRAW also provides a variety of techniques for moving around in documents. This is an important aspect of document management, especially given that CorelDRAW supports documents of up to 999 pages. You need to be able to jump instantly to the page you require.

Applying a layout style New in version 4

CorelDRAW provides six pre-defined layout styles. These are:

- Full Page
- Book
- Booklet
- Tent Card
- Side-Fold Card
- Top-Fold Card

In versions before 8, the dialog which launches here is the Page Setup dialog.
In versions 3-4, it lacks a Preview facility.

Users of version 4 should click Page Setup in the *File* menu, instead.

Users of versions before 8 should omit step 1.
Version 5 users should activate the Layout tab before carrying out steps 2-3 only.

You can also access layout styles within the Print dialog. If you want to do this, make sure you select Full Page in step 2.

Full Page is the default; you'll probably use this most of the time. Book and Booklet include automatic impositioning, the process whereby pages are printed out in the order in which they need to be bound (for instance, in a twelve page A5 booklet, pages 1 and 12, 2 and 11 etc. might need to be printed on the same A4 sheets). The other layout styles are rather exotic.

To apply a layout style, pull down the Layout menu and click Page Setup. Now do the following.

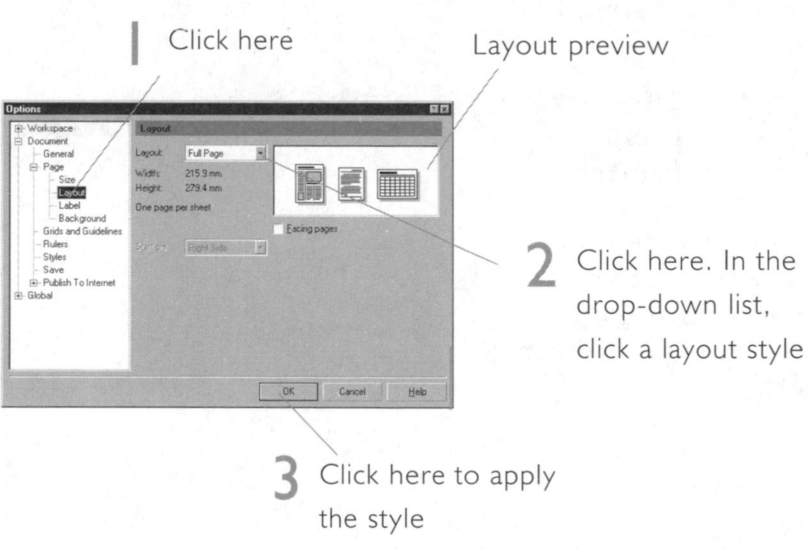

Setting the page size

Users of versions 3-4 should click Page Setup in the *File* menu, instead.

In versions before 8, the dialog which launches here is the Page Setup dialog.
In versions 3-4, it lacks a Preview facility.

Version 5 users should activate the Size tab before carrying out steps 1-3.

Click Set From Printer to have CorelDRAW match the page size to the size specified by your current printer settings.

CorelDRAW comes with almost forty pre-defined page sizes. It's important that you pick the right one for a given document. If you don't, it won't print correctly.

To choose a page size, pull down the Layout menu and click Page Setup. Now carry out the following steps:

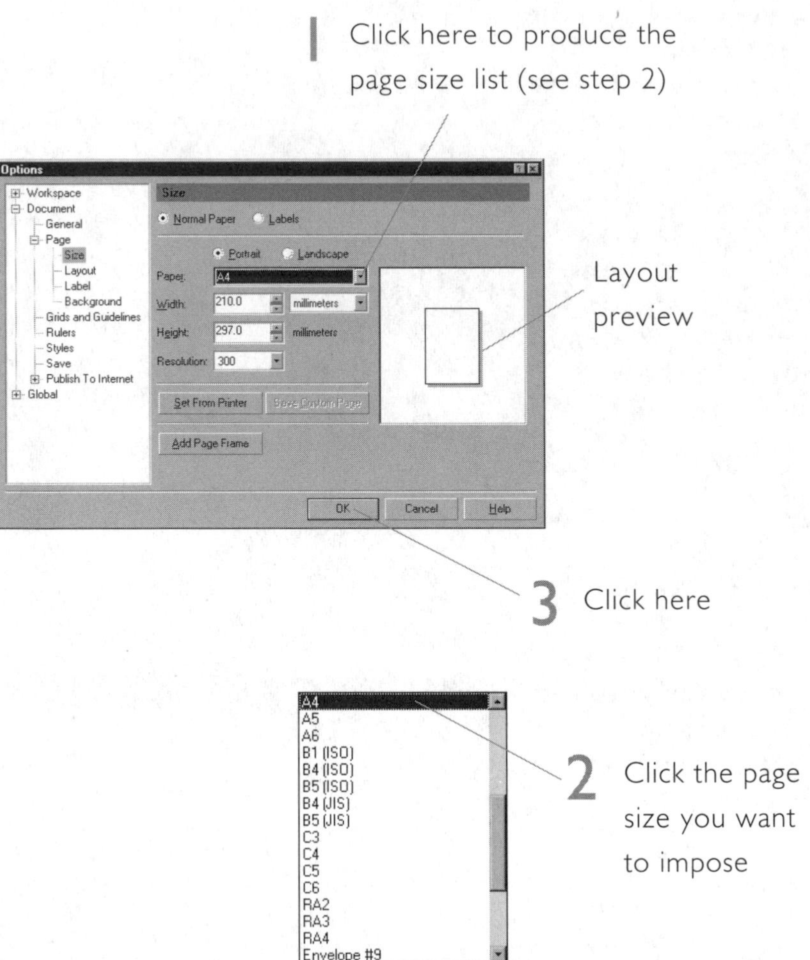

Creating a custom page size

Users of versions 3-4 should click Page Setup in the *File* menu, instead.

In step 1, click a page size *directly* (and omit step 2).

Given the wide range of preset page sizes CorelDRAW provides, it's perhaps unlikely that you'll need to define your own. However, there are times when you may need to do so. For example, you might decide to create business cards. In this case, you could create a suitable page size and then output the result on disk to a copy-shop for subsequent printing...

To specify your own page size, pull down the Layout menu and click Page Setup. Now do the following.

In versions before 8, the dialog which launches here is the Page Setup dialog.

In versions 3-4, it lacks a Preview facility.

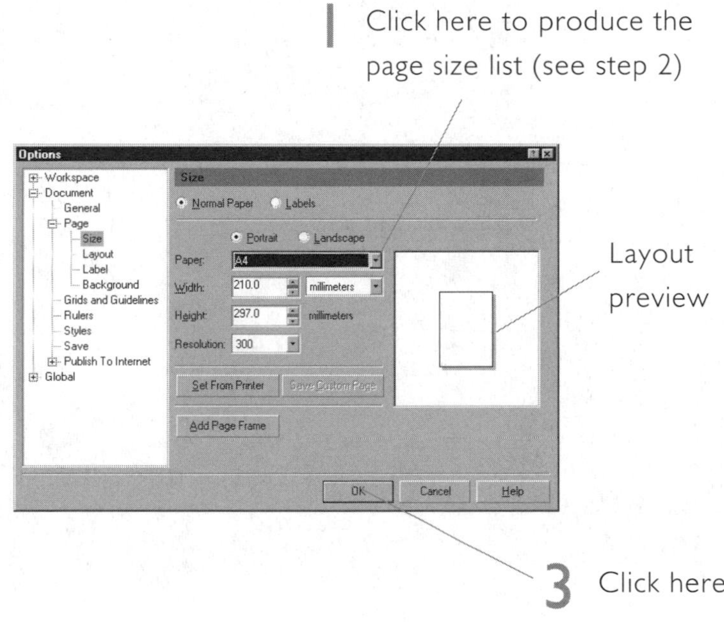

Version 5 users should activate the Size tab before carrying out steps 1-3.

Click Set From Printer to match the page size to the size specified by your current printer settings.

Custom
Slide
Letter
Legal
Tabloid
Statement/Half
Executive
Fanfold
Double
Broad Sheet
A0
A1
A2
A3
A4
A5

2 Click Custom

Setting page orientation

An especially important page layout consideration is orientation. There are two options:

- Portrait
- Landscape

Portrait is the default. With Portrait, the longest page dimension is oriented vertically. With Landscape, on the other hand, the reverse is true. The next illustration makes the distinction clear:

Portrait orientation

Landscape orientation

In versions before 8, the dialog which launches here is the Page Setup dialog.

Users of versions 3-4 should click Page Setup in the *File* menu, instead.

Version 5 users should ensure the Size tab is active before carrying out steps 1 and 2.

To specify a document's orientation, pull down the Layout menu and click Page Setup. Now do the following:

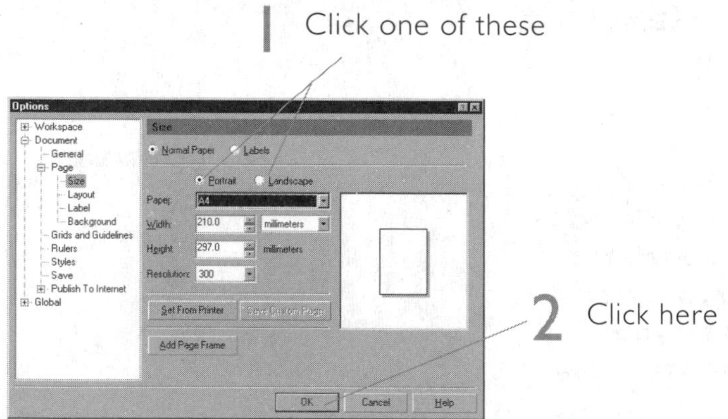

Specifying the background colour

Users of versions 3-4 should click Page Setup in the *File* menu, instead.

Additionally, omit step 1. In step 2, click the Paper Color button. Complete the dialog which launches, then click OK. Finally, omit step 3 then carry out step 4.

You can have CorelDRAW apply any colour to the Printable Area. You should bear in mind, though, that this is for display purposes only: although you can use it to see what your drawings would look like if printed onto coloured paper, the colour won't print.

To apply a non-printing colour to the page, pull down the Layout menu and click Page Setup. Now carry out the following steps:

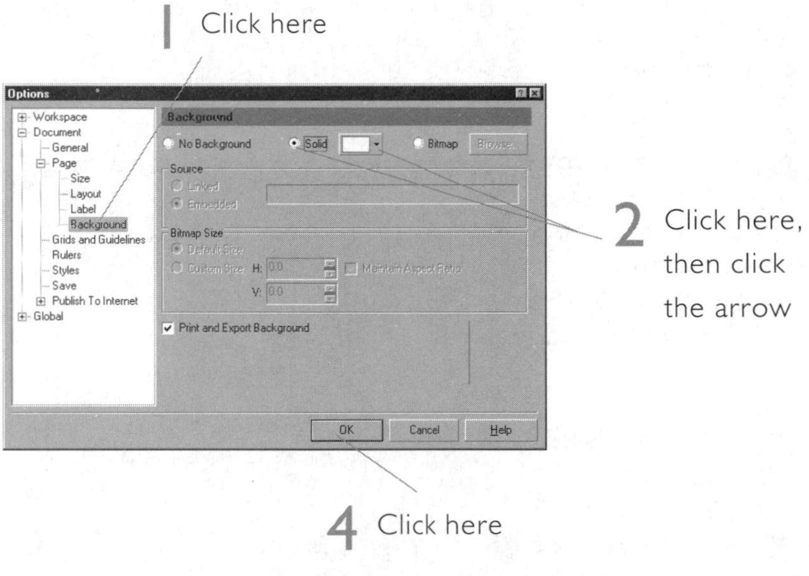

In versions before 8, the Page Setup dialog appears here.

Additionally, the background colour feature is known as paper colour.

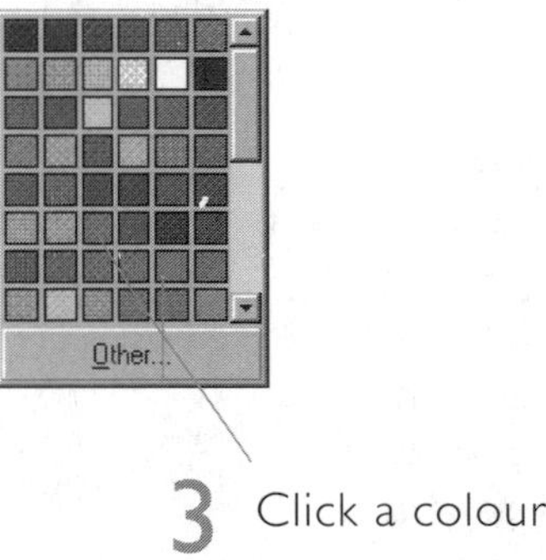

Users of versions 5-7 should omit step 1.

Version 5 users should also activate the Display tab before carrying out steps 2-4 only.

Adding a printable page frame

It's sometimes desirable to apply an outline or fill to the entire working page. You could do this manually, by defining a rectangle of the same dimensions as your current page size and then outlining or filling it. However, you can have CorelDRAW create the rectangle for you, automatically and much more easily – this is called adding a page frame. You should note that whatever outline or fill you impose using this technique *will* print.

HANDY TIP

Users of versions 3-4 should click Page Setup in the *File* menu, instead.

To add a page frame, pull down the Layout menu and click Page Setup. Now do the following.

In versions before 8, the dialog which launches here is the Page Setup dialog.

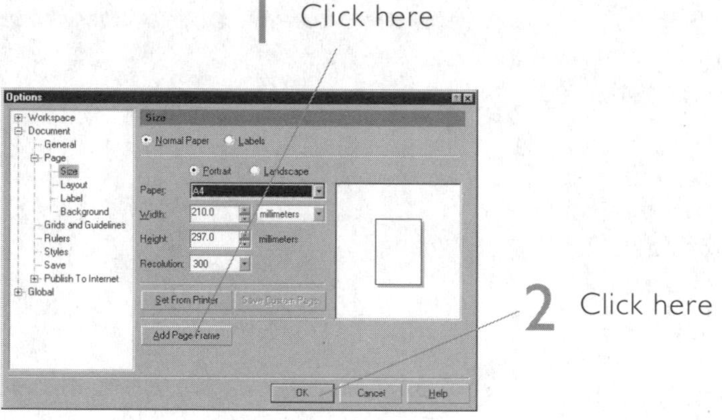

Version 5 users should ensure the Display tab is active before carrying out steps 1 and 2.

The illustration below shows a selected page frame complete with texture fill:

You can manipulate the page frame in the normal way. For example, you can drag it with the mouse to move it...

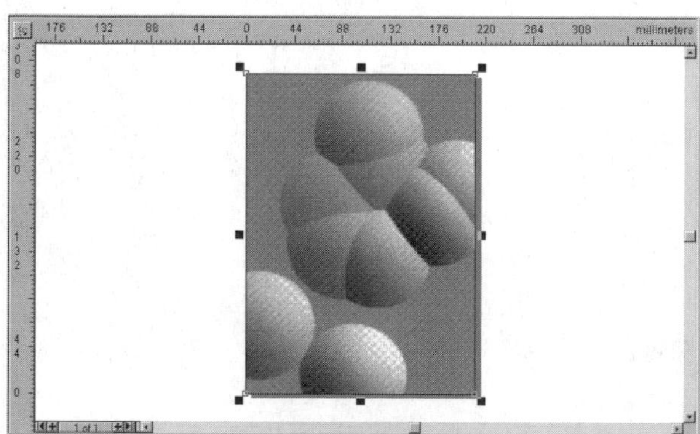

Hiding the page border

By default, CorelDRAW surrounds the Printable Area with a shadowed border:

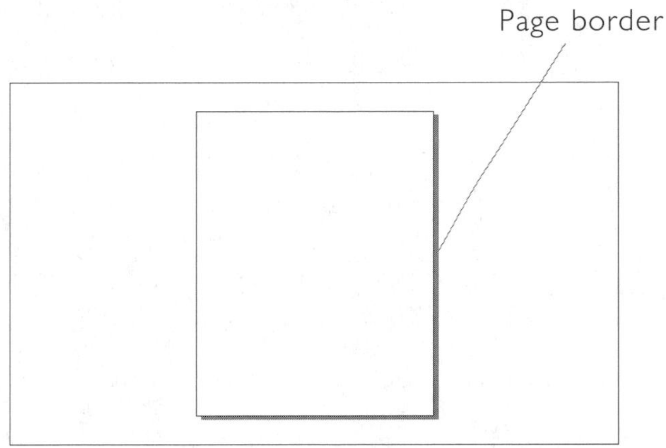

Users of versions 3-4 should click Page Setup in the *File* menu, instead.

This border serves an important function: any drawing objects which lie outside the Printable Area don't print. As a result, it's desirable to leave the border in force. If you want to hide it, however, pull down the Layout menu and click Page Setup. Now carry out the following steps:

In versions before 8, the dialog which launches here is the Page Setup dialog.

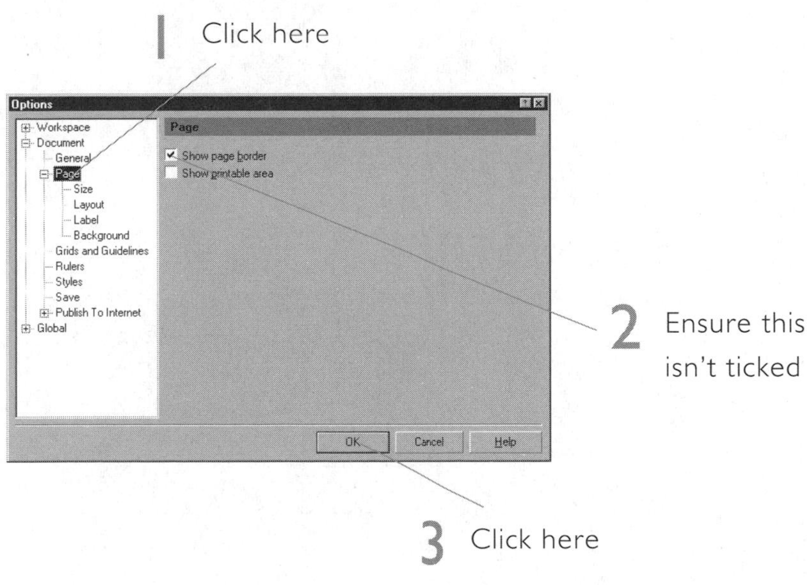

Users of versions before 8 should omit step 1.

Version 5 users should ensure the Display tab is active before carrying out steps 2-3 only.

Using facing pages New in version 4

CorelDRAW provides special layout options for documents with more than one page. These include:

- the ability to work with facing pages
- the ability to specify whether multi-page documents begin on a left or right page

Working with facing pages is very useful, especially (for obvious reasons) if you have graphics which span two pages, or if you need to copy or move graphics to an adjacent page. It's also useful for text work: it provides a useful overview.

Multi-page documents should usually start on a right-hand page.

Look at the next illustrations:

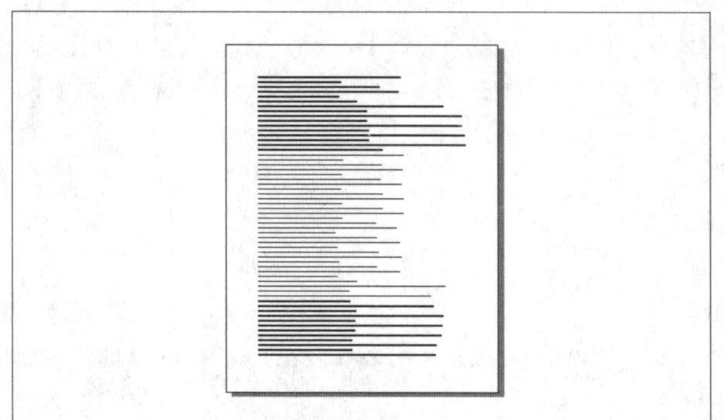

Working with single-page view

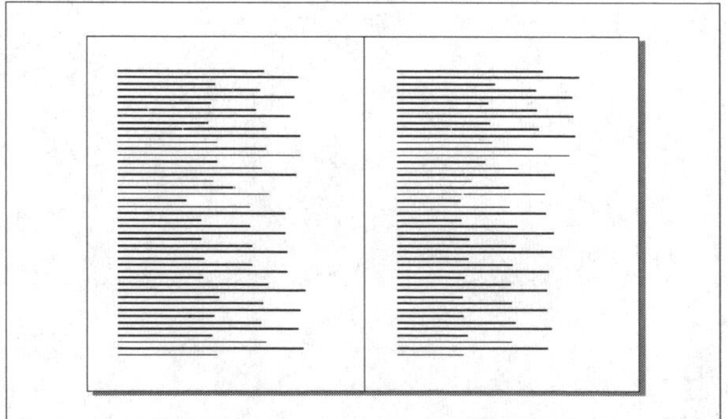

Working with facing pages

Users of version 4 should click Page Setup in the *File* menu, instead.

In versions before 8, the dialog which launches here is the Page Setup dialog.

Users of versions before 8 should omit step 1.

Version 5 users should ensure the Display tab is active before carrying out steps 2-3 only.

Implementing facing pages

To work with facing pages, pull down the Layout menu and click Page Setup. Now carry out the procedures listed below.

1 Click here

2 Ensure this is ticked

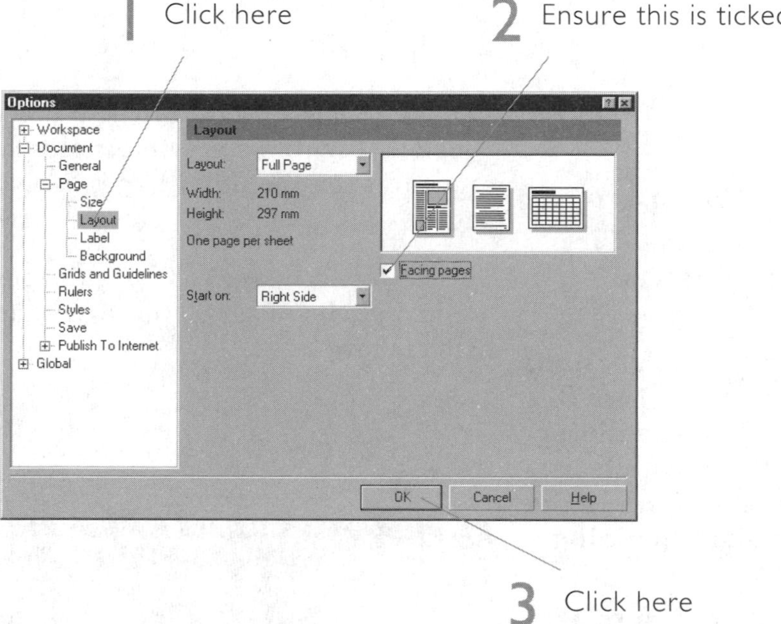

3 Click here

Note that the Facing Pages option is not available for the following layout styles:

- Tent cards
- Top-Fold cards

See page 172 for how to specify start page options.

Setting the start page New in version 4

When you implement the Facing Pages option for a multi-page document (see pages 170 and 171 for how to do this), you can also set an ancillary feature. You can opt to have the document begin on either of the following:

- an odd page
- an even page

Users of version 4 should click Page Setup in the *File* menu, instead.

Use the following as a guide. With most or all books and booklets, page 1 occurs on a right-hand page. With brochures, on the other hand, page 1 is generally an even page.

To set the start page for facing pages, pull down the Layout menu and click Page Setup. Now carry out the procedures listed below.

In versions before 8, the dialog which launches here is the Page Setup dialog.

Users of versions before 8 should omit step 1.

Version 5 users should ensure the Display tab is active instead of carrying out step 1.
Additionally, omit step 2. Finally, carry out steps 3-4.

1 Click here

2 Click here

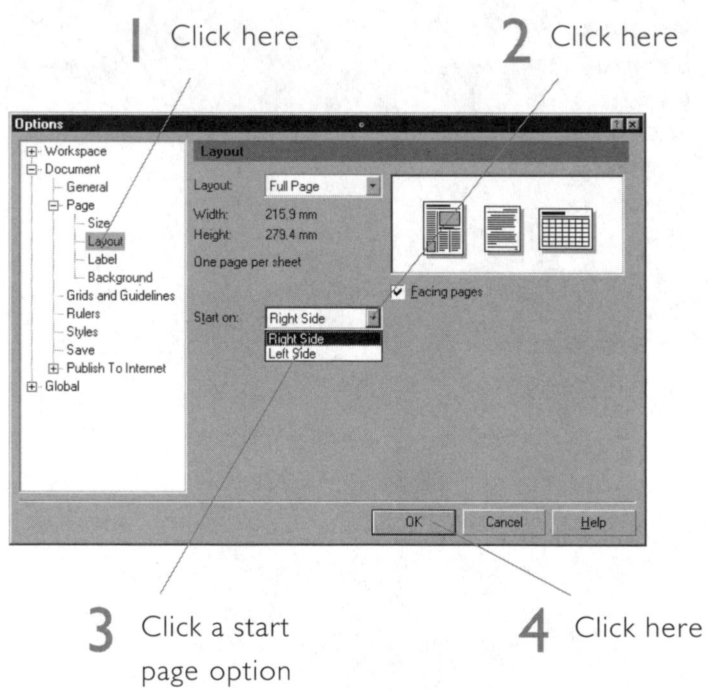

3 Click a start page option

4 Click here

Inserting pages New in version 4

To delete one or more pages, pull down the Layout menu and click Delete Page.

In the Delete Page field in the Delete Page dialog, type in the number of a *single* page you want to delete. If you want to remove multiple pages, also click Through to page (*Thru Page*, in versions 4 and 5) and type in the number of the final page you want to delete.

Finally, in either case, click OK.

When you delete one or more pages, CorelDRAW does not provide a warning that doing so will permanently remove the page contents.

You can, however, undo page deletions in the usual way.

One way to convert a single-page document into a multi-page document is to add one or more new pages. This is a viable option if you want to make room for extra text or additional objects (but you don't need to do this if you're importing a text file – in this situation, CorelDRAW automatically creates as many extra pages as required).

You can specify:

- the number of pages you insert at a given time
- the reference page (the page before or after which you want the new page(s) inserted)
- whether the new page or pages are inserted before or after the reference

To insert a page, pull down the Layout menu and then do the following:

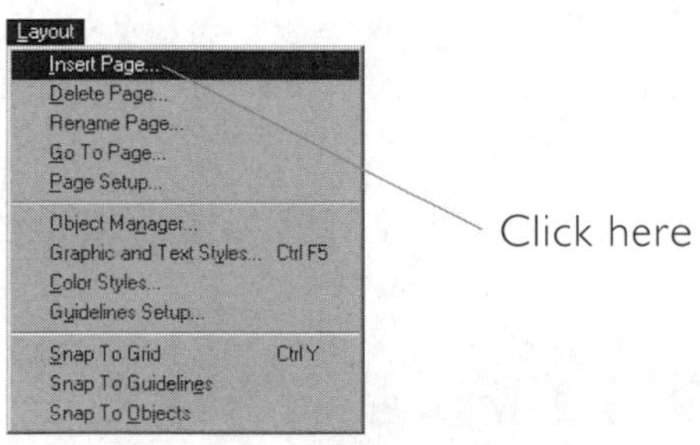

Now carry out the following steps:

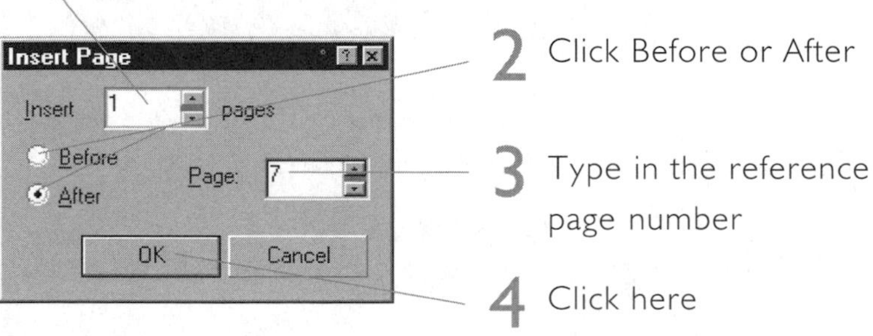

Going to specific pages New in version 4

CorelDRAW provides a variety of techniques which you can use to move from one page to another. You can use (arguably in declining order of usefulness):

- the Page Counter
- the Go To Page dialog
- specific keystrokes

Use whichever method most appeals, or even a combination of methods.

Using the Page Counter New in version 6

See page 10 for how to use the Page Counter to jump to specific pages.

Using the Go To Page dialog

This is arguably the most convenient method for moving around in your CorelDRAW documents. However, it has one disadvantage when compared to the Counter: you have to launch the dialog as often as you need to move to another page.

Users of versions 4-8 can use a shortcut to launch the Go To Page dialog. Click the Page Total area:

2 of 2

in the Page Counter.

First, pull down the Layout menu and click Go To Page. Now do the following:

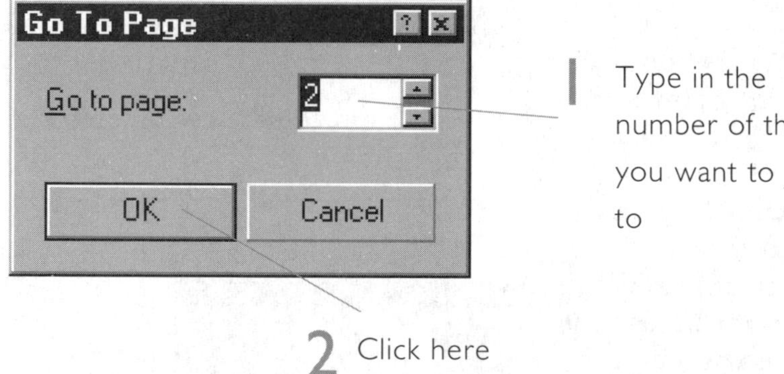

1 Type in the number of the page you want to jump to

2 Click here

Using keystrokes

Press Page Up or Page Down to step up or down through the available pages, one page at a time.

Chapter Eleven

Printing and Publishing

Most or all of your work in CorelDRAW will need to be printed, either on a desktop or higher-end printer. This chapter shows you how to tell CorelDRAW precisely what you want printed. You'll also learn how to preview your output *before* you start printing. Finally, you'll output your work to formats which can be read on the World Wide Web (if you have a modem and a suitable Internet connection) and use a Wizard to prepare files for service bureaus.

Covers

Selecting your printer

In versions before 8, the dialog which launches here is rather different.

Version 3 users should omit steps 1-2.

Re step 3 – in version 3, click the Print Setup button instead.

In version 4, click the Printer button.

In version 5, click the Setup button.

Finally, complete any further dialog which appears.

This is just a sample dialog; your printer's Properties dialog may look rather different.

Before you print your work, you should ensure CorelDRAW uses the correct printer. If you need to proof your work on a desktop printer, select this. If, however, you intend to submit your work on disk to a copy-shop or bureau, you'll need to select another (and see pages 185-186). You should also adjust your printer's setup, if applicable.

Specifying the correct printer

Pull down the File menu and click Print. Now do the following:

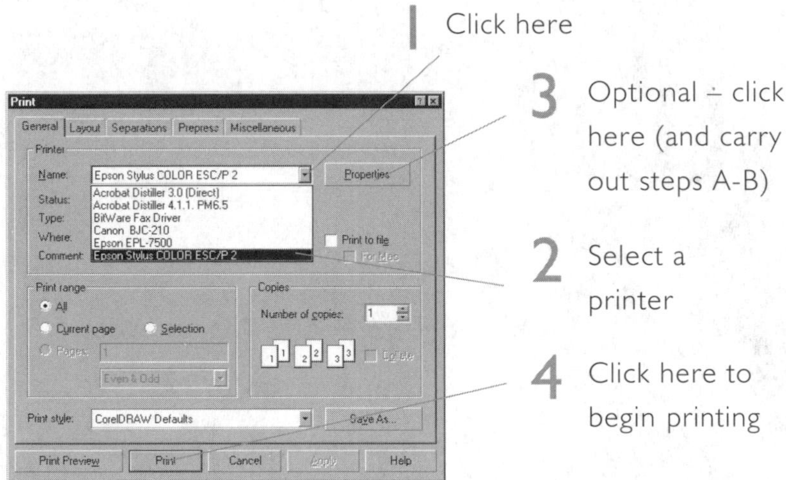

Adjusting your printer's settings

Follow step 3 above to access your printer's native Properties dialog, then do the following:

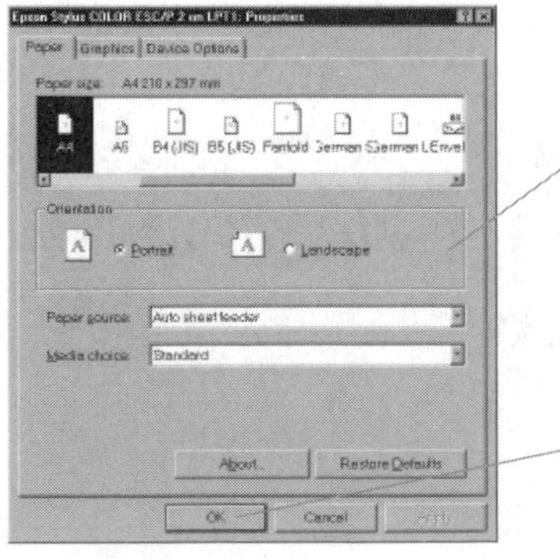

Selecting what to print

Options B, C, E and F on the right are unavailable in version 3.
C, E and F are unavailable in version 4.
E and F are unavailable in version 5.

CorelDRAW allows you to be very specific about what you print. You can print:

A. the whole of a document

B. a page range (e.g. pages 1, 3 and 6 to 10 inclusive)

C. the current page

D. pre-selected objects

E. only odd or even pages

F. specific document components (by type)

In versions before 8, the Print dialog varies.
Select those options which are appropriate.

Selecting which pages to print

If you want to print specific objects, select them first. Pull down the File menu and click Print. Then carry out any one of steps 1-5 below. Follow step 6 to print only odd or even pages. Finally, perform step 7 to begin printing.

Re step 5 – pages are separated by commas, ranges by dashes. For example, to print pages 1, 4, 7 and 9 to 16 inclusive, enter:

1,4,7,9-16

(without a comma or stop at the end).

1 Click here to print all pages

2 Click here to print the current page

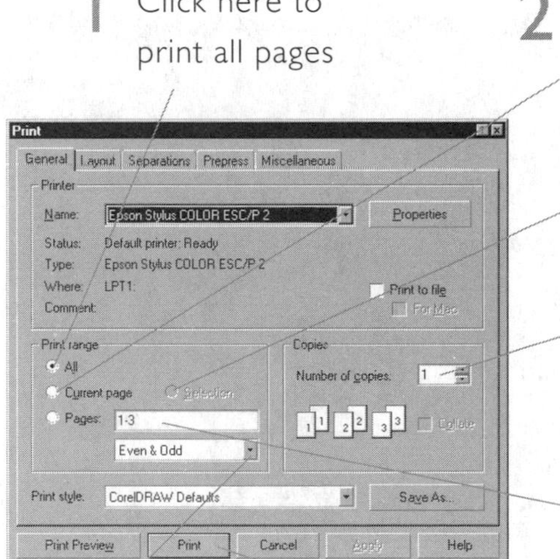

3 Click here to print selected object(s)

4 Type in the no. of copies required

5 Enter a page range (see the HANDY TIP opposite)

6 Click here. In the list, choose Odd Pages or Even Pages

7 Click here

Printing components New in version 6

An interesting and useful feature in CorelDRAW is the ability to include document components in a print run *generically*. By the same token, you can also exclude them. This is very useful for proofing your work. Component types are:

- vector graphics
- bitmapped graphics
- text

You can also specify whether CorelDRAW should print colours faithfully (you need a colour printer for this), in black and white or as greyscales.

HANDY TIP

In versions 6 and 7, follow a slightly different procedure. In the Print dialog, click the Options button. In the Print Options dialog, ensure the Options tab is active. Follow steps 1-3, then click OK or Close, as appropriate. Back in the Print dialog, click OK to begin printing.

First, press Ctrl+P to launch the Print dialog. Then do the following:

1 Ensure this tab is active

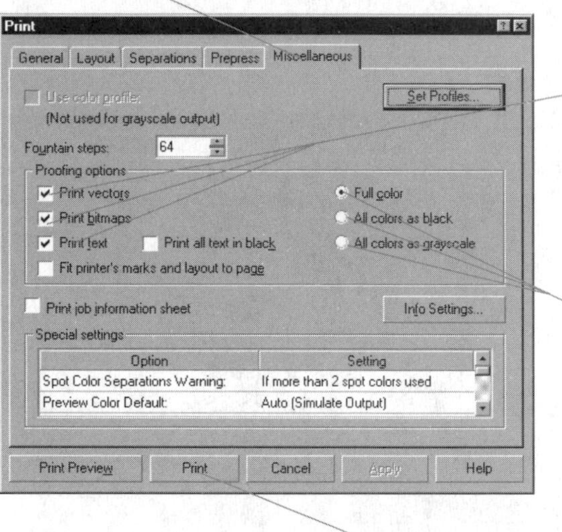

2 Click the relevant component options

3 Click a colour option

4 Click here to begin printing

HANDY TIP

Click Print all text in black to have coloured text print in black.

Print Preview New in version 4

In versions 7 and 8, the Print Preview window is full-screen.

In version 4, however, it's part of the Print dialog, while in versions 5-6 it forms part of the Print Options dialog.

In version 4, the procedure is different.

Press Ctrl+P. In the Print dialog, click Fit to Page or Center. Finally, click OK to begin printing.

In versions 5 and 6, the procedure is different.

Press Ctrl+P. In the Print dialog, click Options. Select the Layout tab. Now carry out steps 1-3.

Finally, click OK to begin printing.

An extremely useful feature is the ability to preview your document before you initiate printing. CorelDRAW's Print Preview facility is very advanced. You can:

- (in the case of multi-page documents) preview successive pages
- print the previewed page immediately
- drag the previewed object(s) to a new location on the holding page
- display coloured objects as greyscales
- have the previewed object(s) centred on the page
- have the previewed object(s) fill the page

To preview the active document, pull down the File menu and click Print Preview. The Print Preview window launches – see page 180. Press Ctrl+L, then do the following:

1 Click here to have object(s) fill the page

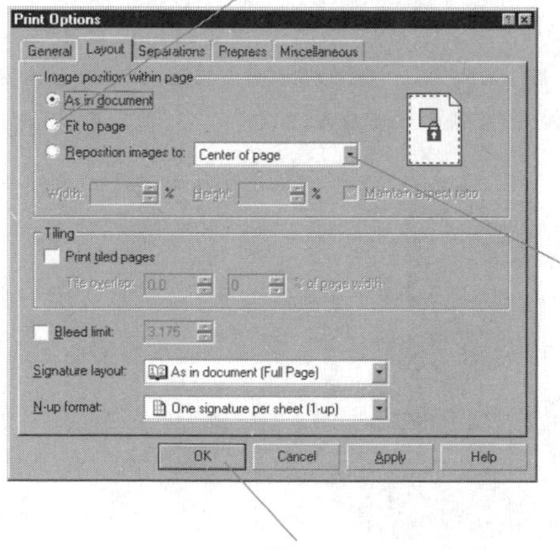

2 To centre objects, click here; choose a centring option in the list

3 Click here

In versions 4-5, you move objects in the Preview window within the Print dialog. To launch this, press Ctrl+P.

In version 6, you move objects in the Preview window within the Print Options dialog. To launch this, press Ctrl+P, then click Options.

In version 6, the actions on the right both require a different procedure.

Move the pointer over the Preview window within the Print Options dialog. Perform the stipulated actions (but note that the menu differs slightly).

To close Print Preview in versions 7-8, press Alt+C. In version 6, press Esc.

Moving previewed objects New in version 4

In the Print Preview window, move the mouse pointer over the object you want to drag; it changes into a cross. Hold down the left mouse button and drag the object to a new location. Release the mouse button to confirm the move.

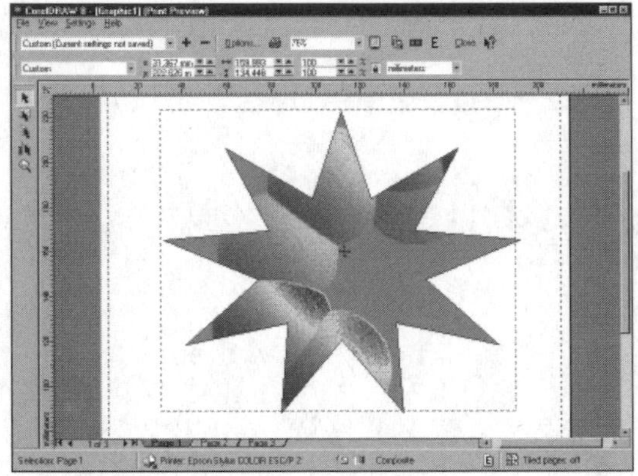

A previewed object being moved

Printing the previewed page New in version 6

Move the mouse pointer over the Preview window and right-click once. Click Print This Sheet Now.

Displaying in colour New in version 6

By default, in the Print Preview window coloured objects display as greyscales. To have them display in colour, move the mouse pointer over the window and right-click once. Now do the following:

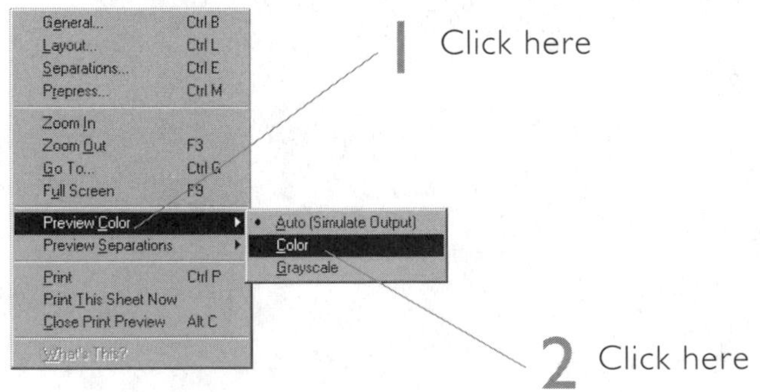

Using print styles New in version 6

CorelDRAW uses the concept of styles (collections of associated formatting commands) in several ways. We've already covered:

- text styles – see pages 80 and 81
- layout styles – see pages 163 (and 183)

However, CorelDRAW has a further additional, and innovative feature: print styles. You can impose printing parameters and save them as a style. This means that you can apply these settings to subsequent print jobs with just a few mouse clicks.

Creating a print style

In version 6, the procedure is rather different.

Press Ctrl+P. In the Print dialog, click Options. Do the following:

Click here

Now follow steps 1-3 on the right.

Pull down the File menu and click Print Preview. Make any relevant layout adjustments (see pages 179-180). Press F12. Finally, carry out the following steps:

1 Name the new style

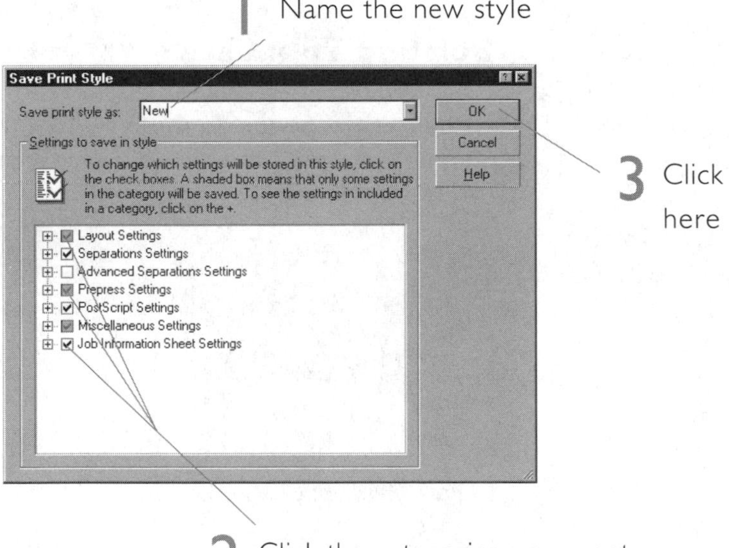

3 Click here

2 Click the categories you want included in the new style

Re step 2: categories which have been selected have: ☑ against them.

In version 6, the procedure is rather different.

Press Ctrl+P. In the Print dialog, click Options. Do the following:

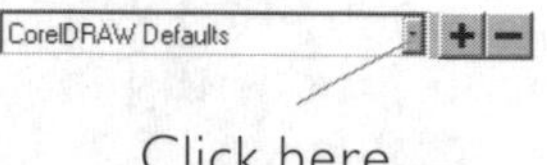

In the list which appears, click a style. Click OK, (followed by Cancel in the Print dialog)

In version 6, the procedure is rather different.

Follow the procedures in the tip above (but *don't* yet click OK in the Print Options dialog). Now do the following:

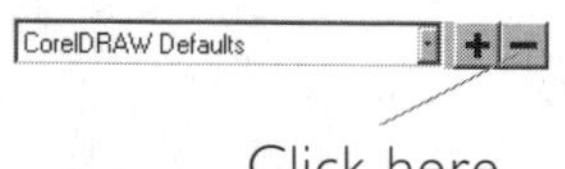

Follow step 2 on the right. Finally, click OK (followed by Cancel in the Print dialog).

Applying existing print styles New in version 6

Pull down the File menu and click Print Preview. Carry out the following steps:

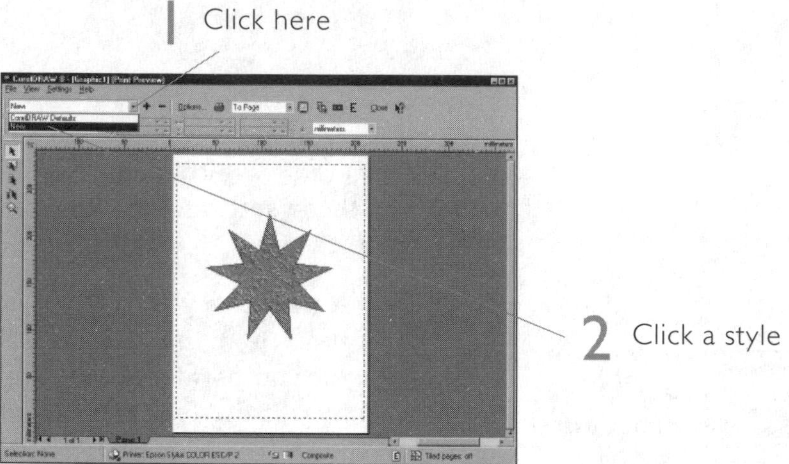

Deleting a print style New in version 6

For housekeeping reasons, it's sometimes useful to delete an unwanted style. To do this, first follow steps 1 and 2 above. Then pull down the File menu and carry out the following steps:

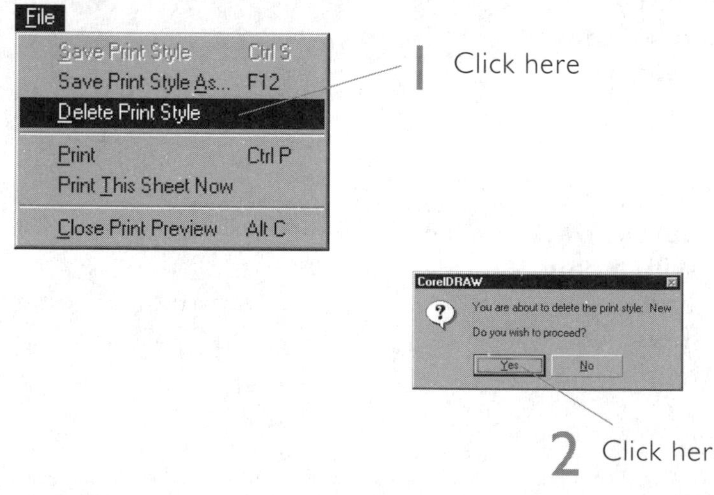

Using print/layout styles New in version 5

In version 4, you can only apply layout styles from within the Page Setup dialog (see page 163) . . .

In versions 5- 7, the procedure is rather different.

Press Ctrl+P. In the Print dialog, click Options. Ensure the Layout tab is active. Click the arrow to the right of the Layout style field; in the list, click a style. Click OK, followed by Cancel.

In version 8, layout styles accessed from within the Print dialog are called Signature Layout styles.

In Chapter 10, we looked at the use of layout styles from within the Page Setup dialog. In versions 5-8, you can also apply layout styles from within the Print Options dialog, just before you print.

If you choose to do this, there are certain points you have to bear in mind. When you use the Page Setup dialog to implement a layout style, this setting is automatically carried through to the Print Options dialog. With one exception (which we'll discuss shortly), any layout style changes you make now will result in your document not printing correctly. If you've already applied a layout style, leave well alone.

The exception? If you applied the Full Page style from within the Page Setup dialog, you can – if you want – apply another style in the Print Options dialog.

To apply a layout style, press Ctrl+P to launch the Print dialog. Then carry out the following steps:

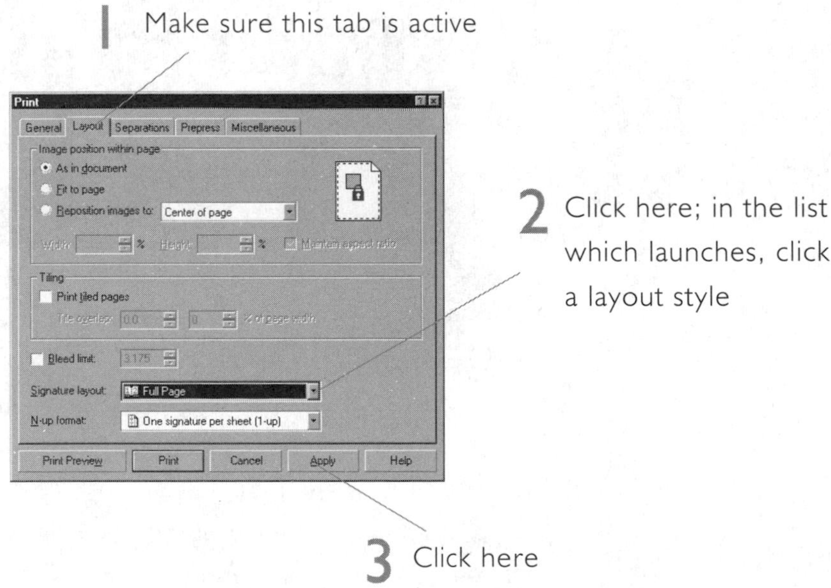

Proofing aids New in version 4

You can have CorelDRAW append a variety of additional material to your printed output. This is a valuable technique for proofing your work.

The most frequently used examples are:

1. file information – i.e. the name, date, time and filename (if applicable) at the foot of each sheet
2. page numbers
3. crop marks (alignment aids which you can use to trim your output)
4. registration marks (guides which help you align colour separations)
5. a colour calibration bar across on each sheet (you can use this to proof coloured or greyscale output)

A magnified view of the colour calibration bar (and crop marks) in Print Preview mode

Using proofing aids

Pull down the File menu and carry out the following steps, as appropriate:

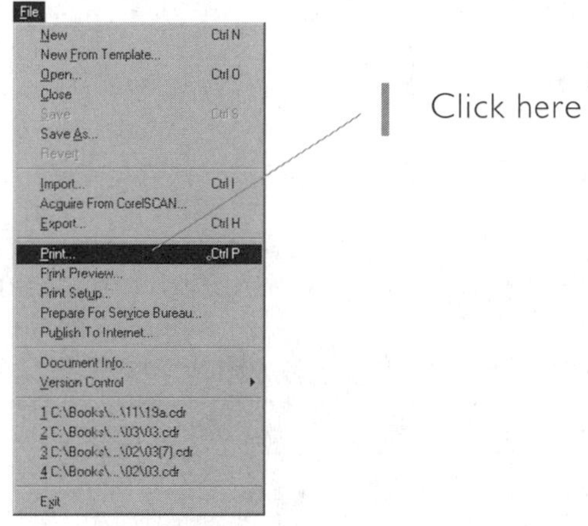

1 Click here

2 Ensure this tab is active

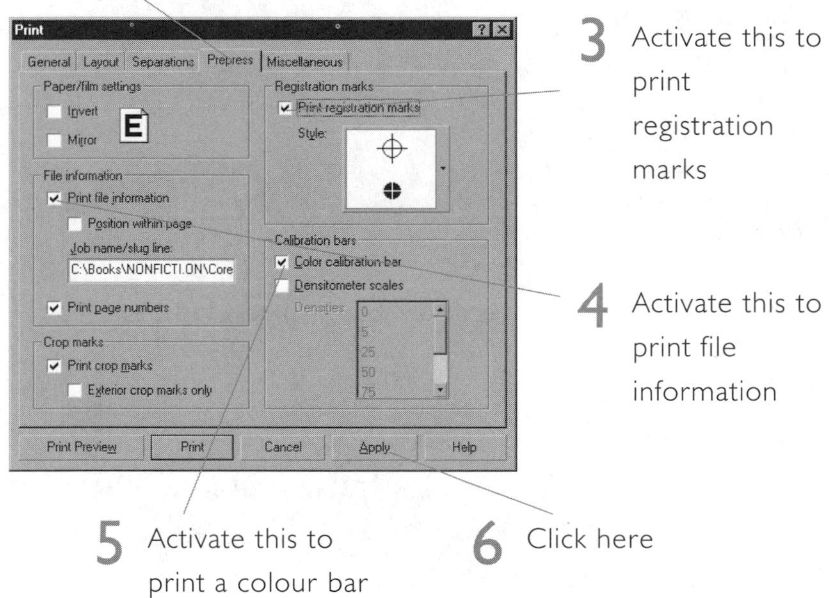

3 Activate this to print registration marks

4 Activate this to print file information

5 Activate this to print a colour bar

6 Click here

Version 4 users should press Ctrl+P. Click Options. Complete the resulting dialog. Click OK.

Users of versions 5 and 6 should press Ctrl+P. Click Options. Use the Pre-Press Bar at the base of the dialog to impose proofing aid settings. Click OK.

Users of version 7 should press Ctrl+P. Click Options. Select the Options tab, then the Marks and Prepress button. Complete the resulting dialog. Click OK.

Activate Print page numbers and/or Print crop marks.

Printing to a file

Consult the copy-shop or bureau – *before* you print your work to file – to avoid snags.

You can have CorelDRAW print a file to disk rather than directly to your printer. This may be useful if you intend to have your work printed by a copy shop or service bureau. You simply take the disk to them and they should be able to output the document more or less automatically.

When you choose to have CorelDRAW print a file to disk, it produces a PostScript file with the extension .PRN. This should be usable by any bureau.

To create a print file, press Ctrl+P. First set all other appropriate print options. Then do the following:

Re step 1 – in versions 4-8, click For Mac if your print file will be used on an Apple Mac computer (frequently the case with bureaus).

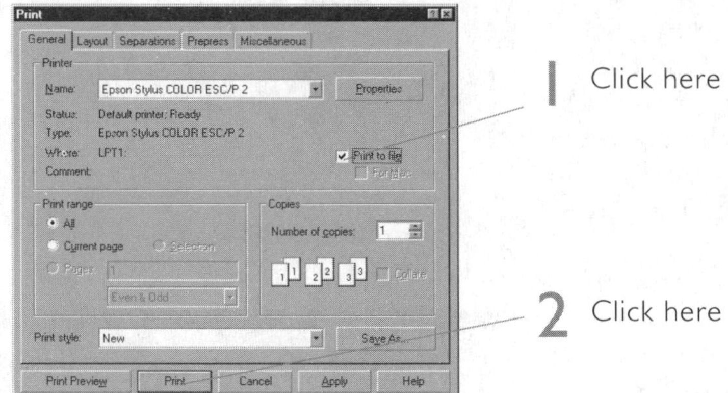

1 Click here

2 Click here

3 Click here. In the drop-down list, click the drive you want to host the print file

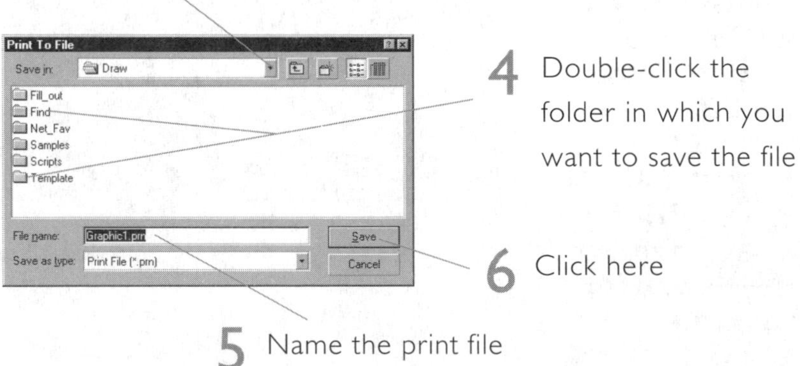

4 Double-click the folder in which you want to save the file

5 Name the print file

6 Click here

The Bureau Wizard New in version 8

The Prepare For Service Bureau Wizard leads you through the process of producing output files.

Use it to make sure you don't omit any information which is vital to your service bureau.

Formats 1. & 2. are both editable.

The Prepare For Service Bureau Wizard produces .PRN, .CDR **and** .EPS **files, according to which profile you choose in step 1.**

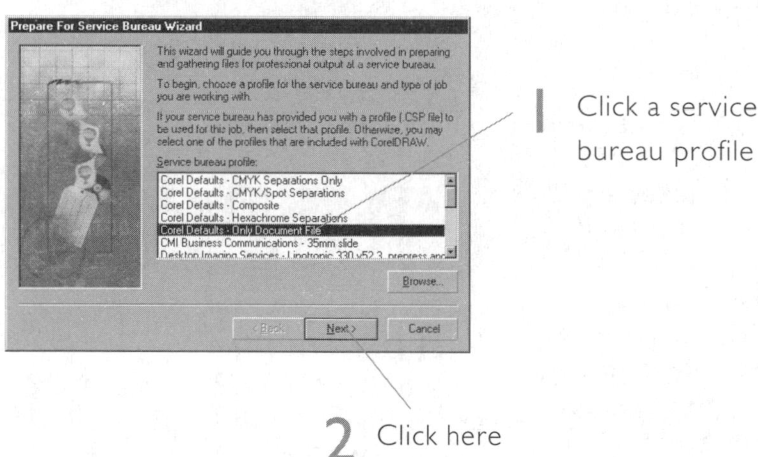

We saw on page 184 how to create a .PRN file for transmission to a copy-shop or service bureau. However, this has disadvantages, chief of which is that the .PRN file can't be verified by the bureau before printing, or amended if faults are discovered.

There are other options, though. You can send your work:

1. as a .CDR file (though not all copy-shops or bureaus welcome these)
2. as an .EPS PostScript file

Although you can use the techniques discussed on page 160 manually to export your work as an .EPS file, the best method to use for both 1. and 2. above is the Prepare For Service Bureau Wizard.

Running the Prepare For Service Bureau Wizard

Pull down the File menu and click Prepare For Service Bureau. Do the following:

The dialogs which now appear depend on the profile selected in step 1. Complete them as appropriate.

Re step 1 – version 8 comes with numerous pre-defined profiles.

You may find that your bureau will be able to provide you with additional examples . . .

Publishing to the Internet New in version 7

HTML (Hypertext Mark-up Language) is the standard Internet file format. However, it supports limited formatting options.

Files in Corel Barista format, on the other hand, can contain much more formatting. For example, if you set text in multiple columns in CorelDRAW and then publish to the Internet, the columns will reproduce . . .

You can publish your work in HTML or Barista (Java) formats, for use on the Internet.

Pull down the File menu and click Publish to Internet. Now do the following:

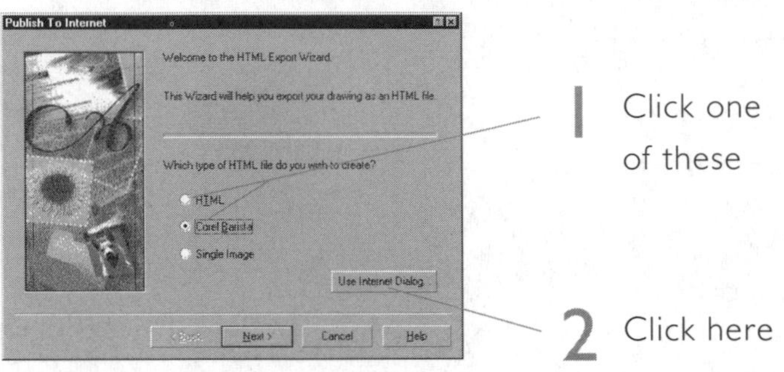

1 Click one of these

2 Click here

3 Type in the destination folder

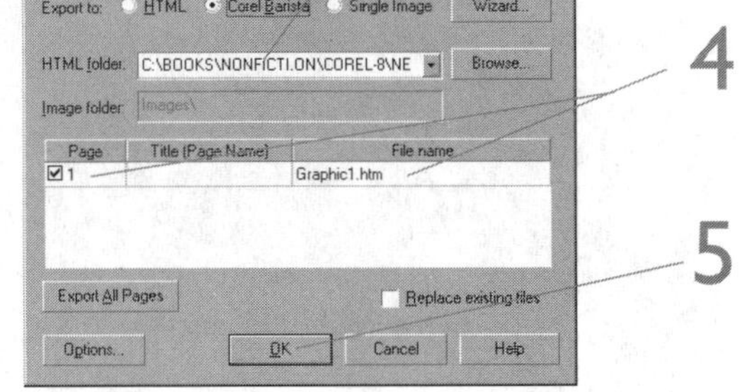

4 Complete these fields, as appropriate

5 Click here

HANDY TIP

In version 7, omit steps 1-2. Instead, in the Publish to Internet dialog (slightly different), select a destination folder. In the Save as type field, click the relevant format. Allocate a filename.

Finally, click Export.

Corel Barista files

For Internet browsers to read Corel Barista documents, certain files must be copied *to the same folder as the documents*. These files are located in the following folder:

*/Corel/Draw70/Barista — in version 7

*/Corel/Graphics8/Barista — in version 8

where * is the hard drive onto which CorelDRAW was installed.

Index

P

R

S

T

U

V

W

Z